GEN. MIRABEAU BONAPARTE LAMAR

Pgs. 3
6
36
98
105
108
109
140
145
158

Samuel H. Walker. This is a photograph of Walker in the uniform of a Captain, U.S. Mounted Rifles. It and a companion shot in civilian clothing are the only known photos of Texas Rangers taken during the Mexican War. Original in the Walker Papers, Texas State Library.

The Highly IRREGULAR IRREGULARS

TEXAS RANGERS In The Mexican War

By

Frederick Wilkins

EAKIN PRESS ★ Austin, Texas

FIRST EDITION

Published in the United States of America
By Eakin Press
A Division of Eakin Publications, Inc.,
P.O. Drawer 90159 ★ Austin, TX 78709-0159

ISBN 0-89015-716-2

Library of Congress Cataloging-in-Publication Data

Wilkins, Frederick, 1916–
The highly irregular irregulars : the Texas Rangers in the Mexican War / by Frederick Wilkins. — 1st ed.
p. cm.
Bibliography: p.
Includes index.
ISBN 0-89015-716-2 : $17.95
1. United States — History — War with Mexico, 1845–1848 — Campaigns. 2. Texas Rangers — History — War with Mexico, 1845–1848. I. Title.
E405.W55 1990
973.6'2dc20 89-16856
CIP

This is for Frances.

A Texas Ranger. Copied from Pictorial History of Mexico and the Mexican War *by John Frost (Harrold & Murray, Richmond, Virginia), 1848.*

— Courtesy The Institute of Texan Cultures

Contents

Texas Rangers and a Mexican volunteer force attacking a Mexican garrison at Laredo, Texas, 1841. On horseback (left) is John Coffee (Jack) Hays and (right) Captain Antonio Perez. 1970s watercolor by Bruce Marshall.
— Courtesy The Institute of Texan Cultures

Preface

There are few people in America who have not heard of the Texas Rangers. Many may have nothing more than a vague recollection of one man and one mob, or of a few men fighting impossible odds. Usually the extent of familiarity is that Rangers have something to do with police work. Not many know that the Rangers go back before the Texas Republic, or that they fathered the use of Colt five-shooters. Almost no one knows that they were soldiers at one time, fighting in a war as part of the United States Army.

The Mexican War (1846–1848) is one of America's forgotten conflicts. It was not popular at the time, creating bitter political struggles at home. While the South generally supported the war, other sections were lukewarm or refused to take any substantial part in it. Even some of the officers who fought with distinction did not believe in the justice of the fighting. The regular army fought bravely and well.

The war produced some striking victories, against great odds. However, some of the volunteer regiments had mixed performances, and some of their actions did not reflect great credit on the volunteer system. Along with this, the mounted units from Texas performed without uniforms, furnished their own horses and weapons, and acted in a manner that amazed their friends and terrified the enemy.

The sterling performance of the army in Mexico was overshadowed by the oubreak of the Civil War. Compared to the hundreds of thousands fighting in that struggle, the small numbers of the earlier war seemed trivial. Even in veterans' benefits and pensions, the Mexican War soldiers were forgotten. Everything seems to have gone against these men.

The popular trend in modern historical studies has been to distance ourselves from any acts of aggression, even to the point of making American forces the villains in whatever struggle — whether it involved Native Americans, Mexican nationals, or Vietnamese. We judge the past by present morality and eagerly accept a few or isolated incidents as cause for blanket indictments. Even reputable historians have taken this course, with the result that entire units have been branded villains and written out of the history books.

They deserve better.

This book is neither whitewash nor hero worship. Neither is the task of history. The volunteers from Texas would not have wanted one or felt comfortable with the other. They would have wanted the facts as we can determine them, and nothing more. My intention is to tell the story of the almost forgotten mounted riflemen from Texas — the Rangers. The Ranger myth has never died, but we think of them only as lawmen of the Wild West. This is the story of those earlier Rangers, the only Rangers to be American soldiers. These were men who truly could be classified as highly irregular irregulars.

Ranger weapons. Top — Walker Colt. Colt Patterson with loading lever. Fighting knife, usually classed as the Bowie Knife. To the left, copper powder flask.

— All weapons from the Texas Ranger Hall of Fame, Waco, Texas.

Acknowledgments

I would like to acknowledge a great debt to C. D. Sporlin for his work in printing the muster rolls of the Texas units and to Henry W. Barton for his research in the formation of the various units. Without them, it would have been difficult to complete this book. Donaly Brice and the staff of the Archives Division of the Texas State Library provided valuable assistance and support. Richard L. Fritz, curator of the Third Cavalry Museum, furnished Walker's service record and other data. They are too many to mention individually, but the staffs of the Main Library at San Antonio, the University of Texas at San Antonio, Trinity of Texas, and the Daughters of the Republic of Texas, San Antonio, made the research for the book possible. I am forever grateful. Tom Burks, of the Texas Ranger Hall of Fame in Waco, Texas, provided the photographs of Ranger weapons and equipment.

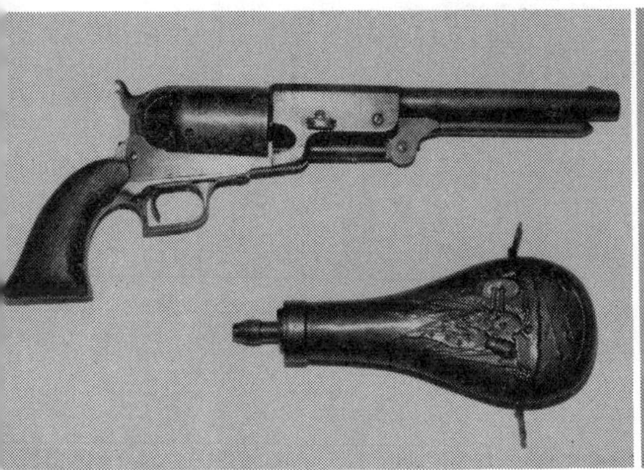

Walker Colt — the Model 1847 — with powder flask.

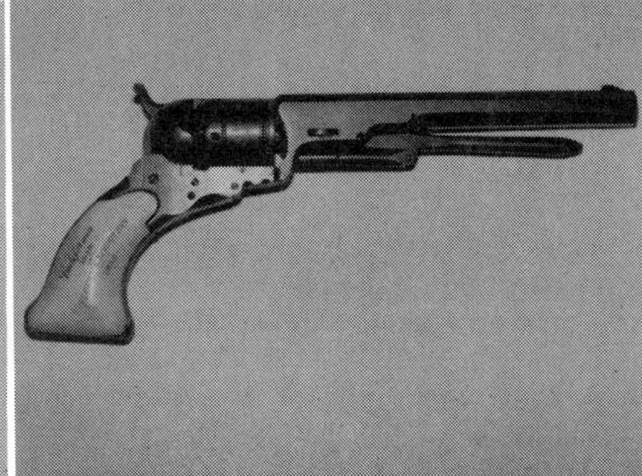

Colt Patterson. This model has the loading lever patented in 1839. Most Pattersons used by the Rangers did not have this feature.

"We had a little shooting match . . . and they lost!" — *A Texas Ranger's report to his captain.*
— Courtesy The Institute of Texan Cultures

ONE

The Legend Begins

During the Mexican War, volunteer cavalry units from Texas joined the United States Army and attracted national attention. It seemed to the writers who described these bearded, uniformless men that they were seeing something larger than life, and in most cases they so described them. The name "Ranger" became forever associated with Texas, another part of the mystique of the Lone Star State. To the correspondents who sent stories back to home papers and the men who wrote their memoirs in later years, the Texans seemed to spring full-grown from the brow of some mythical god, armed with rifles and repeating pistols, as likely to slay friend as foe. Whatever they were, the Texans were "good copy."

But even legends must start somewhere.

The Ranger legend, myth or fact, began years before the Mexican War. The Rangers evolved out of the conditions of the Texas frontier. Originally, the settlers who came to Texas settled in grants, mostly on individual farm units. As more came into the country, they organized a few settlements and small towns. From the very first, they were in danger of Indian attack, initially from tribes already in the settled areas, and later from Comanche raiders who sought horses.[1]

Early Spanish efforts to control the Indians had been unsuccessful. With Mexican independence, little else could be done to furnish military support for the colonies. The settlers had not come to a new land to be driven out, and so they began developing their own local protection. They had an earlier example to go by: the minute company of American colonial days. Militia companies were formed. Some of the settlements and farms constructed typical log forts in a central location and gathered there when raiders were sighted.

The Anglo settlements and farms were in East Central Texas, a heavily wooded country. The settlers mostly served as footmen, and when they divided up the settlements into six militia districts the defenders were basically infantrymen. Texans during the fighting in 1835–36 that led to independence and the establishment of a free nation were largely foot soldiers. Sam Houston had over 900 men at San Jacinto, where he defeated Santa Anna, but only a handful were horsemen.[2]

For the most part, the Texans were armed with flintlock rifles of the "Kentucky" type.[3] This long rifle dated back several generations and was a woodsman's weapon. The Texans were also equipped with big knives, both for general camp use and for fighting. The tomahawk was used sparingly. The tactics and weapons did not differ from those of frontiersmen in the revolution.

Such strategy worked fairly well against the Indians they first encountered. The natives were mostly unmounted, and the settlers were not handicapped in fighting them. With independence, the Texans had to contend with Mexican invaders, and the Mexican forces contained mounted units, or were entirely mounted raiders. Comanches had raided into Texas since Spanish days, but they had attacked the original towns. Initially they tried to be on good terms with the Texans, even though they came to steal horses. The Texans did not understand this form of friendship. By the mid and late 1830s, the Comanches and the Texans had begun a war to the death.

The Comanches were the finest horsemen of their time, and their small tribal units developed into a warrior society. They were relatively few in number, or they might have destroyed the Texas settlers. As it was, they managed to prevent westward movement beyond a certain line for decades.[4]

Infantry units could not possibly fight these invaders. Something besides the assembling of militia companies was needed to defend Texas. As early as the 1820s, Texans had seen the need for mounted units that could "range" the country between block houses. They would get away from a passive defense, useless against swift raiding

Comanche bands. These companies could move fast and either attack raiders or trail them as they retreated and punish them. The germ of the Ranger system was in place by the time of the Texas Revolution, though the companies played no real part in the actual fighting.[5]

An important step in the first development of the militia system was naming more or less permanent commanders for each area. In this way a group of leaders developed. Certain men were able to spend more time outdoors, and they had an opportunity to develop skills in tracking and living on the frontier.

The new Republic had some grand ideas for military forces. An army was created, at least by law. A navy was formed and even put to sea. But the Texas of the late 1830s was a poor country. The only resource the nation had was land. Payment for just about anything was in land. There was one other resource: men. Hundreds of footloose idealists, adventurers, and on-the-run outlaws traveled to Texas to help fight for independence. With freedom won, most stayed, and thousands more followed to seek their fortunes. For the first time, there was a pool of single men who were not tied down by family and farms — men who could serve for extended periods of time in quasi-military companies.

It was obvious that there would have to be some form of civilian-military response to the Indian threat. Texas simply could not support an army. Sam Houston, the first president of the Republic, did not like the idea and was opposed to a hard-line policy against the Indians.

The next president, Mirabeau B. Lamar, believed in a drastic program to drive all Indians from Texas. However, he had no more money for an army than before, and the threat was still present and growing. By about 1840, the Texans began taking formal steps to create mounted companies to defend against increasing raids.[6] A series of external threats led to what would become the Rangers.

While they had made raids earlier, the Comanches began a systematic assault on the Texas settlements. Normally, Comanche raiding parties consisted of a few braves out to steal horses and kill anyone who was unlucky enough to be caught in the open. Only once did they depart from this pattern and wage full-scale war. In early August of 1840, a force that has been estimated as high as a thousand braves came down from the Comanche lands and struck through the heart of Texas. This was invasion. Historians believed that the Great Raid was made in reprisal for the slaughter of the Comanche chiefs in San Antonio in the so-called Council House Massacre. This undoubtedly played a part, but it is now known that Mexican agents were active in inciting the Indians to raid.[7]

This war party, the largest ever assembled from the Comanche tribes, struck straight through the settlements, all the way to the Gulf Coast. Fortunately, they were more interested in horses and plunder than killing or taking towns. As the alarm went out, militia companies began forming and trailing the broad path of the invaders.

Details of the chase and final battle are interesting, as they show how the militia organization handled an emergency of this nature. Capt. Adam Zumwalt gathered thirty-six men and started following the trail. Each party sent out scouts to alert other settlements to the danger. Capt. John Tumlinson, the first Ranger commander, who had served during the Revolution, gathered sixty-six men and started after the Comanches. He attacked, found out he had more than he could handle, lost a man, and fell back, sending out word of the size and direction of the war band. Next Ben McCulloch rode in with two dozen, and Zumwalt caught up. Clark Owen arrived with another forty. Individuals and small groups were coming in as they got the word and saw their families safe. The companies picked Ben McCulloch to command. It was his first Ranger service, though he and his brother had fought at San Jacinto.

These were old-time local militia units forming and moving to the scene of danger. Only now, the units were mounted, highly mobile, and getting ready to fight the Comanches on their own terms. They were men who now had some years of experience. Though still armed with single-shot rifles and pistols, the mounted men were brave, not rash, and they made no attempt to engage the main body of Comanches.

Gen. Edward Burleson, an experienced Indian fighter, was gathering forces. The whole area was alerted. It was decided the Indians would be brought to battle along Plum Creek, near present-day Lockhart.

The Comanches had captured several thousand horses and mules, along with some prisoners, and were heavily loaded with all types of clothing and anything that had caught their attention as they sacked individual homes and the small settlement of Linnville on the coast. If they had not slowed to save their horse herds, they would have gotten back with scant loss.

Burleson came up to the militia forces with his men and thirteen Tonkawa Indians who had run thirty miles on foot to keep pace with the mounted Texans. Gen. Felix Huston, who represented the regular army, such as it was, was in command, but the actual fighting was done by the company commanders, men who understood Indian fighting.

They had developed a rough system of tactics, based on their weapons and the character and weapons of their foes — which is about the way it has been done since the first war. The Comanches were masterful horsemen, skilled as mounted archers. Their weapons were crude compared to the medieval archers of the Middle East, but they were quite effective at close range. At longer distances the rifles of the Texans could outshoot them. However, if the Indians got close and the Texans had empty guns, it was a decided mismatch. Besides his bow, each brave carried a long lance, and he had the courage to charge home and use the point. The only way the Texans could win a fight, unless they heavily outnumbered the Comanches, was to always have some men with loaded rifles. For the Indians, fighting became a game to entice the Texans to fire all together, or too soon, and then charge home. The Texans had to fire in relays and always have shot in reserve, constantly reloading. This was not simple, as the long rifles were slow to reload, and almost impossible to load on horseback.

A number of men who fought at Plum Creek later wrote accounts of the battle. One, John Holland Jenkins, described how the Texans deployed for battle, using a rudimentary tactical system.[8] They came up in columns of two, which in those days was called double file. One man held both horses, while the second file was free to fire. It would be nice to say the Texans invented this method for fighting horse Indians. They did — in Texas. At the same time it was being "invented" in many other places as trappers and explorers encountered the Plains Indians.

Plum Creek was a Texas victory. The Comanches lost most of their captured horses — about 2,000 by some accounts. The body count was considerable. There never was another raid of this size, nor was there ever again a major penetration into the heart of the country. The Comanches simply returned to small but endless raids.

In many ways, 1840 was a critical year in Texas. If possible, the new Republic was in worse shape than when independence was won in 1836. Most of the old tribes had been driven from Texas, but the Comanche threat was as real as ever. Not even the great victory at Plum Creek or Moore's campaign later in October removed the danger. Mexican attempts to create Indian troubles were always facing the Texans, and there was the constant threat of a major Mexican invasion to restore Mexican rule. The country was too poor to support any decent military force.

What was needed was a force that could scout the borders and spot invasions, harry them, and allow time for the militia companies to form. There were enough single men to fight in the units, providing they could be paid, and the Texans were beginning to know how to fight in frontier fashion.

During 1840, John Coffee Hays's name appears officially for the first time. He had been in Texas two or three years, coming from Tennessee. On February 15, 1840, C. Van Ness wrote to President Lamar suggesting Hays as a surveyor to locate the northern boundary of Travis County.[9] Hays apparently had been working at this trade the previous two years. He was a volunteer in the fight at Plum Creek but had attracted no special mention. Already a number of men had made names as captains, but young Hays would become the premier partisan leader.

The Texas government decided to form standing companies that year to patrol the frontiers. While little documentation has survived showing exact dates and names, Hays was one of the men selected as a captain.[10] A half dozen men had already made records as commanders and were well known, but they were not selected, for whatever reason. If Hays's appointment seems strange, it was one of the most fortunate events in Texas frontier history.

Half a country away, another young man would have an equally marked impact on Texas, his name entwined with Hays. They would never meet, but between them they would influence frontier history. Samuel Colt patented a new revolving firearm in February 1836.[11] He managed to form a company and began manufacturing rifles, carbines, and pistols in a factory in Paterson, New Jersey, known as the Patent Arms Manufacturing Company. Colt sold his new weapons from 1836 to 1842, when the company folded. He did, however, retain his patents.

The concept of a revolving firearm is as old as gunpowder. Because of production and ignition problems no practical repeating weapon was possible before Colt's day. He was able to use the relatively new percussion cap to ignite his powder charge, doing away with the capricious flint ignition. The Industrial Revolution provided machinery and factory assembly methods, crude as they were, to mass produce weapons. And he came up with the only really new idea: how to turn, align, and lock a cylinder in line with a stationary barrel, using a ratchet and pawl.

From a modern perspective, it seems incredible that his new pistols did not become an overnight success. All the user had to do, once his weapon was loaded, was point and cock the hammer, squeeze the trigger, and repeat until all five charges had been fired. Not only did the user have five charges that could be fired in rapid order, but the bullets were fired with greater accuracy and at longer distances than the common single-shot, muzzle-loading pistol.

True, there were some drawbacks. First, the weapons were costly. Second, loading was slow and cumbersome and involved taking the pistol apart. The fastest way to reload was to carry a spare cylinder and change cylinders, rather than recharge the individual chambers. Last, and this was the major fault found by the military, the pistols and rifles had a considerable number of parts. It was feared they would not stand up to the hard use of campaign conditions.

Colt was a salesman as well as inventor, and he spent a great deal of time and effort advertising and selling his new weapons. During the next several years, advertisements for his Patent Arms weapons appeared across the country. A New York dealer was selling his rifles for $150 in 1838.[12] They were advertised in New Orleans, and Colt personally went to Florida to sell rifles to the troops fighting the Seminoles. He did not sit by and await results from army testing or contracts that might never come. Just how the new weapons spread from New Jersey will never be completely known. Many early Colt records were lost in later fires. It is not known how many revolvers were manufactured before production stopped in 1842. Current estimates put the figure at only 2,800.[13]

William S. Harney, lieutenant colonel of the 2nd Dragoons, wrote Colt in February 1839 that his men had used Colt rifles for a year and that only two of fifty were not in service.[14] However, he gave no combat details. A year later, the sergeant of the fifty-man detachment Harney spoke about wrote to Colt and praised the rifles. He described the extensive target practice and field use given the weapons, but he did not mention any combat use.[15]

The main combat use would be in Texas. Most of the early trade in Colts is obscure, but it seems the first documented introduction of the new weapons was by John Fuller, who tried to sell the new rifles to the Texas Army, or what passed for an army. Again, it would seem that there would be little contest between repeating arms and single-shot muskets, much less flintlocks. But the army turned down Fuller and purchased Tyron manufactured arms, saying Texas was so dry that caps were not necessary and the soldiers could get by with cheaper flintlocks.

Records show considerable numbers of these muskets being purchased. However, in some manner, some of the new Patent Arms guns were acquired. An item in the *Journals of the Texas Fifth Congress,* April 1840, mentions the payment of $3,282.50 (charged to Colonel Hockley) for patent rifles purchased from Charles D. Sayre.

The major sale of Colt pistols was to the Texas Navy. This took place before the mysterious buy of carbines. The handguns were authorized April 29, 1839, and the first group was shipped on August 3. John Ehlers, Colt's partner and manager, signed the invoice sending the first 50 five-shooters to Texas. These Colts cost $55 for carbines and $35 for pistols, including spares and accessories. At least some of these pistols were equipped with loading levers.[16]

Records show that 180 pistols and a like number of carbines were ordered. But arsenal records indicate that by July 1, 1840, 230 pistols had been issued, with no more weapons in storage. So many records have been lost in various Adjutant General Office fires that the exact details of how many Colts were bought may never be known. What is important is that a substantial number *were* bought, and they would change frontier combat.

Some revolvers came to Texas through dealers. One report of a fight in Brazoria in 1842 said a man used a Colt. The man, named Stewart, fired three shots from his new Colt revolver at a man named Allston, wounding him. Allston then used a rifle and a shotgun to kill Stewart. A number of the local citizens then took Allston out and shot him.[17]

Colt also had some success in his own state of New Jersey. In 1841 the Citizen Volunteers of Paterson had thirty-five Colt rifles and used them in target exhibitions. The prize was a Patent Arms pistol, probably donated by Colt.[18]

Some of the revolvers got out to the frontiers. Colts probably were available in some quantity in 1838. By 1839, Josiah Gregg had some of these weapons on a trading trip to Santa Fe. A year or so later some trappers used them in scattering an Indian attack. George Wilkins Kendall mentions his experiences with Colt rifle and pistol during the

Santa Fe expedition. There was no combat use on this ill-fated and ill-conceived fiasco, and the weapons were destroyed to keep them from falling into Mexican hands.[19]

At this time Colt pistols sold for forty to fifty dollars a set, including pistol, mold, and powder flask. Pepper boxes, multiple-barrel revolving pistols manufactured by Allen, sold for a fraction of this. The Allen weapons were not suited for anything other than close-range civilian use, but they captured the Eastern market and continued to do so for years.

So, while there were Colts in Texas, they were not used in battle on any scale for a number of years.

The Texans were convinced that reacting to raids was not the solution to the Indian problem. Some pressure had to be put on the Comanches in their own territory. In October 1840, Col. John H. Moore led a force north and struck a major Comanche camp on the Red Fork of the Colorado River. The Texans had learned not to leave their horses. They attacked mounted and completely surprised the camp. In a running battle, they inflicted heavy losses on the braves and took women and children as prisoners. Much of the camp loot had been captured in Linnville, showing that this band had been one of the participants in the Great Raid.[20]

This was a major victory which displayed the developing skill of the Texans as they adapted to mounted combat. It has another important aspect that has been generally overlooked. During this fight, one of the Texans used a new Colt repeating rifle. It is the first documented combat use of a repeating arm in Texas.[21]

A few Colt rifles were in the hands of the Texans who attacked Mier in 1842.[22] They may have been used, but the surviving accounts stress the usual deadly accuracy of the Texan rifles and do not mention any Colts. Other than the almost universally overlooked first use at Moore's second fight, there is no mention of Patent Arms use in Texas.

The basic weapon was still the long rifle, though this weapon was changing. The early Texans had fought with a flintlock long rifle, as mentioned before. By the late 1830s and 1840s, this Kentucky Rifle was being modified to meet the conditions of the Plains and Rocky Mountain hunting. The buffalo hunters and Rocky Mountain trappers were horsemen, and the old form of stock was difficult to handle on horseback. The rifle barrel was too long and the caliber too small for the bigger game of the West.

A weapon we now call the Plains Rifle evolved.[23] This was the basic rifle, loading the same, but with a shorter barrel and larger caliber. The drop to the stock was not as pronounced, and mostly they were half stocked and finished with plainer hardware. In time, they would be iron mounted, replacing the fine brass ornamentation that was a characteristic of the earlier rifles. Flint was being replaced with percussion caps, but this was a slow development. Caps were expensive and hard to come by on the frontier. For a long time, flint would be the popular form of ignition.

As the newer rifles were introduced, the old powder horns began to give way to copper or brass powder flasks. As caps were introduced, a new accessory — the cap box — was added. The earlier hunting pouch, which carried everything from food to spare clothing, continued in use.

A lot has been made of Bowie knives; every man on the frontier carried some form of large knife to prepare game, perform camp chores, and serve as the main eating tool. It doubled as a fighting weapon as necessary. There was no pattern to these weapons, merely whatever the individual could find or afford. Each had a large blade, usually single-edged with a part back edge. Blacksmiths made them, and many were imported from England.[24]

Each man carried one or two single-shot pistols, again simply whatever the Ranger could find or afford. They were large-bore, useful at very close range.

These pistols and the knife were carried from or stuck through a waist belt. When revolvers were introduced, they were probably stuck in the same belt. The military used pistol holsters attached to the saddle, but civilians preferred to keep their pistols at hand. The pistol holster, as we think of it today, developed later in the revolver era. The Rangers probably just stuffed the first Colts in their belts. This was a dangerous way to carry a valuable weapon, and holsters attached to a belt probably came into use fairly early in the game.

By the early 1840s, the Texans covering the frontier were a completely mismatched group of uniformless individuals who were armed in no set fashion, other than some form of rifle. A careful examination of tactics from Plum Creek, 1840, through the Mexican invasions of 1841 and 1842, shows a consistent pattern in the way the Texans fought. The single-shot, muzzle-loading rifle was the basic weapon.

When possible, the men dismounted and used a natural terrain feature, preferably a creek bank, as a shelter. They fired in relays and always kept some rifles charged. This method was used whether fighting Indians or Mexican cavalry. It was a perfect defense against Mexican artillery. The classic example of a large-scale fight was the battle along the Salado in 1842. The pursuit of the retreating Mexican forces following their withdrawal from San Antonio continued to show the normal tactics of the day.[25]

Small-scale Indian fights during the early 1840s show the same pattern. The Texans were flexible. When confronting groups on more equal terms, they would often change the pattern and rush the Comanche and keep on him so closely that the Indians could not use their bows to advantage, if at all. The fight in Sabinal Canyon in July 1841 is a good example of how this new tactic worked.[26]

Fighting on whatever scale into 1843 is pretty well documented by a number of participants, who were specific about weapons and their use. Not one mentions Colt pistols or rifles.

The introduction of Colt revolvers on a considerable scale took place late in 1843. A great deal of supposedly factual data on weapon use in this period is subject to doubt, but one of the men who was among the original Ranger users is the authority for this statement.[27] He also categorically stated that the weapons came from the old stocks of the Texas Navy. Other statements from former naval personnel support this position. Also, there simply are no documentary sources to show any other sizable quantities of the revolvers coming into Texas other than through the Navy contract.

One story claims Colt presented a Texas merchant with a pair of his pistols before he went out of business. The merchant returned home and eventually gave or sold the weapons to Hays. This could be true, but the supply of five-shooters was from ex-Navy sources. Such would have been a change in policy, as the Rangers furnished their arms and horses. Someone was impressed enough with the new pistols to give them to the men who needed them the most. Someone — possibly Hays — saw the possibilities and adopted the revolvers as well as a new fighting tactic.

Threats to the frontier did not diminish during the mid 1840s. On January 24, 1844, the Ninth Texas Congress authorized the formation of a company of mounted gunmen to act as Rangers on the western and southwestern frontier.[28] John C. Hays was the commander. The company was recruited and operating by March 15, and was retained in service throughout 1844 because of the threat of Mexican invasion and constant Indian raids.[29] It was the closest thing to a regular military force that Texas possessed, and it may have been the finest Ranger company ever. This company would put the final polish to the developing Rangers. Personnel must have changed to some degree, but a significant group remained on the rolls over much of the year and became very professional in their skills. They still looked like bandits.

The only difference between this company and earlier units was in weapons. This Ranger company had a number of Colt five-shot revolvers. The Rangers had them long enough to become accustomed to their use and to develop confidence in the vastly increased firepower they provided.

During the spring of the year there were the usual Comanche raids, though efforts were being made to form some kind of truce. Reports were made of a Comanche raid in the Hill Country, and Hays took fourteen men and rode north from San Antonio to check on the possibility of an attack. Just why he took this number, rather than the entire company, is open to speculation. There were never enough Rangers to patrol all of his territory; the rest of the company could have been on other missions. Or he may have been confident in the extra power of his new arms. Sam Walker, one of the company, later said they had confidence enough to tackle several times their strength.[30]

The detachment moved north to the Pedernales River and halted; Hays did not wish to go farther north and possibly compromise any negotiations that might be going on. The Rangers went back to the Llano and then to the Guadalupe River. They were a little above the San Antonio Road, about sixty miles from San Antonio.

Hays and most of the Rangers had dismounted along a creek, with some of the horses unsaddled to rest them. A rear guard was coming up to join the others. Long before they got into the temporary camp, these Rangers saw they were being followed. A small party of Indians had cut their trail and were staying just out of rifle shot. The Texans hurried ahead and told Hays. Quickly, the Rangers saddled and turned back along their old trail. They soon saw about ten Indians, who turned and retreated, though not in full flight.

Inexperienced men, outnumbering the Indians, would have galloped full tilt after them, confident their extra numbers would give them a victory. The Rangers had been at the game too long. They knew that ten Indians would have run. The Comanche was brave, but he did not look for fights when outnumbered. A deadly game was being played; by now each side knew the rules.

The Comanches stopped before a large stand of trees. Once again the Texans did not rise to the bait, and the retreat continued. Sometime later, they came to a ridge and it all became clear. While the Rangers waited, a large war party formed on the hilltop, joined by the other Indians. As usual, the braves dashed about. One would ride to the front and halt, shaking his shield and lance, shouting threats and telling of his kills. Others rode from side to side, trying to draw fire, but keeping out of rifle range. The Rangers counted as best they could, somewhere between sixty and seventy. With all the movement it was hard to get an exact count. At the best, there were four to one, probably more.

A year earlier, the Rangers would have looked for a place in which to make their defense: a creek bank or heavy woods. But this was different. This was a day they had been expecting. Today each man had at least one of the new Colt five-shooters, and they were going to see how well they worked in battle.

Hays gave a command and the detachment walked toward the hill. The braves on the crest were shouting insults, challenges. It seemed the whites were going to walk into the trap. First they would fire their rifles; then the Comanches would rush before they could reload. They may have wondered why the Texans remained mounted. Usually, when outnumbered like this, they would dismount and use the horses for shelter, if they could not find a river bank, or boulders or trees. There must have been a feeling of great anticipation on the hill that this would be a great victory.

The Rangers advanced at a walk until they were at the foot of the hill, where they were out of sight for a moment. Hays signaled, probably having explained what he proposed, and the line changed to column, broke into a gallop, circled the side of the hill, and then dashed up the slope and caught the Indians in the flank. The Rangers fired their rifles and dropped a number of the surprised braves. Then the entire group ran down the slope onto more level ground, and the battle began.

Assuming each Ranger had brought down a man with the opening volley, the Texans were still outnumbered three or four to one, and the Comanches had no intention of running. The Texans slung or dropped their rifles, depending on how closely they were pressed, and started firing with their Colt revolvers. This must have caused something close to panic among the braves — for a time. They were used to single-shot pistols, which were about as deadly as firearms when used as clubs. Now the Texans were firing and firing, the braves dropping right and left, their shields pierced. The fight drifted along the open country, a small group charging, being repulsed, reforming, rushing again. And the little guns kept firing. It was not a continuous fight, and some of the Texans managed to change cylinders, difficult as that was in a mounted fight. Some even managed to reload their rifles, which proved most fortunate.

A few of the Rangers got too far ahead of the others and were cut off and lanced, but escaped. Somewhere in the melee, Peter Fosh was killed. Hays reported that after the third round the Indians began to break and retreat, but they reformed and one of the chiefs was making every effort to rally them for a final change. Fosh was already dead. Sam Walker, W. B. Lee, and R. A. Gillespie were seriously wounded. Andrew Erskine had a slight wound. Most of the revolvers were probably empty, as well as their rifles. A third of the men had casualties.

Hays asked if anyone had a loaded rifle. Gillespie called out, and Hays told him to drop the chief. Badly injured, Gillespie dismounted and steadied his rifle and took careful aim. The sharp crack of the rifle drowned out the yelling of the chief. For a moment the remaining braves stared at the body and then began to drift away.

There was not much pursuit.

Hays had three seriously wounded men and probably a number of horses had been injured; all were winded from the moving fight. The Rangers camped where they fought since the Comanches had gone. It must have been a shattering experience, something the Indians had to think over. They made no effort to pick up their dead from the field, which was almost unheard of. Hays counted twenty-three bodies and estimated thirty had been wounded, most badly.

The second day after the fight, while Hays was getting his wounded in shape to travel, the Rangers spotted four Indians riding toward the camp, evidently trying to find relatives or wounded. Hays ordered six men to chase them. At a dead run, the two groups rode for about a mile, where the Comanches were overtaken and three were killed. One escaped in the brush. That ended the fight at Walker Creek. Hays returned to San Antonio, where he wrote a report to the secretary of war and marine, dated June 16, 1844.[31]

This was the first real battle involving Colt pistols, and it is very likely that the Rangers entered the fight because they were so armed. Hays made an interesting statement: ". . . closed in with them, hand to hand, with my five-shooting pistols, which did good execution. Had it not been for them, I doubt what the consequences would have been. I cannot recommend these arms too highly."

It was rather an historic affair, even though, like many earlier Texas battles, few men were involved. There was no doubt after this about the capabilities of Colt revolvers.

Word of the battle evidently spread rapidly, considering the limited communications of the day. There was great interest in San Antonio when Hays returned. Mary Maverick described how Hays visited her and told of the battle. She was the only one who put a specific date on the fight — June 8. Her version, in her memoirs, agrees fairly well with other accounts, though she talks about six-shooters.[32]

T. G. Western talked about the fight in a letter to Sam Houston, dated June 16, the day Hays wrote his report. From details in his letter he had spoken either with Hays or members of the patrol. Since he suggested that the Indians had cut the Ranger trail, he could only have gotten this information from a participant and not from reading the report.[33]

A correspondent was in San Antonio and claimed to have been given a lengthy description of the encounter. On June 29 the *Morning Star* in Houston published a complete story. This version is in agreement with most accounts and goes into full detail, which Hays's report does not. It is much like slightly later accounts based on eyewitness versions, such as that of Samuel Reid,[34] who would chronicle Ranger history in the Mexican War. The only feature of the newspaper account that is open to question is the range at which Gillespie killed the chief. It is likely that most fighting was at eight or ten paces, even closer, but highly unlikely that Gillespie fired at only thirty paces. The Comanche bows could easily cover thirty paces. Had they been that close, Gillespie would not have gotten off a shot, nor would the other Rangers have survived.

There are a few other accounts, though these were all written long after the event and did not influence the use of repeating arms. J. H. Jenkins told of hearing about the fight from Rufus Perry, a member of the Ranger company and supposedly in the fight. There are some variations in Perry's recollection and other versions. Time can do this to the best of memories. His version is the only one that states: "Here Colt's five-shooter was first used."[35]

Another supposedly eyewitness version has many details but claims the Rangers fought 200 Indians. This is a case where time makes a good story better. None of this is really of great moment, other than to historians and those who delight in catching them in error. The fight did take place, with results generally as described. There was a victory, though not without considerable injury, and the repeating pistol became a part of Ranger equipment.

There must have been a concerted effort to buy any Colt revolvers available, but there are no definite accounts of who was selling how many or at what cost. The cost, probably, was whatever the buyer could afford. At any rate, by November 1844, when an inventory of all Texas arsenals was published, not a single Patent Arms weapon was listed on hand. There were all varieties of small arms, numerous land and naval cannon, but not a single Colt.[36]

Walker Creek did not stop Indian raids, nor eliminate the danger of Mexican invasion. Soon after the battle, in August, Hays reported he was keeping an eye on a force across the river that could contain 600 men. He was using spies to track the enemy. A Mexican attack was a constant threat, while Comanche raids were an endless occurrence.

Interestingly enough, the Mexicans were having their own problems with Comanche raids. On March 20, 1845, *Semanario Político del Gobierno de Nuevo León* reported that the incursions of wild Indians were hampering the reconquest of Texas. The paper suggested the "perfidious Texans" were behind the raids. This showed the willingness on each side to blame the other for Indian attacks and marked the further growth of mutual hatred. The feeling was so intense and the perceived danger so real, the Texas Congress managed to keep the Rangers on duty during the remainder of 1844 and well into the next year.

Fortunately, a few muster rolls of this command survived fires and the years. For the period June 27 to October 28, 1844, Hays is shown as captain, with Ben McCulloch as lieutenant. There were forty-eight names in all, including that of Sam Walker. Hays received $75 a month; McCulloch was paid $50. Privates drew $30.[37] These were good wages for the day, and the Rangers worked hard and suffered greatly in earning them.

One example of patrol life on the frontier shows the kind of men who made up the early Rangers. They were very tough and not always heroic. In August 1844, Hays sent a four-man patrol to check on rumors that Mexicans were stealing horses along Turkey Creek between the Rio Grande and the Nueces. Rufus Perry was in charge and had ordered the others to go ahead and select a campsite on high grounds, where they could have a commanding view. As Perry was riding along, checking the trails, he discovered he was being followed. When he reached camp, he found the others had camped along the river bank, in brush country. Before he could move, they were attacked by a large force of Indians. Two of the men had undressed for a swim. The Rangers fired and scattered.

Hit by an arrow, Perry still drew his five-shooter and got off a few rounds but was hit again. Somehow he managed to get to the river and was joined by the two naked members of his patrol, who had lost everything but their horses. Shortly they were found by the fourth man, Kit Acklin. He asked the two mounted men to take Perry up on one of the horses and head for San Antonio, but they refused. Perry had been hit by several arrows and appeared dead, or about to die. They argued he would only hold them back. The two dismounted and took his shoes and weapon and rode off, leaving Acklin with the body.

Another Indian charge caused Acklin to run, but the supposedly dead Perry sat up and managed to hide in the dense brush. For some reason the Indians did not push into the thicket, maybe thinking he was armed and would die anyway. Perry did not die. He managed to stop the bleeding by packing moss and dirt in his wounds. He walked and crawled for 120 miles to San Antonio, reaching the town on the seventh night of his ordeal. He had lived on a few mesquite beans and some prickly pear apples. It took him three months to recover, but he would live to fight again.

Acklin also walked back to San Antonio. Though not wounded in the fight, he took two weeks to recover. The other two had horses, but the long ride, naked, without food, under the hot August sun, burned them to a crisp. They were berated by Hays and the San Antonio citizens for abandoning their comrades, but evidently received no other punishment.[38]

The two men who ran were not cowards. Both had served with distinction in numerous battles and one would go on to serve in the Confederate army — and die in combat. It was a very rough era, and then, as always, today's hero could be tomorrow's coward.

The company was still active a year later. The last surviving muster roll, August–September of 1845, shows about the same enlisted ranks. Walker is still a private, but McCulloch is no longer with the command. R. A. Gillespie is listed as lieutenant.[39]

Events taking place far from the frontier would soon change the company into a regiment.

John Coffee Hays became a legend in a few years. The overworked phrase "born leader" comes to mind, but he was no more that than others so classed. Jack Hays had the gift and worked at it. First, he was available, while some others, who had served earlier and with distinction, had to worry about families. He liked the wild life and had the will to be a leader. Hays was not a commanding figure. At five feet eight and perhaps 150 pounds he certainly did not lead by presence. He was undoubtedly brave, or controlled his fear, which is much the same. He was able to adapt to frontier fighting and learned his lessons well, from both Comanche and Mexican raiders.

Early on, he understood the necessity for discipline in the Rangers. This was not the drill-ground obedience of a regular army command, but the unquestioned obedience of a battlefield command. The men who began to make up the bulk of the Rangers understood that orders given by a competent leader were the difference between success and failure, living or dying. This had nothing to do with dressing, camp living, or how they talked to each other when not fighting.

Hays must have been involved in more fights than have been documented. Several battles are generally accepted as having taken place, as more than one person made mention of them. He could not have molded his reputation on the few scouts and fights that can be proven by combat reports. Certainly by 1845, when Texas was going into the Union, Hays was the best known Indian fighter in the Republic. He was not only the senior company commander, but the commander of the Southwest frontier.

Hays had another leadership quality: the ability to work with diverse groups. During the early periods, the new settlers from the States and the native-born Mexicans worked well together. Unfortunately, this has been forgotten to a large degree. Most of the immigrants settled land away from the few Mexican towns and had little contact with the original inhabitants. When the American Texans began to come to San Antonio after independence, they had their first extensive contact with the *tejanos*. Hays worked closely with them, as he needed men and they were superb horsemen who knew the country.

When Hays went south after bandits who were robbing on the San Antonio–Laredo road, he took with him thirteen Mexicans commanded by Capt. Antonio Perez. Hays, incidentally, took only twelve Rangers. Perez and his men performed well. Later, at Sabinal Canyon, in an Indian fight, Hays again had more Mexicans from San Antonio than he had Anglos. He also used friendly Lipan Indians as scouts and fighters.[40]

This cooperative spirit began changing, very gradually, in 1840–1841. Antonio Canales started an aggressive raiding campaign into Texas. Various incidents showed that the Mexicans were encouraging Indian raids. One of the causes of the break was an unfortunate series of events involving a prominent family in San Antonio. The Seguins, father and son, played a distinguished role in early Texas, supporting Anglo immigration, fighting an oppressive Mexican government, and taking a major role in fighting during the revolution. Appreciative citizens of Walnut Springs changed the name of their settlement to Seguin, which it bears to this day.[41]

In January 1841, the son, Juan Seguin, was elected mayor of San Antonio. Some jealousy and a degree of dissatisfaction among some citizens was created by this honor. Still, he was popular enough to be reelected in 1842, but opposition to his tenure had grown. There was some dispute about property and land. Seguin finally resigned and went to Mexico, and from then on his story is unclear. He said Santa Anna gave him an option of prison or joining Mexican forces. When next he was in San Antonio, it was as part of Woll's invading force. However he may have been coerced, even his old supporters now considered him a traitor. He returned to Mexico and would be a prime target for revenge-seeking Rangers during the Mexican War.

Two invasions of Texas led to a counterinvasion of Mexico, the abortive Somervell Expedition. Led by Alexander Somervell, a considerable force of Texans captured Laredo and Guerrero and went on downriver to Mier. Here the command began to break up. The leader saw the expedition could not really accomplish anything, and the experienced men such as Hays and McCulloch turned back. Some refused to return and vowed to capture Mier. They crossed the Rio Grande and fought a considerable Mexican force in the town for two days. Casualty reports cannot be trusted, but the Texas rifles must have taken quite a toll. The Mexicans gave the Texans the chance to surrender, which they did.

Then began the terrible ordeal of the Mier prisoners. After a long march, the surviving Texans were quartered near a *rancho,* called Salado, where they escaped on February 11, 1843. It was nearly impossible for them to get back to Texas from deep in Mexico. Four did manage to return, but the rest were eventually recaptured. Santa Anna ordered their execution, but the governor of Coahuila, Francisco Mexia, refused. A compromise came in the form of the old Roman decimation. Every tenth man, who drew a black bean from a pot, was shot in the back.

The survivors were sent on to Perote Castle, where they were kept, along with the survivors of the Santa Fe Expedition, until they were gradually released. The last was set free on September 16, 1844. The horror tales of their captivity and the execution of the "black bean" holders had a great deal to do with changing attitudes among the new and old Texans. A number of the Mier prisoners would serve during the coming war. Men who had lost relatives and friends on raids across the Rio Grande would be in the war. The earlier cooperative spirit was gone.[42]

Hays still used native *tejanos* as spies in checking on Mexican troop movements, but there were no longer large contingents of San Antonio men on his scouts. He and the other Rangers, or mounted gunmen, were probably too busy to worry about changing conditions in the Republic.[43] Nor did they likely spend much time thinking about the changing conditions that were moving the Lone Star into the Stars and Stripes of the United States. Annexation and war were ahead. The Texans were ready, with a large number of skilled horsemen who were accustomed to outdoor living and familiar with weapons, and they had a lean, mean motivation that other volunteers would lack. The war ahead was not a patriotic event to them — it was personal.

TWO

First Service

There had been a strong annexation movement in Texas from very early days. Still, the sentiment for annexation in the States was divided. The various moves and countermoves for Texas to join the Union and the efforts to block this action are not part of this narrative. Suffice it to say that by 1845 most people agreed that the joining of the two countries would happen. It was also generally accepted that such a move could lead to war with Mexico.[1]

In order to be prepared for such an eventuality, the U.S. government began shifting forces to meet a possible attack. A large portion of the regular army was concentrated at Fort Jessup in western Louisiana. Commanding this provisional force was Col. Zachary Taylor, 6th Infantry.[2]

Taylor was selected partially because of geography. He was nearest to the scene and was the senior officer in the area. Also, he had a good record as a soldier. It had been a long time since he had commanded any sizable force; nor had any other American commander. The forces used in the Seminole War of the 1830s had been more detachments than commands. By June 1845, Taylor had the 3rd Infantry, eight companies of the 4th Infantry, and seven companies of the 2nd Dragoons — the largest American force since the War of 1812. On June 15 he was ordered to New Orleans and then to Texas.[3]

By July, Taylor had reached Corpus Christi and set up a camp with about 1,290 troops. The place was little more than a dot on a map, a sandy beach area facing the Gulf of Mexico. Offshore were islands of sand stretching as far south as the eye could see. Inland was a dense brushy area called the chaparral, an area that ranged from difficult to impossible for travel.

On August 6, 1845, the adjutant general wrote Taylor and told him to contact the Texas authorities and see what local forces could be raised. This was merely exploratory, as the adjutant general cautioned there were no provisions for paying any Texas troops yet. The units would be organized and mustered into service only to help repel invasion.[4]

In the meantime, additional American units kept arriving to reinforce the little army. Seven companies of the 7th Infantry and two volunteer artillery companies from New Orleans arrived in camp, as well as some Texas mounted men, but Taylor could not accept the volunteers. At the time, he probably did not see any need for volunteers, and the officers of his command were against the idea.

The enlisted men in the regular army were heavily foreign-born, as native Americans had an aversion to service during peacetime. The officers, however, were an exceptional group, especially the company-grade officers.[5] A markedly high percentage were graduates of the Military Academy, trained in the most current military tactics. They were the lieutenants and captains who would command the armies of the Civil War. Now, they set about drilling the units making up the American army, worrying that they would not be able to finish the war before a horde of lowly volunteers filled the ranks and casting disparaging remarks about their rather nondescript commander.[6]

The young company-grade regulars looked on war as their special preserve and did not want a lot of volunteers to spoil the game before they could defeat the enemy. Some wrote down their views on the volunteers in diaries or letters. George B. McClellan had nothing but pity for the poor volunteers at first, as they had exceedingly high sickness rates. Later, he found other excesses: "You never hear of a Mexican being murdered by a regular or a regular by a Mexican. The volunteers carry on in a most shameful and disgraceful manner. They think nothing of robbing and killing the Mexicans."[7]

Young George Gordon Meade was even more outspoken, castigating the volunteers for every form of excess, especially their lack of discipline and the almost complete lack of control by their officers.[8]

All of this was true, but it was the system and not the volunteers that was at fault, and it would take another war or so to find the solution.

And as is often the case, McClellan and others saw things as they wished to see them. His suggestion that the regulars fought one war and the volunteers another is false. There was a war going on, and the Mexicans did not make these subtle distinctions. Their country was being invaded, and they fought the invaders with any weapon or tactic they could find. The Texans knew there was a war in progress, a continuation of one they had been fighting for a decade. There were few rules to the game, other than survival.

So, whether the regulars liked it or not, they would have to have the volunteers, and they came by the hundreds and thousands. Although they caused a lot of trouble, they also fought well. The Rangers attracted a lot of attention, for many reasons, and they received much praise and a lot of blame. At the time, all they were interested in was fighting.

Taylor received another message from the adjutant general written on August 30, gently chiding him for not writing more often and stressing the need for communicating regularly. Included was a mission-type directive giving Taylor authority to take any action necessary to repel invasion or attempted invasion.[9]

If he had not been keeping Washington informed, he was at least communicating with the Texas government. On August 16 he wrote Anson Jones, president of Texas, stating his willingness to keep the volunteers, or spies, now in service and offered to muster them into Federal service at the wages Texas was paying.[10] He must have heard about the constant Indian raids and the possibilities of Mexican raids. It was the beginning of an on-and-off policy that would last the war.

A few weeks later, September 6, Taylor wrote saying he doubted the possibility of war.[11] An agent had returned from Matamoros and reported everything was quiet in that town and along the border.

By September 14, he was changing again, maybe to mollify President Jones and to hedge his bets. Taylor informed the adjutant general that he had received some more Dragoons and didn't think he would need any mounted units from Texas. However, he continued, since he had asked Jones about troops, he would muster in a "few companies of rangers, amounting in all to about 300 men, as proper to be mustered into the service for the protection of the frontier." He went on to state he didn't really need them but would keep them as a matter of policy for three months. He concluded: "The commander of the rangers at San Antonio, Major Hays, has reputation as a partisan."[12]

The Texans were chomping at the bit. Hays's old company was out of service, but other Ranger units were formed to meet Taylor's call. Richard A. Gillespie organized a company in San Antonio, the Texas Mounted Rangers, and they were mustered into service on September 28, 1845.[13] He evidently picked up a number of men from the old company. Michael Chevallie was first lieutenant, and Sam Walker was one of the privates. This company was in Federal service, defending the frontier.

Another unit that would serve with distinction was formed from Victoria and Goliad counties. John T. Price was captain, with four sergeants, four corporals, a bugler, and sixty-four privates.[14] This unit was mustered in several days before Gillespie's company.

For the time being, these companies stayed in place, ready to protect the frontier. The two countries were neither at war nor quite at peace. Gradually, most of the regular army was concentrated in Taylor's camp on the Gulf Coast of Texas. He has been severely castigated by modern writers for not doing more during this period of several months at the end of 1845. Actually, checking contemporary accounts, considerable drilling was done up to the regimental level.[15] The troops, huddled in a tent camp, were subjected to a miserable fall and winter, with heavy rains. Insects were bothersome; illness began to plague the command. When the campaign finally ended, battle casualties would be moderate, but sickness would cause astounding death rates.

Shortly into the new year, on January 13, 1846, the adjutant general sent Taylor a copy of a letter that had been sent to the new governor of Texas, J. Pinckney Henderson, stating that Texas could now be called upon to fill quotas for troops for Federal service. Since the former Republic was now fully incorporated into the Union, there were no longer any legalities to prohibit Federal mustering of Texas troops.[16]

On February 2, Taylor received orders to move to the Rio Grande. It took until the twenty-fourth for the command to actually start marching. The move was welcomed by the troops; anything was better than the confining camp between the Gulf and the dense, inland chaparral thicket. The army marched by easy stages and encountered the enemy on March 21, 1846, at a stream crossing.

As the advance guard came to the bank, they saw Mexican troops on the south side. They were told there would be a fight if the Americans tried to cross. This was Taylor's forte — a fight, *any* fight. He galloped up, brought some artillery, deployed his advance, and ordered them into the water. The troops cheered and advanced. The Mexican troopers watched for a moment and vanished.[17] The first encounter of the war ended in nothing, but it cheered everyone. Perhaps, they thought, there would be a fight after all.

The army continued south toward Matamoros, about thirty miles away. On March 28 Taylor was in sight of the Mexican town, their first objective.[18] He had less than 3,000 men. His infantry regiments, the bulk of his army, were highly trained and commanded by excellent officers; his cavalry was exercised in European tactics. However, the horses were not accustomed to the climate and the officers and men had no experience in partisan warfare. Taylor did have an ace-in-the-hole with his artillery. While he had a few heavy caliber guns, most of his artillery was small-bore, mounted on special carriages. The crews all rode and had been trained to move and fire in a most original manner by Maj. Sam Ringgold. They were literally "flying artillery."[19]

The army was about to face a new form of combat.

The same day they reached Matamoros, the terms of enlistment of several of the Texas Ranger companies expired. Sam Walker and others headed south for the Rio Grande and a chance at fighting. A considerable number of footloose Texans followed the army. Some, like George Washington Trahern, were making a living of sorts catching wild cattle for the army, acting as mule drivers, helping with pack trains — anything to eat and live, or maybe get in on a fight.[20]

Taylor had resisted signing on any Texans earlier, but he gave Walker authority to raise a company. On April 21, 1846, Walker's company was mustered into Federal service, with J. P. Wells as first lieutenant. It was a large company — ninety-one privates — gathered from men at Corpus Christi and Point Isabel. The term of enlistment was three months.[21]

Samuel Walker had been a member of two of Hays's Ranger companies. Before the Walker Creek incident, he had considerable service. He had fought in the regular army during the Seminole War and was evidently familiar with the supply system. Walker had written a monograph on the command and commanders in the war and was a trained soldier before he became a partisan and frontier Indian fighter.[22] During 1842 he served in the fighting against the Mexican invasion of

Texas and went on to join the expedition to take Mier. Unlike Hays and McCulloch, Walker stayed and became a prisoner in Mexico. He was released in 1843 and returned as another man seeking vengeance.

He must have had something more than casual contact with Taylor for the general to authorize him to raise a company. Taylor had heard of Hays, but he could not have known Walker. At any rate, he did authorize the new company, and Walker went to work on the depot at Point Isabel.

On April 20, the day before his company was officially mustered into Federal service, Walker drew thirty-two Colt revolvers with accessories, eight Hall carbines, and six North rifles.[23] Probably buried somewhere in the National Archives are the issue slips for these. Fortunately, Walker, with his military training, kept copies of his turn-ins, and they remain today in his papers at the Texas State Library. He didn't stop with weapons; he got axes, shovels, halters, blankets, percussion caps, forty pounds of lead, even several tents. He drew property on April 22, April 29, and as late as early May, when he got eight bridles, eight martingales, and a surcingle. Walker signed these slips as captain of the Mounted Rangers, and the slips usually show the unit as Texas Mounted Rangers.

Besides giving an idea of how units were equipped, these documents throw light on the arming of the Rangers. Many contemporary writers speak of the Texans as having a variety of arms: a rifle and several pistols, usually two Colts. Obviously, this is not true. Perhaps there were *some* Texans who had two Colts, but this was rare. Most did not have even one revolver. If every pistol Colt had manufactured had come to Texas, it would not have been enough to arm each Ranger who served in the various companies. Walker probably drew all the Colts on hand and issued them to his men. He had seen what the new weapons could do in battle. Most of the men had their own rifles and horses. He evidently drew the best long arms in the depot for men who did not have rifles, or had poor weapons. One interesting fact should be noted: *none* of the Colts were turned in, and one lieutenant was charged with two when he was mustered out.[24]

The situation of neither war nor peace was continuing. Earlier, on March 29, Taylor had decided on the construction of a large, bastioned fort opposite Matamoros, as the Mexicans had cannon implaced south of the river and he wanted some secure base if he moved his camp opposite the city.[25] His main depot was at Point Isabel on the Gulf, a good distance away. With a fort, he could move his field forces as necessary and still have a strong anchor to fall back on. Work began at once, with the infantry regiments taking their turn as pioneers.[26]

South of the Rio Grande, a change had taken place in the Mexican army. Gen. Mariano Arista had assumed command of the forces around Matamoros, some 5,000 in all, with 1,600 lancers under Anastasio Torrejón. These two commanders were skilled and aggressive; the peaceful days were over. Arista sent Taylor a note informing him that hostilities had commenced, and he dispatched Torrejón and his horsemen across the river.[27]

Taylor learned of the crossing and sent out a party of Dragoons under Capt. Seth Thornton to locate the lancers. The American detachment had a Mexican guide and rode through the trails in the dense undergrowth for some twenty-five miles. The guide, either too frightened to go further or finished with his job, then left. Thornton and his men believed they were a match for any number of horsemen in the world and continued to a ranch on the river. Having dismounted, they were checking the buildings when the lancers attacked, opening fire from the chaparral. Mounting again, the Dragoons tried to charge, but the muddy grounds slowed them. They tried to reach the river but were turned back. Thornton was wounded and sixteen Dragoons were killed; the rest surrendered.

Two days later, Taylor wrote the adjutant general, describing the incident.[28] He continued: "Hostilities may now be considered as commenced, and I have this day deemed it necessary to call upon the governor of Texas for four regiments of volunteers, two to be mounted and two to serve as foot. As some delay must occur in collecting these troops, I have also desired the governor of Louisiana to send out four regiments of infantry as soon as possible." It had taken a few rounds to change the old general's mind on volunteers.

In the meantime, Torrejón's lancers and guerrillas were roaming the American side of the Rio Grande. Walker had split his command into three detachments and was out most of the time scouring the chaparral. He went out on April 27, leaving a fifteen-man detachment in camp. Early the next day a large force surprised the fifteen men and overran the camp.

George Trahern told about it years later: "We didn't apprehend any danger, but they attacked us and we just jumped for our guns. We hadn't pulled off any of our clothes, just our boots and shoes . . ."

Trahern was not a former Ranger, but he had spent a lot of his young years chasing cattle in the South Texas brush and was not the kind to be taken easily. He and a friend grabbed their weapons and slid into the thicket. The little camp was in a state of confusion: yelling, cursing, screams of pain, horses running wild, and shots could be heard. He continued: "So I had my five-shooter with me, and I went out and got in the thicket."[29]

As he recalled, it was no great thing. Trahern thought he was the only one left alive, and all he was concerned about was staying hid until he could get to some careless Mexican with a good horse. He described how he could hear the jubilant Mexican lancers stripping the camp, noting with wry satisfaction they didn't have much to steal. He had several narrow escapes and twice almost caught a Mexican off guard. Finally he worked his way back to the main force and found that four others had escaped. Six were dead, and four were prisoners. The latter were fortunate; it was early in the war, and they were exchanged.

Although the overruning of the camp was a major embarrassment, it did not seriously affect the performance of the Rangers. No one ever completely agreed on what happened, but there was definitely some failure in security. One version has it that the lancers followed the pickets into camp at dawn and surprised the camp. Taylor, in a report on May 3, mentions the overruning of the Texas camp and states the men were careless. Had those who had left "obeyed the instructions of the captain, a tried frontier soldier, they would never have met such a disaster."[30]

Evidently, the incident did not undermine Taylor's confidence in Walker. In the same report he describes how difficult it was to get an idea of the enemy because of the nature of the country and the lack of light troops. He goes on to tell how the Rangers had been scouting and discovered the enemy on the road and engaged them on May 2.

Others in the army were noticing the Texans. Capt. W. S. Henry mentioned the arrival of Walker and the formation of his company. Henry described the April 28 attack on the Ranger camp and thought that five men were killed and four were missing.[31] During the next few weeks his recollections would contain numerous references to the Texans.

Volunteer units were arriving in camp, but the Texans were a breed apart. They signed on with whatever they were wearing and stayed that way. Mostly they had their own arms, though Walker was not above supplementing private arms with whatever the depot could supply. They had their own horses, and from the first days began to demonstrate their own brand of mounted skills. They were not shy about showing how well they could ride.

One of the young men with Walker put on a show one day. Riding at full gallop, he leaned down from the saddle and picked up three coins from the ground as he dashed along. It was the first of many such exhibitions. Young Trahern, during the course of his service, often showed other mounted troops how the Texans rode and even explained why they were so good. Part of it was their heavy bits, which enabled them to control their mounts with one hand while riding at a dead run.[32]

The Texans had been receiving instruction in horsemanship from skilled instructors in a very harsh academy. By now, they had developed their own brand of riding based on what the Comanches and raiding Mexicans had shown them. These two were among the best in the world; if you failed an examination in their school it usually cost you your life. The Texans had one advantage: their horses. They stuck to their big thoroughbreds and crosses, which by now were accustomed to the climate.

John S. Ford, writing in the 1880s, says the Texans were unlike contemporary cowboys and few people then alive knew what the Rangers of the 1840s looked like.[33] Very little actual gear from the period has survived, and the men who left diaries and memoirs make almost no mention of clothing or equipment. There is one account of their saddles, which are described much like Indian saddles.[34]

A few artists of the day gave some idea of what these men wore and the saddles and equipment they used. Most of these painted trappers and Western types, but one actually was in Texas for a time during the Revolution and was personally acquainted with equipment in use during the 1840s. William T. Ranney painted a number of scenes of trappers and scouts during the 1840s and 1850s, using gear he brought back from Texas. The chief difference between the old and later saddles is in the much lower saddle horn of the 1840s. At that early date working with cattle was not so prevalent, so there was no need for the special horn of the 1870s. A common practice was to spread a skin or a blanket over the saddle to soften the ride.[35]

These paintings also show some version of Ranger dress, though most of the figures are dressed in buckskin. While common in the Republic, buckskin had gone out of favor by the late 1840s. It was not a good material for summer use. The frequent red flannel shirts depicted by Ranney and other artists were certainly in wide use, continuing into the Civil War. Interestingly, Ranney also depicted most rifles as flintlocks.

There was more to the Rangers than trick riding and wild yells. An event that would make the Texans and Walker nationally known was in the making. Taylor had been before Matamoros for some time and had to return to Point Isabel to replenish his supplies. On May 1, 1846, the United States Army fell back toward the coast, leaving the 7th Infantry to hold the nearly completed earthwork. They were not far down the road before Fort Texas was under siege.[36]

On May 2 the garrison worked to complete the fort while watching the preparations taking place across the river in Matamoros. There was no doubt that the Mexicans were going to attack the fort. What they could not see was the deployment of the Mexican forces on their side of the river. That day, the main Mexican infantry force crossed the Rio Grande and cut the road between the fort and Point Isabel, too late to cut off Taylor. From the signs, the Mexicans knew the Americans had passed, and they took positions to block their return. The next day the siege began with a steady bombardment, answered by the cannon in the fort. The firing could be heard in Point Isabel.[37]

Taylor was in a quandary. If he marched before his troops had been resupplied, there would be unnecessary risk. Should he wait too long, the fort might be taken. The key to the puzzle was the condition of the fort and the garrison. Could they hold out? There was no easy answer. The Mexican lancers were combing the brush, controlling the only road. If he sent his entire mounted force, it was doubtful they could cut their way to the fort.

He decided to try. By now it was May 4, and the dull booming of the cannons had not stopped. There was great concern about how much longer the garrison could hold out under such punishment. He sent out a squadron of Dragoons, but they never got through and returned without any information on the defenders. On May 5 he reported the unsuccessful mission and added that a party of Rangers under Walker had gotten through and returned with news that the garrison could hold out.[38]

A brief mention in an official report cannot begin to describe what must have happened. Walker and six men had gone toward the fort with an escort of Dragoons, who halted at the edge of the chaparral. The Texans went on. This was their game. Major Brown, commanding the fort, reported that Walker slipped inside the walls at between 2:00 and 3:00 in the morning, leaving at about 4:00.[39] He returned at reveille. Evidently, he had been scouting outside. With assurances that the garrison was in good shape and would not be starved out or blown away, he started back toward Point Isabel.

Despite the constant bombardment, the defenders had suffered only one death. Walker was convinced they would hold out. All he had to do was get through to Taylor. No one left any records of what happened. The only written record is a turn-in for lost property, the various supplies and arms lost when his camp was overrun on April 28 and a carbine lost "unavoidably in swimming the Lake while carrying Express from Fort Brown."[40]

Sam Walker became the first hero of the war. He was Western and fit the popular concept of the lone American facing terrible odds. The novels of James Fenimore Cooper had prepared the way, as well as the stories of the Western explorers, from Lewis and Clark to the more recent Fremont. The time was ripe and Walker and the Texans became the favorites of the day. His name traveled across the country in a remarkably short time. There was even a play on the New York stage extolling his deeds. When correspondents began following the army, they would add to the fame of the Rangers. A short time later, when Walker lost his horse, citizens of New Orleans sent him a replacement mount as a gesture of their admiration.[41]

Taylor must have been even more impressed with the young captain of the Rangers. In June 1846, when openings for captains in the newly formed Regiment of Mounted Riflemen were being considered, Sam Walker was selected to be commander of Company C. The wild volunteer had finally become a captain in the regular army. As might be expected, this surprising move met with a cry of outrage by numerous company-grade West Point graduates, who signed an indignant letter of protest. The letter would somehow end up in the Walker Papers.

There is more to the incident, a further intertwining of the major players in this story. Walker did not immediately accept the appointment, and his refusal must have been mentioned in the press. Sam Colt noticed the seeming refusal and wrote at least two letters asking for the appointment.[42] The matter was resolved and Walker did accept; however, he stayed in his position as company commander of Rangers, for there was a war where he was.

Taylor started back on May 7 and encountered the Mexican force across his path at Palo Alto. For some unexplained reason, Arista allowed the American force to deploy. He had a lancer force half the size of the entire force Taylor commanded. His cavalry could have created a great deal of damage, possibly prevented the Americans from deploying. Neither the horsemen nor the implaced infantry made a move, while Taylor almost leisurely prepared for combat. The Americans refilled their canteens, selected position, forced their way through brush and high grass, and made ready their artillery.[43]

In the end, it would be the new tactical system developed by Maj. Sam Ringgold that would decide the battle. Palo Alto was a forerunner of the open-field battles of the northern campaign. The highly maneuverable batteries moved about the field, engaging the enemy at critical locations, tearing the enemy infantry formations to pieces with canister. For almost two hours the Mexican infantry was held in position while the American batteries moved close and cut the packed lines into shreds.

After an hour, Arista turned the lancers loose and they charged down on the 5th Infantry, formed in square. These were well-trained and well-led, and no cavalry could ever beat infantry under these conditions. The 5th waited until the lancers were at point-blank range and opened fire. Shattered, the lancers fell back and came under fire from two guns that had come up to aid the infantrymen. This further smashed the horsemen, and they retreated, this time for good.

There would be more fighting, but the little six-pounders seemed to be all over the field, while the big eighteen-pounders in the American line continued to batter the enemy infantry. Ringgold was mortally wounded late in the battle, but the day was won. The fight gradually stopped about dusk.

Taylor would be criticized for not pursuing, but he had a huge wagon train and all his supplies to consider. He did not have enough cavalry to mount an effective pursuit, and they were not suited for the terrain. The next day, early, Walker and his Rangers and the Dragoons confirmed that the Mexican army had retreated.[44] It was the first of Taylor's victories.

Arista fell back to a better defensive position, based on one of the old cutoffs of the Rio Grande — a *resaca,* or ravine. He considerably outnumbered Taylor, as neither army had suffered heavy casualties. Some of Taylor's staff officers were dubious about attacking such a strong position, but the old general seemed to think the best way to move was to go ahead. The Americans deployed again and attacked the

Mexican forces. Again, it was a difficult advance, moving through shoulder-high grass, through sand, and across ravines, with cannonballs plunging the earth.

The Mexican center was their strong point, with their best infantry and a well-served group of guns. Charles May and his Dragoons charged the center and overran the artillery. By the time they had their mounts under control, the Mexicans had reformed and were again firing on the American infantry. Among that infantry were junior officers who would become Civil War generals. At the time, all they could think about was staying alive and moving their men forward.

These were the best infantry in the Mexican army, and the fighting about the guns came down to a bayonet fight. Very slowly the enemy center began to fall back. Then the men, instead of making an orderly retreat, turned and ran. Arista made an attempt to rally his lancers; then he ran.

This time there was plenty of light, and the Americans began a vigorous pursuit. They were yelling and screaming, firing, rushing to the river bank. The Mexican infantrymen jumped into the water and tried to swim to the opposite bank. Hundreds drowned or were shot. The battle ended in a complete rout. It was Taylor's second victory, more decisive than the first; between them he was a national hero. The actions gained him a brevet promotion to major general.

There is no clear indication what Walker and his men did during the two battles.[45] They were busy enough afterward. Taylor reported that he sent light infantry companies across the river, along with mounted volunteers — the Rangers — and some regular cavalry to scout toward Matamoros.[46] The enemy had certainly fallen back on the city and perhaps into the interior. Taylor turned down Arista's request for an armistice and began moving his army across the Rio Grande. He occupied Matamoros without incident. The only Mexican troops were 400 wounded in makeshift hospitals. The Americans assumed the care of these troops.

By May 20, Taylor was complaining that only Price's company of Rangers had reached him in answer to his call for four Texas regiments.[47] This company had been protecting the Victoria area and hurried to the army when his call went out for Texas troops. Among other matters, Taylor complained that the volunteer units now coming in had exhausted the supply of tents. The next day, May 21, he reported he had dispatched his cavalry, regular and volunteer, after the enemy, under the command of Lt. Col. John Garland. Several days later, he reported they had returned with no sign of the enemy and with exhausted mounts.[48]

Though no one ever described all that must have happened, there was more to the story. Again, Captain Henry had a few more details, almost diary-like entries.[49] He noted that Walker and the Dragoons started on May 19 to check the retreating enemy. He says there were two Ranger companies, which means Capt. John T. Price and his men must have started on a mission as soon as they hit camp. The horsemen followed the retreating Mexican army for close to sixty miles and actually caught up to the rear guard. They were outnumbered and on tired mounts but engaged in a fire fight. Two of the Rangers were wounded before they broke off the pointless engagement. They had found out what they needed to know: the Mexican army was not making a stand at any point.

They returned to Matamoros, and most people believed the war, such as it had been, was over.[50]

THREE

★ ★ ★ ★ ★ ★ ★ ★ ★

The Regiments Form

War was a reality in May 1846, and Taylor again requested troops from Texas — and elsewhere. He was now dealing with a state, not an independent republic, and his message went to the new governor, J. Pinckney Henderson, on April 26, 1846. H. G. Catlett took the letter to Austin, his arrival being mentioned in the local papers in early May.[1]

When he asked Texas for two horse and two foot regiments, Taylor started a complicated chain of events. Much of the raising and planned raising of companies in the following months is of interest only to historians and people tracing ancestors. Henderson replied to Taylor, saying he doubted the state would support two infantry regiments, but he knew Texas could easily furnish forty companies of mounted men — four regiments.[2]

Not having been a state for any period of time, Texas did not have a militia organization as did the rest of the country. It was never formally established in the Republic, where the men nearest the scene of danger formed and fought. But now the militia concept had some decided advantages. The governor reasoned that four regiments equaled a small division (a proper command for a major general). Henderson figured that he was the logical man to command, complete with staff. Naturally, the papers, highly partisan, had a grand old time with this concept. One suggested that if Texas raised enough generals, they could fill at least one of the companies requested by Taylor!

None of this bothered the governor. He turned the state over to the lieutenant governor, A. C. Horton, and went off to war. He did all this as a major general of militia, not volunteers, a technicality that allowed him to go and take along a full staff. Mirabeau Buonaparte Lamar went as inspector, the senior staff member. Henry L. Kinney was division quartermaster, and Edward Burleson and Edward Clark were aides. So, a governor, a former president of Texas, and several distinguished citizens went off to fight — under highly questionable authority — and performed admirably.[3]

Normally, volunteer regiments were formed by calling the local militia companies into service. Since there was no militia system, the best that could be done was to place a company quota in the counties. This was spread about so that twenty companies would be raised, but it was not really that well planned. For example, Henderson, as he went south with his staff, ordered Hays to gather all the ex-Rangers he could and meet him at Point Isabel, which was designated the rendezvous point for the Texas companies.[4]

The governor did not know, or else forgot, that Hays and a lot of the former Rangers were already in Federal service from earlier calls. The Ranger leader, along with Michael Chevallie, had enlisted as privates to get on the rolls. They had to stay, guarding the frontier, until the enlistment was up. The rules were different now, with Uncle Sam saying who could be where, and with officers in volunteer units elected. Hays knew this, and his actions for the next few weeks showed a definite plan. He, Chevallie, and enough men to form a company rode south. This group was sworn into service on July 4, 1846, as Company B of the 1st Mounted Rifles.[5] Christopher B. Acklin was elected company commander. Hays and Chevallie were still privates, but it was a mere technicality, necessary to get them into service and eligible for election to senior ranks.

Meantime, other companies from the western part of the state had been formed. A company from Colorado County was mustered on June 10, to become Company E. Major General Henderson was doing some pretty keen bookkeeping to form his regiments. On July 11 another company arrived and was mustered in. This became Company F, with Frank S. Early commanding.[6]

When seven companies from the western counties had arrived and were mustered in, an election was held on June 22 to select regimental officers. It was no great surprise when Jack Hays was selected as colonel. Sam Walker was picked to serve as lieutenant colonel, and Michael Chevallie was major. The 1st Regiment, Texas Mounted Rifles, was officially in service, less three companies.[7] Some of the companies from the eastern counties were showing up at the rendezvous, but Henderson managed to keep them apart, rather than fill the missing units in the 1st. He did juggle some men and transferred a few, and on July 13 was able to organize Company H of the 1st.[8] This left Hays shy two companies, but they would be added to his regiment later.

One of these companies, subsequently mustered in as Company A, would have a distinguished history. It was already on the scene when the others started marching south. When the call came to form a company from Gonzales County, Ben McCulloch reversed the procedure a little and raised his own company, not waiting to be elected.[9] In thirty-six hours, he collected his men along the Guadalupe River and was on the way south. McCulloch was one of the most experienced frontier fighters in Texas, being a captain years before, and he had no trouble attracting experienced fighters.[10] The company was formed on May 11, was in San Patricio two days later, struck the coast below Corpus Christi and forded to Padre Island, then made the long trip down the island, reaching the tip of the sand pit on May 19. By May 23, the company was on the Rio Grande, where they were billeted near Walker and Price, near the recently named Fort Brown.[11]

They were the third Texas unit to reach the army, too late for the initial battles, but their turn would come. They attracted as much attention as had the earlier Ranger companies, and any doubt about the way the Texans dressed and operated was laid to rest. McCulloch's men were no different from the others. They began to give new meaning to the term "irregular." Fortunately, an outsider had joined McCulloch's company and recorded his experiences. Samuel Reid, a lawyer from Louisiana, became a Ranger in name and fact.

When McCulloch was assigned "quarters" under the walls of Fort Brown, it was little more than someone pointing to a spot on the ground. Reid picked up the story:

> Here we found Walker's and Price's companies of Rangers encamped, and here we *constructed* our tents for the present, — constructed, we say, because the government never furnished us, during our whole term of service, with a patch of canvas large enough to keep out a drop of rain, or shield us from a ray of the scorching sun. Whether it was because they thought the Texan troops were accus-

> tomed to, and could endure more hardships than any other troops in the field, we do not know. One thing is certain, they gave us as ample an opportunity to evince our greatest powers of endurance and fortitude as the disciples of Diogenes could have desired . . .[12]

In all fairness, it should be noted that not all Ranger companies lived like this. Walker had drawn some tents, though he didn't seem to use them. Taylor did make efforts to get tents to as many units as possible, especially in the 2nd Texas.[13] Walker, Price, and McCulloch were on the move most of the time; they would not have been able to use tents. Later, when two regiments of Rangers would be serving, they were often away from the base on scout, wagon escort, or courier duty, with little opportunity to use tents. Actually, Taylor *did* think they were hardy and could get by on little and so stated.[14]

Life in the Texas camps was informal, to say the least. Reid described one of his earlier experiences with his new companions: "While standing in the midst of a group, talking to the captain, a young fellow came into camp with a rifle on his shoulder, and a couple of ducks in his hands, and addressing the captain, said, 'Ben, if you haven't had dinner, you'd better mess with me, for I know none of the others have fresh grub today.' "[15]

This tells something of the rather informal mess arrangements, especially where the officers were concerned, and a lot about the first-name basis among officers and men in the same company. The companies were largely raised from one area, with the members knowing one another. This informality had nothing to do with discipline. A captain might tell a man to do something, using his first name, but the man would obey the order without question, using the captain's first name in reply. Casual was not the same as sloppy. Informal was not insubordinate — no matter what the regulars thought.

Much of the initial — and later — impression of the Rangers was caused by their clothing. It was next to impossible for trained, disciplined, *uniformed* troops to look at the men from Texas and see anything other than a mob. If there were sixty men in a company, there were sixty outfits. They wore civilian clothing that was comfortable, rough, able to take abuse. Reid could find nothing uniform, other than their slouch hats, which were broad-brimmed to shield against the Texas sun.[16] A lot of these had rounded crowns, though not all. Most of the men were bearded and had mustaches, even the young ones. That and a fine horse, a good rifle, and pistols (many with five-shooters) was the extent of their uniform. Volunteer regiments came to duty with a variety of uniforms. As these wore out, they were replaced with regular issue uniforms, though the volunteers did not always wish to give up their distinctive state uniforms. When the Ranger clothing wore out, they patched it some more and kept going.

One of the differences between the soldier of 1846, regular or volunteer, and today's soldier was in feeding. There was no regular mess, as the term is used today. Then, each company was given a certain number of rations — whatever food was available — and the men in the unit prepared it in whatever fashion they desired, or could manage. "Messes" usually consisted of four or more men, with one preparing the food for the day. Generally, the system worked well enough, if the quartermaster or commissary could provide the basic ration. For a large part of the time, the Ranger companies were on scout, and they bought what they could find along the way. McCulloch's men used their own funds, to some degree at least.[17] On other occasions, the army furnished one of the officers a sum of money to defray meal costs and forage for the horses.[18]

The system did not always work, even for other volunteer units. B. F. Scribner, in his *A Campaign in Mexico,* mentioned that his company messes got by in the earlier stages of the campaign by hunting cattle, fowl of all kinds, wolves, and snakes. He described one mess serving a seven-foot rattlesnake! Scribner was quite surprised to find out that other companies in his regiment were eating well from army rations.[19]

Ranger camp routine differed from the other units in the army. Scribner detailed his daily company activities. The men rose at daylight and had company and squad drill for two hours. Each day eight men and one noncommissioned officer (NCO) were detailed for guard duty. At 4:00 in the afternoon, they went through company drill, with regimental drill at 5:00. The time between morning and afternoon drill was for washing, cutting wood, possibly hunting game, and taking care of weapons and equipment.[20]

Like the rest of the army, the Rangers were up at daylight. The day started with groups taking the horses out to graze, if there was grass nearby. Often, they had to go a mile or more, and they went prepared. They always went fully armed, loosening saddle girths and slipping the bridles down about the necks of the horses. Each man had a *cabaristas,* a form of halter copied from the Mexicans. This was twenty to thirty feet long and gave each animal room to browse. Each Ranger kept the loose end of the rope in his hand while his horse looked for grass. With guards out, it was difficult to surprise or stampede the horses.[21]

There was no drill in the Ranger companies. Being cavalry, their "drill time" was devoted to care of their horses. They had the same need to keep as clean as possible, draw rations or buy food, gather wood, and patch their clothing, but the main part of the day was given over to grazing their mounts, grooming them, checking for worn shoes, hoof cuts, or anything that would impair the health of the animal — and ultimately their own.

Reid gave an account of a typical afternoon:

> Many of the men had just come in from grazing their horses, and were now occupied in grooming them; others were cooking over fires, and preparing supper. At sundown we were invited by our mess to take a cup of coffee, out of a tin pot, and reminded by them, after our hearty meal, that our *cook-day* would come on Monday. Rations of corn and oats were then served out for our horses — the guard was paraded, and the sentinels posted. It was a fine evening, and the Rangers sat round in groups listening to the song and stories of their comrades.[22]

The Texans provided their own entertainment, which was usually storytelling.[23] The state reputation for throwing the bull goes back to the beginning. However, the tall stories cut off early. By 9:00 the camp was quiet, the men asleep on their blankets. It didn't take them long to settle into a routine.

The three Ranger companies in the army were not figured in the quotas for Texas. The time of enlistment was about up for Walker and Price, and Taylor needed all the cavalry he could get. He must have been a happy man when McCulloch showed up with his men, and Taylor kept them apart from any regimental assignment for the time being. When Sam Walker heard about his election as lieutenant colonel of the new 1st Texas Mounted Rifles, he resigned his position as company commander and began clearing his property accounts. He signed his turn-in as lieutenant colonel and went to join his regiment and his old commander, Jack Hays. The first lieutenant of the company, J. P. Wells, became captain, with George Trahern as the new senior lieutenant, dating from June 30, 1846. It was little more than a courtesy appointment. The company was mustered out of service on July 16, when their enlistment was up.[24] One of the privates in the company was Mabry B. Gray, who would shortly reenter service and make a considerable, if not entirely praiseworthy, name for himself.

In the meantime, Capt. John T. Price had been busy. His enlistment was almost up, but his company escorted a battalion of the 1st Infantry to Reynosa and guarded the trains on the return. This regular command was led by Lt. Col. Henry Wilson, who would become well acquainted with the Rangers. Special Order 78, of June 4, 1846, directed this move, with Price returning a week later.[25] His company was mustered out of Federal service on June 25 at Matamoros.[26]

Taylor knew that considerable mounted reinforcements were on the way from Texas, but for a time he had McCulloch's company as his sole Ranger unit. Price had been called in from Victoria, and the area from there to Corpus Christi was unprotected. Taylor authorized another Texas company, apart from the two regiments. This outfit was formed on July 21 at Matamoros from recently discharged Texans, with Mabry B. Gray as captain. It had no numerical designation, being carried on the rolls as the Texas Mounted Volunteers.[27] They signed on for a year.

While out of chronological sequence, it is desirable to mention the last two companies in the 1st Texas before going on to the 2nd Texas. R. A. Gillespie had already formed a company largely from San Antonio. When the new call came, his company went through another reorganization and marched south, to Laredo, not to Point Isabel, as had all the others. They did not reach the army until August 30, mustering in at Camargo. [28]

The last company to join the 1st was formed around June 11 at Wheelock. They elected Eli Chandler as captain. An experienced Indian fighter, Chandler was probably the oldest man in the command at forty-six — a year over the enlistment limit. K Company, as it became, joined the army at China, Mexico, on August 30, though they were credited with service from July 18.[29]

So the 1st Texas, which, because of fate and experience of its commanders, would be the most famous of the Ranger units, was assembled in bits and pieces. They had an army organization chart for a volunteer regiment:[30]

1 Colonel
1 Lieutenant Colonel
1 Major
1 Adjutant — a lieutenant from one of the companies
1 Sergeant Major
1 Quarter Master Sergeant
2 Principal Musicians

10 companies, with:
1 Captain
1 First Lieutenant

2 Second Lieutenants
4 Sergeants
4 Corporals
2 Musicians
80 Privates

There were enlistment restrictions as well. No man over forty-five or under eighteen could be accepted, and all had to be in good health. A company was required to contain at least sixty-four effective men to be mustered into service.[31]

Naturally, it didn't always work out that way. Chandler was overage, and it is likely that a number of men listed their ages as eighteen on the muster rolls, when they were younger. One of Chandler's privates was forty-two; the youngest was eighteen. Five of the men were in their thirties; all the rest were in their twenties, mostly low twenties. It was a young regiment of officers, noncoms, and privates.

There were fewer men in the western counties, and the company strength reflected this. McCulloch had forty-one privates; B mustered sixty-two. Company C brought sixty-seven, while Chandler had only twenty-nine for a time.

Not much attention was paid to other ranks. Originally, Company A had four sergeants; Company D a first sergeant; and C Company carried four sergeants and four corporals. D Company showed up with everything: sergeants, corporals, and buglers.[32] Where they got bugles, if they had them, is a mystery.

Raising the second mounted regiment was easier in the more heavily populated eastern counties. As an example, George T. Wood raised a seventy-four-man company in one day! Most areas had no trouble in filling their quotas, and during May and early June the companies were forming and electing officers. By mid-June they were ready to start south for Point Isabel. Six of the companies marched pretty much together, with two others close behind, reaching the rendezvous a day after the others. Henderson and his staff were waiting. Taylor wrote on June 10 that the governor and "large numbers" had arrived.[33] Most of the entire regiment was assembled by June 25, 1846.

Regimental elections were held early in July, with George Wood selected as colonel. The lieutenant colonel position went to John E. Myrick, and William R. Scurry became major. There were the necessary elections to fill their vacated posts, and the regiment was mustered into service July 10, 1846.[34]

Historians have somewhat neglected Wood and his 2nd Texas,

since the 1st was commanded by Hays, with Walker, Chevallie, McCulloch, Gillespie — all famous names. In fact, it would be hard to find two more dissimilar commanders than Hays and Woods. Hays had grown up on the frontier and probably had his life savings in his saddlebags. Wood was a well-to-do plantation owner, active in politics, and a Texas senator.[35] He had, however, fought in one of the many Indian wars and was a company commander of a militia company when he was nineteen. Genteel background or not, he would serve well, as would his less celebrated Rangers. While the Texans from the eastern counties on the whole did not have the Indian fighting experience of many from the 1st, they were still outdoorsmen, farmers, good horsemen, and good riflemen.

James K. Holland, a lieutenant in the company commanded by his uncle, kept a diary, one of the few written accounts by a Ranger.[36] He reported that the good gentlemen of the more settled areas had a perfectly normal thirst and took joy in helping the soldiers along the way show their appreciation for their patriotic service. Some of the celebrants consumed huge amounts of whiskey, and it was fairly common to leave men behind when the column moved out each morning, most of whom managed to rejoin when they sobered up. Each settlement tried to show admiration for the heroes marching to war. These were the glory days, with banners, pretty girls, good food, and much whiskey. When they passed below the settlements and got into the brush, things began to change. By the time they reached Point Isabel, war did not seem so pleasant. Young Holland was not accustomed to the exposure and hardships of campaigning, but he reminded himself that he had come to "see the elephant."[37] They had come to fight.

One regiment of infantry was raised, commanded by Albert Sidney Johnston.[38] This unit also marched to the rendezvous point. It would not have a happy history.

FOUR

★ ★ ★ ★ ★ ★ ★ ★ ★

June 1846

The inactivity that followed the occupation of Matamoros ended in June. Taylor was receiving reinforcements in dribbles, and he knew the two mounted Texas regiments were on the way to meet him. But as June began all he had was three companies, two about to be discharged as their enlistment was up. This left him with McCulloch's company, the Texas Militia. He decided to hang on to them. They looked good, and in a short time they would be the only Rangers in the army.

Ironically enough, the first official mention of the Rangers for the month was Taylor's response to the War Department, acknowledging the return of a muster roll for Gillespie's company, dated May 9.[1] He admitted it was not properly completed. It would be the first of a continuing series of letters and acknowledgments, explanations and entreaties, which were often complaints, about the Texans.

On June 8, Secretary of War William Marcy wrote Taylor, asking for his views on conducting the war.[2] It was one of many diplomatic letters the secretary would have to write to his two major field commanders. He still gave Taylor complete freedom, but he did tactfully suggest that it might be wise to move to a healthier location, possibly Monterey. If both banks of the Rio Grande could be secured, the river would be available for free movement of men and supplies. And, he added, considerable reinforcements were on the way to Taylor, to total about 20,000 men.

The United States had sent Taylor south with no clear strategic plan. In those days there was no such thing as contingency plans to fight anyplace on earth. Actually, few people in the States had even been in Mexico. There was no clear idea about the country, the road system, population centers, or water locations. Taylor was sent down to repel an invasion of Texas and occupy the disputed territory in South Texas. He had done that and invaded Mexico — and now something else was happening.

Taylor had already begun to move part of his command. Order No. 78, June 4, 1846, directed a battalion of the 1st Infantry to proceed to Reynosa on the sixth. Price's Rangers were sent as escorts and scouts and to guard the train on its return, as mentioned earlier. Already the general was depending on the Texans for this kind of work.

He had other plans afoot. Order No. 85, on June 15, directed a lieutenant from McCulloch's company to draw funds for supplies for the company on its current route.[3] An explanation for this move followed several days later when Taylor wrote the adjutant general that Lieutenant Colonel Wilson had occupied Reynosa without opposition. Also, volunteers were coming in, "and twelve or fifteen companies from Texas; others from Texas are continually arriving." He went on, "A portion of these volunteers have been lying in camp for nearly a month, completely paralyzed by the want of transportation. Exposed as they are in this climate, to diseases of the camp, and without any prospect, so far as I can see, of being usefully employed, I must recommend that they be allowed to return to their homes."[4]

He said that he had dispatched Captain McCulloch and his company to Linares in order "to gain information touching the number and position of the enemy, and the resources of the country." McCulloch and some forty of his company had left their camp near the fort, now named Fort Brown, on June 12.[5] Someone in the staff evidently didn't get around to seeing that the men had money for supplies until June 15; by then they were well away. It didn't make any difference, though. The Rangers were accustomed to living off the country, or taking along what few things they required.

Starting in the morning, the Rangers had crossed the river on what leaky ferries were available and marched into Matamoros by noon. They went through and turned onto the upriver road to Reynosa, the route taken by Price and Reynolds. McCulloch was too experienced in border fighting not to know that any of the indifferent inhabitants watching them might be spies.

The detachment stayed on the road until dusk, camping near a *rancho.* Samuel Reid remembered it was the Rancho de Guadaloupe, a place with excellent melons and vegetables, including roasting-ears. "The most of us had a little pocket change, and we drove a lively trade with the Mexicans, for all the eatibles they could bring to our camp," he wrote. This was one of the first mentions of buying food from the inhabitants, but all eyewitness accounts of the war would mention it.[6] The government was convinced that the northern provinces would not fight and might even break away from the central government. Accordingly, strict orders had been given not to take anything from civilians without proper payment. Reid explained this policy and continued: "How absurd that policy has been, the experience of the campaign has since exhibited."

McCulloch's scout was the first time the Texans had been on an extended mission without other troops. It was an excellent chance to act as they did on the frontier — and take whatever they needed. To their credit, they followed orders and paid for every bite of food they ate, usually at double value. Reid mentioned that 2nd Lt. James Allen had joined them, with his saddlebags full of specie, and acted as commissary officer.[7]

After a night at Guadaloupe, the Texans waved goodbye and started up the road. After a time, they cut across country to the Linares road. Taylor had given them the mission of covering the road, deep into Mexico, to see if it could be used as a route to attack Monterey. The Mexican army had used the road, falling back from Matamoros, but they had little baggage and no artillery. The American force was tied to decent roads, burdened as they were with artillery, a long wagon train, and a sizable pack mule train.

The Rangers were not traveling in a complete void, even though they had never actually seen the country. In the baggage train General Arista lost at Resaca de la Palma was an excellent map of the country from the river south through Linares. While it did not show land forms with the accuracy of a modern map, the large ranges were indicated, with passes, and the major *ranchos* and water holes were accurately located. Evidently, several copies had been made, for McCulloch had a copy and it was eagerly studied by everyone in the company. This was invaluable when a man had to leave the company and return to the main camp. Such an event happened the day after leaving the first *rancho,* when a horse became lame. A Ranger was as good as his mount, and when a horse went lame, horse and rider were sent back. This was not too deep in enemy territory, but it must have been a lonesome feeling for that poor Ranger to watch the column move out.

McCulloch had a mobile column with a few pack mules to carry forage, as this was more critical than food. There were no tents or camp utensils, and the mules might have carried extra water, as well as forage. Water and forage were the key elements. They moved rapidly, checking the poor Linares road and the country near the road. Signs of Arista's army were still on the ground: broken weapons, packs, discarded shoes, lost playing cards.

The country was mountainous, dry, and the road was miserable. Certainly, the first stretch was not suitable for wheeled transport. When it began to rain, the Rangers decided it was not suitable for people or horses. Fortunately, this was in early summer; when the rains soaked them, they were warm and their spirits were not dampened. They camped each night near the road, but with the main body well into the brush. Sentinels covered the road and the sleeping Rangers, and pickets also guarded the camp.

The third morning out, the road guards heard horsemen approaching, going toward Matamoros. McCulloch and a few early risers were saddling horses when they heard the noise. Immediately he mounted, followed by a growing number of the Rangers. The advancing party of Mexican riders had halted when they saw the sentinels. It must have puzzled them to see unknown horsemen so far south. Evidently, there had been no alarm spread through the interior. The Texans did not dress too much differently than they, and it was still half light.

"Quien vive?"

McCulloch rode up then and answered, *"Amigos."*

The Ranger spoke Spanish and evidently read the language, but he had an accent that gave him away.

The leader of the *rancheros* aimed his musket at McCulloch. *"Los americanos malditos!"*

"Follow me!" yelled McCulloch as he charged, followed by the men who were riding over from the camp.

A few strangers suddenly changed into a yelling, charging group, and the *rancheros* turned and fled for the chaparral, a few hundred yards away. They had a good start before McCulloch and his party reached the road and took after them. They all hit the brush in the half light, the Mexicans splitting right and left. The ground was rocky and filled with holes. The half dozen men behind McCulloch found the going treacherous; several horses fell, one throwing its rider. In the dense brush, the Rangers had to rein in. It was difficult to walk a horse through most of the thorny bushes, much less gallop. The *rancheros* dismounted, dropped their weapons, slid into the bushes, and vanished.

The disgusted Rangers gave up the chase and walked back, picking up spurs, guns, and several abandoned horses and pistols. It was small consolation for missing a fight. On the way they found that one Texan had been hurt when he fell on his knife; he could not ride without assistance.

By now the Rangers had passed a number of ranches, and the alarm was certainly out. McCulloch was afraid to let another man go back alone. He picked an escort to go with the injured Ranger, probably men with the poorest horses. Reid recalled that this reduced the detachment to thirty-five. Originally forty men had been selected, those with the best horses.

McCulloch knew what could happen, and so he kept the strongest mounts. Now, with the alarm out, he never stopped or rode long in any direction. He never approached a ranch or settlement from the north, the direction expected of an American attack. He and his men always circled in the night and rode onto the places from the south or west. Everywhere their appearance was a complete surprise. They so terrified the local inhabitants by these moves that the people answered all their questions, probably expecting death if they did not. At one place they found enough corn to last the horses two days, and the unwelcome news that this was the last place on the road where they could expect to find forage in any quantity.

There was no reason to doubt this intelligence, and McCulloch had to make a decision. His mission was to see if the Linares road was suitable for an advance inland. Clearly, it was not. The night of June 20 the party camped in a mesquite grove, a place that afforded ample grazing for the mounts. It was one of the more enjoyable memories of the long march. Some shepherds had told the Texans that this was the last place that had water until Linares, which was probably another sixty miles.

While the bulk of the Rangers stayed in camp, McCulloch sent Lt. John McMullen and ten men to see if the report was true. McMullen rode south to the point where their map showed a water hole. For once the map was in error. To be certain, the lieutenant continued another thirty miles, halfway to Linares, and found no water. He returned with this unwelcome news. It was another example of a skilled commander operating in hostile territory. While the map had been accurate so far, McCulloch had the word of locals that there was no water. If he took his entire detachment and did not find water, they might lose their horses, which meant losing their lives. Eleven men could carry enough water to go and return, even if the well was dry. All he would risk was losing a few days. Both parties were strong enough to handle any *ranchero* groups that might show up. He also had confidence in young McMullen, a veteran of Mier and frontier fighting. The confidence was not misplaced.

They could have returned, but McCulloch had other plans. From what they had learned along the way, Arista had moved his battered forces from Linares to Monterey, and the way to Monterey by Linares was impossible for wheeled transport. There was also talk that Canales, the most famous of the *ranchero* chiefs, was recruiting men along the Monterey to Matamoros road. So, it was decided to accomplish two goals: dispose of Canales and scout out the country and roads farther west toward Monterey. On June 21 the detachment turned at right angles and cut across country to the west.

There was a road of sorts that an impressed guide insisted they take. Having little trust in the man, McCulloch placed him at the head with likely orders to shoot him if he had been lying. This part of Mexico was largely open plain, with lovely stands of huisache just beginning to bloom. The Rangers could see the bright yellow blooms for miles; the soft scent seemed to say this was peace, not war. But then there was the sun, and the sun said war.

Expecting water, the Rangers had finished their canteens and gourds early in the day. Now men and horses began to suffer. It is difficult to understand how hard campaigning is on horses. One may picture the animals at a gallop, forever strong, eternally swift. This image is inaccurate; the horse is relatively fragile. By afternoon, the Rangers were having to stop and rub down their mounts, unsaddling to dry the backs of the animals. The good-natured joking that usually filled the air gave way to cries for water and what to do with the guide if a spring or stream was not found.

McCulloch had them scatter in groups along the sides of the road and sent scouts well ahead to locate a water hole. The sun was still about an hour in the sky when one man galloped in with news that a water hole had been found a half mile off the road. Experienced or not, the Rangers wheeled and galloped their tired mounts toward the water. Fortunately, McCulloch was off to the side nearest the water and reached it well before the first riders. When they dashed up, their captain was standing before the muddy pool. He halted them and waited as the others came up, many with badly winded mounts. He told them calmly that he would shoot the first man or animal that rushed into the water.

Had he not stopped them, a few of the animals would have run into the water and fouled it so much it would not have been drinkable. With care, the men going a few at a time and carefully filling their canteens and gourds, all had water. Then they led their horses, again a few at a time, taking care not to get into the already muddy water. Finally, the pack mules were allowed to drink, but the beasts were not easily controlled and several rolled over and over and turned the pool into thick mud. By then it did not matter.

During the day some of the men, while scouting for water, ate prickly pear. It was a juicy fruit, but not for men unaccustomed to the country. By next day a number of the Rangers had fever and ague. There was nothing to be done; they simply kept up as best they could. By nightfall they were sick and bedded down with the others, wrapping in their blankets to cut the chills that followed the fever.

It did not seem possible that a day that had been so hot and dry could be followed by a night so wet. During the night, the cloudless sky turned black and a thunderstorm drenched the camp. Samuel Reid tells a tall story of bedding down with an old Texan, since he had a waterproof ground sheet and the Texan liked this modern convenience. When Reid awoke they were in a puddle of water, and he suggested they had better move to higher ground. The old man told him this was silly, as they had already warmed *this* puddle. If they moved, they would have to warm a second puddle. This bit of frontier logic did not impress Reid. He left and spent the rest of the night sitting upright against a tree. He learned a lot from the experience: care in selecting a sleeping spot, and, more important, keeping your powder horn stopped.

It was well into the morning before the Rangers had dried out their clothing and blankets enough to continue. They were now in a more barren country, hilly and rocky. About noon they were lucky to find a pool of water collected from runoff in a rocky basin. It was hot and covered with scum, but they strained it as best they could and drank it. From the pond they could look down on the Monterey road. As they moved out, a small group of carts was seen. Riding down, they surrounded the man, a merchant who was taking his produce to Monterey to sell.

The poor man was terrified at the sudden descent of armed men. Certain they were bandits, he knew his life and possessions were lost. Much to his surprise, the men turned out to be Texans — which may not have reassured him at first — who then offered to buy corn. In addition to the corn for the horses, they bought some dried beef.

The Rangers were taking the noon break when they spotted a horseman farther down the road. For a moment this man was on the point of running, but the Rangers were too close and too many, and he waved and rode up to them.

"Mail rider!" one of the Texans yelled, and they surrounded him and took the big leather bag he had with him.

McCulloch took the bag and read through the contents. The mail rider was certain his official position would result in a terrible death. As the Ranger glanced at the various documents and divided them into two groups, his confidence gradually came back. McCulloch sorted the mail into private letters and those that seemed of an official nature. He returned the first to the bag and gave it back to the rider. The other communications he kept for Taylor. He motioned the man to proceed, and the fellow waved and rode off, undoubtedly taking with him great tales of his adventure with the hated Rangers, and how he had bested them.

They met a few more people along the road, but information on Canales was of little value. Some said he had been in the vicinity about a week before. There was no point in riding about looking for him. McCulloch had too much information about roads and the country to waste more time. The company turned north toward Reynosa.

The ragged Texans traveled up the road from the south, from Monterey, and caused a great alarm in the garrison. From a distance they could see the white walls of the town, the roof tops filled with soldiers, officers with spyglasses trying to make out the identity of the advancing column. Drums were beating the call to arms. It must have amused the Texans, as they rode into the plaza and dismounted, to see the commotion they had caused. As the officers came up and greeted them, they were told that a warm welcome had almost been extended. Later, they learned more fully why the garrison had been so edgy.

This was the end of the first extended scout by a Ranger company. It made a name for McCulloch and added further luster to the Ranger legend. George Wilkins Kendall had ridden every tortuous step of the way, and he wrote the first of his dispatches extolling the Texans. Kendall described the twisting and turning of the column that tried to locate Canales:

> I say hurried and complicated movements of the Texians, because from the time of our leaving Matamoros, to our reaching this place, the men never took off their coats boots or spurs; not an extra or second shirt was carried by one of them; and although the weather was rainy much of the time, and two heavy northers visited us while encamped, there was not a minute when any man's pistol or rifle would have missed fire, or he would not have been up and ready for an attack. I have seen a goodly number of volunteers in my time, but Capt. Ben. McCulloch's men are choice specimans.[8]

All in all, allowing for some slight journalistic freedom, he was pretty close to the mark. The Rangers probably weren't interested in praise. They went outside the town to a shady grove and made camp and rested.

A Dragoon company could not have made this scout. They were not trained or equipped for this duty; nor were their horses up to the job. The Texans had found a niche that others could not fill — and didn't want to. The regulars found the escort duties along the roads not to their liking, and they simply did not operate in the chaparral.

The Rangers had a quiet time in Reynosa. It was before the main rainy season, and the camp outside town was dry and shady. Men and horses welcomed the rest. The only disturbing note came from constant prophecies of doom made by the local citizens. Soon it was clear why the garrison had been under arms when the Texans rode up from Monterey. Reid recalled with some humor how the Mexicans came to the camp and told the Rangers in strictest confidence that Antonio Canales, the great *ranchero* leader, would raid their camp that very night. Next day a massed assault by forces would be led by Juan Seguin. The well-staged bit of psychological warfare didn't work with the Rangers. After a while the people gave up in disgust and concentrated again on the regulars.

What did not cease was the muffled boasting of the Mexicans who had raided the country north of the Rio Grande. When the Mier prisoners had marched to captivity in central Mexico, they had spent a particularly difficult time in Reynosa. The entire town had made a concentrated effort to mistreat and humiliate the Texans. Lieutenant

McMullen had been a prisoner, and he certainly told the rest of the company of his experiences. A brutal raid had started from the town, and some of the men who had taken part in this massacre were brazen enough to brag about the deed within earshot of the Rangers.

The reputation for cruelty that would later taint the Texas Rangers probably began in Reynosa. A few of the more notorious bandits were found shot to death. Pickets and foraging parties would find a man hanging from a tree — all very mysterious and unexplained. Reid mentioned these strange occurrences, without any direct accusation, but he left little doubt who was responsible. While he did not have the frontier upbringing and first-hand ill feelings of most of the Rangers, the adopted Ranger sided with their reasoning. He said, from the side of his mouth, that the Mexicans probably committed suicide from remorse over raiding into Texas![9]

Supplies were being carried upriver by steamboat, and a few days after reaching town one of the boats docked and unloaded cargo. McCulloch decided to go downriver and bring back the rest of his company from outside Matamoros. Kendall went along with others from the garrison. While not a part of the Texas story, the use of the steamboats would become a major point of friction between Taylor and the War Department. The general saw the advantages of using the river as much as possible to ease his lengthy supply line, a line that would stretch with each advance west and south. Soon Taylor had the department buying boats wherever possible. The correspondence generated by these transactions would fill a decent-sized volume.[10] The amount of anguished conversation and cursing can only be imagined.

Life picked up a little when two Mexican officers were captured in town. They pretended to be innocent citizens, but Lieutenant Colonel Wilson, the garrison commander, was certain they were spies and asked Lieutenant McMullen to send them to Taylor. Sgt. Archibald Gibson and five men took the prisoners and dispatches and left for Matamoros and headquarters. This reduced the detachment to twenty-five men.[11]

It was now late in June, and the rains began. The lovely grove, near the river, was starting to be more a mud field than a campsite. McMullen went to see Wilson and had the first of a series of unpleasant encounters with the regular. The town had several empty buildings suitable for housing men and horses, but Wilson refused to allow the men to take refuge there. He haughtily informed the Rangers that in time of war, the quarters of a soldier were in the field. All of which was well and good, but the colonel was living in the best house in town, and the Rangers could not see the justice in that. McMullen came back and reported the army position, and the Texans spent another day and night in the rain and mud. The camp was renamed "Camp Nasty."

The Rangers didn't give a damn about government policy. They probably recalled that when the Mexican army captured San Antonio in 1842, they took whatever they could carry. There was a large cotton shed nearby and they saw no reason why they should sleep in the mud when there was a vacant shelter. McMullen suggested they move inland to higher and drier ground, but Wilson refused. He wanted them available in case of attack. McMullen then made a formal request to make use of the shelter, and Wilson had the good sense to give in. The shed was large enough to house men and horses, and the detachment would look back on this as the most comfortable time during the campaign. A few days later, a scouting party had to swim over their old campsite.[12]

The part of the company in Reynosa had achieved wide renown for the long scout toward Linares. Meanwhile, the remainder of the Texans were moving slowly toward Matamoros. James K. Holland noted in his diary that they passed the battlefields on June 25. The war was beginning to get close now. Even this late there were still signs of the fighting. And the same rain that was causing problems in Reynosa was plaguing Holland's regiment. He wrote that it had been raining for days and they slept as best they could in the mud. They had slaughtered cattle for food, augmenting what the commissary orderly could get.

The rain and possibly bad water were beginning to cause more than normal sickness rates. Holland wrote: ". . . your humble svt. never was as sick in his life — never thot of dying before — scared to death."[13]

The three weeks the detachment at Reynosa spent was not entirely a long *siesta,* but there they probably spent less time in the field than in any other comparable period. Lieutenant McMullen was not entirely passive during this period. Reid recalled how the lieutenant came one night and told twenty men to get their horses and make no noise.[14] The puzzled men asked no questions and assembled out in the dark, ready for whatever lay ahead. McMullen told them nothing and led them off into the night. Well away from town, he informed them that they were going after Canales. He had overheard a rumor that the noted bandit chief was to be at a *rancho* near the town that night. Unfortunately, they didn't know where the *rancho* was located. The problem was solved when they came across a boy who was familiar with the place. For a dollar he promised to guide them to the location. They rode for some miles through the night, and finally the boy pointed to some lights ahead.

McMullen halted the column, while the youngster vanished into the darkness, not wishing his people to know he had guided the Americans. McMullen had the men count off, each fifth man to serve as horse holders. They continued on as quietly as possible and scattered out, surrounding the ranch buildings. It was simple enough, as a party was filling the night with music, and no one had any thought of twenty Texans appearing out of the dark. Lanterns lighted the open patio, where numerous couples were dancing; others were eating and drinking. There was so much noise, the Rangers could have walked their horses onto the patio and not been heard.

When his men were in place, McMullen walked calmly onto the patio and greeted the startled guests. The women started screaming, and the men turned to run or find weapons, but there seemed to be someone with a rifle everywhere they looked. Whatever they had been celebrating had turned to dust. Most expected death from the silent, unkempt men with the rifles and strange pistols. One old man, drunk and trying to be brave, kept shuffling about, crying that they were poor folk and had nothing to fear from their enemies.

McMullen made no explanation and began searching the house. He found that if Canales had ever been there, he was long gone. Finally, the lieutenant came out. He smiled and told the group they had been riding by and heard the music, so they stopped. Now the party must continue, he said. The relieved Mexicans invited the Rangers to stay and have food and drink. The music started again, and while some quietly stood guard in the shadows, a few of the party folk in the detachment took off their weapon belts and powder flasks and joined the dancers.

The long white dresses of the young girls made a stark contrast to the somber-clothed, black-booted Texans. What the young Rangers lacked in sartorial elegance they made up in dancing skills. They immediately adapted the music to frontier steps — or ignored it. The entranced Mexican girls did not know that the outlandish steps they tried to mimic had equally strange names: Arkansas hoedown, Kentucky heel tap, double shuffle, and back balance lick. Their former dance partners were jealous almost to the point of challenging the Rangers.

McMullen finally broke up the party. They had a final glass of wine and vanished into the night as quietly as they had appeared.

If the nighttime dance seems an oddity during wartime, it was nothing compared to the almost comical events that took place in town on June 24, the feast day of San Juan. The day was celebrated in almost medieval fashion. No person on foot was allowed in the town streets. Everyone who had a horse of any kind paraded through the various streets and about the plaza. Each man wore his best clothing, displayed his finest horse equipment, and decorated his mount with ribbons. All of this was to impress the ladies of the town, who watched from the roof tops. There was another feature to the promenading — manly courage. No man could give way to another. If two horsemen met, one had to be ridden down. There were contests, with two groups charging one another, seeing who could overthrow the other.

It was naturally more than the Texans could bear, without taking part. Knowing how the day would be celebrated, twenty carefully groomed their horses and rode into the main plaza. There was one reason they could be so carefree: The garrison was in full evidence, most of the plaza being occupied by artillery, with some side streets barricaded. For once the Texans didn't have to worry about ambushes. They didn't even carry rifles or gear, though it would be safe to assume plenty of pistols were hidden away.

The seemingly innocent Texans rode into the plaza and formed a loose line at one end. Immediately everything stopped, and the town gallants gathered and formed at the other end. As was customary, the group offering a challenge rode by the Rangers. The Texans pretended not to understand and stayed in place. It was too good to be true, and the town cavaliers formed again at the opposite end of the plaza, then wheeled and charged the line.

The rushing horsemen outnumbered the Texans, but most of them were riding ponies and the Americans were on larger, heavier mounts. Just as the mass of ponies was about to crash their line, the Rangers wheeled right and left and opened a wide gap. The yelling attackers screamed in derision as they rode by, up a side street. Some distance up the narrow way, they began pulling in their horses. By then the yelling Rangers had formed a solid column and were charging them at a gallop. The heavy horses struck the lighter formation and scattered them against the walls of houses, into the dirt, and completely smashed the group.

Those not unhorsed broke into whatever side streets were near and did not gather until the laughing Texans had reformed and started making the rounds of the town, throwing kisses to the young women on the roofs or in the doorways. The bowled-over riders — those not hurt, that is — took it with good grace and followed the preening Rangers at a respectful distance.

Thinking to retrieve some degree of honor from the disaster of the day, one of the Mexicans who spoke some English suggested a chicken race. This consisted of one man trying to carry a chicken from one point to another. The men of the town would try to take it away from him — by whatever means. This seemed more fun than the collision of groups, and the Rangers immediately agreed. Clinton DeWitt volunteered to carry the chicken from a spot in town to the Ranger camp, some two miles distant. The route selected was full of holes and scattered with loose rocks. While the rules were being explained and a chicken found, a number of the Reynosa gallants were riding out to take ambush positions. No weapons would be used, but anything else was legal.

DeWitt had one of the best horses in the company, and Samuel Reid said he was a wild young man. In that company, this was *wild.* DeWitt grabbed the chicken and started out at a run. After a time, the chasers followed, but his mount was so swift that they never came close. However, at several places he was intercepted by the hidden riders. This added spice to the chase. Single riders were simply ridden down, or wisely wheeled and let the heavy mount go by.

DeWitt managed to avoid small groups and was almost at the Ranger camp when he was overtaken by an equally wild man on a spirited pony. The man grabbed the chicken by the neck and for a moment they rode side by side, neither man being able to tug the bird free. The Ranger soon noticed his opponent was allowing his bridle to fall free as he used both hands to grab for the now strangled fowl. Grabbing his own reins and the bird in one hand, DeWitt reached over and grabbed the attacker about the neck and tugged his mount to a sudden halt. The man's pony kept on at a gallop, while the startled rider was tugged loose and smashed to the ground. Yelling in triumph, DeWitt rode the few yards into camp, his trophy held high in the air.

Neither side was willing to stop with one, and the game went into a second round and a third, all with the same result. Finally, the game was called. As one of the townsmen explained: *"No mas gallenas en Reynosa."* There were no more chickens in Reynosa.[15]

And so, June came to an end. The United States Army was beginning to advance, slowly, on Monterey. The Ranger regiments were still marching to catch the main force, and McCulloch had made a name to add to Walker's exploits.

FIVE

★ ★ ★ ★ ★ ★ ★ ★ ★

Toward Monterey

By the beginning of July, Taylor seems to have decided how he wished to prosecute the war. On July 2 he wrote the adjutant general explaining his views, including an expedition to capture Chihuahua. He was concerned about supplies and the difficulties of obtaining intelligence. His plan was to move the regulars to Camargo and establish a main depot, then move to the mountains, on to Saltillo. This, he explained, was the only artillery route. The country could support no more than 6,000 men, and he would not need all the thousands promised by the secretary of war. There was no way to attack Mexico City from the north, crossing a thousand miles of impossible country.[1]

This was all beyond the basic interests of the Texans. They had come for a fight, and the broad picture was not that interesting. James K. Holland's diary shows how much he knew or cared about strategy. He mentions they were mustered in for six months on the second of the month. There is also this entry: "Nothing of interest occurred up to 1st July — and that day was a memorable epoch in my existence — for it was *wash day with me* and I done it tolerably well too — this thing of washing is a dirty business anyhow — and I am going to quit it."[2]

The 2nd Regiment celebrated the Fourth of July in traditional fashion. Holland said that the main address was given by a Dr. Smith and was well received. General Henderson read the Declaration of Independence. According to the young lieutenant, he did a creditable job and most of the men were impressed.[3]

Upriver, the detachment of McCulloch's company held their own celebration. Someone managed to get two horse buckets of whiskey, which were sweetened by a generous helping of sugar and watered down to go around. Lieutenant McMullen, a talented leader, found other business that day, and the Rangers were left alone.

As Reid remembered the glorious day, any stray chickens or pigs that wandered into the camp area were caught in the numerous salutes the Rangers fired. There were many speeches, though fewer listened as the day wore on. The Texans made an exception to the custom of *siesta* for such a marvelous holiday, and the orations and salutes continued throughout the afternoon. The noise became so loud, the good Colonel Wilson was awakened a half mile away and thought an attack was taking place on the Rangers' shed. He dispatched a file of soldiers to investigate.

Finding no assault, but plenty of whiskey, the regulars joined in the celebration and eventually took back an invitation for Wilson to join the party. He came, probably out of curiosity, but stopped when he could not see any officers present. He thought he was hiding, but someone had seen him. As he began to slip away, one of the men proposed a toast to the colonel. All present joined in a wild cheer. Wilson got the joke and left them alone for the rest of the night.[4]

No one wrote how the other Rangers spent July 4. Back in Matamoros, McCulloch and the rest of his company were probably getting ready to leave. It is hoped they had time for a toast to the flag in the bars of the city. On the fifth, they started out with the rest of the 7th Infantry to join up with the Reynosa garrison and move on to Camargo.[5]

McMullen's detachment continued to have the place of honor, not always to their liking. A few days after the great celebration, they were told to chase some bandits that had been raiding in the vicinity. It was not a duty they relished; most of them were perfectly content to let the Mexicans kill each other. Orders were orders, though, and they picked up a guide to lead them to the bandits. Their guide was a poor man who had been mutilated by the outlaws and was barely alive. He led them to a place outside town where he had been tied to a tree and left to die. It was in the center of what had been the outlaw camp, some ten miles from Reynosa.

The trail was still fresh, and the Rangers pursued the bandits, but soon found the men had split into groups and scattered into the chaparral. The Rangers divided and checked the various trails, but they were too late and gave up the chase. While still scattered, some of them heard a party coming from up the river. Then they could see a group coming over a hill some distance away. McMullen collected his men and had them hide along the road. He galloped off to draw the advancing party into the ambush. In a short time he was back, accompanied by the rest of the company. McCulloch had his unit together again.[6]

Reid wrote that McCulloch had the confidence of the general, more so than any of the other Rangers. This seems true, but it is often difficult to see how Taylor felt about the Rangers as a group. He undoubtedly had mixed feelings — wanting them for their skills, but only in a fight. In a letter to a surgeon friend on July 7, he discussed the Texans. One sentence has been often quoted to damn the Rangers. The entire passage is somewhat different:

> I agree with you in doubting the reorganization of the Texans, I feel but little interest in the matter: altho I expect if they could be made subordinate they would be the best, at any rate as good as any volunteer corps in service; but I fear they are & will continue too licentious to do much good. I hope you will give them all the medical aid in your power as well as supply them with medicines and hospital stores as long as they can be spared. I hope the tents have arrived are now & that those people have been supplied with enough to protect them from the weather; I am please to learn the Gov is satisfied that all that could be done for them —[7]

Taylor starts out with high praise and then tempers it a bit. An old meaning of "licentious" is "disregarding accepted rules and standards," which would not be too inaccurate when talking about the Texans. The more accepted usage — "morally unrestrained, especially sexually" — somehow does not seem to fit what Taylor had in mind. At least the passage shows he did have some concern for their well-being, and indicates, as do other comments, that some of the Texas units were supplied with tents. Another interesting sidelight is his use of "Governor" when writing personal letters. In his official papers, Henderson is always "Major General" or "General."

Whatever he thought, Taylor made full use of the Texans. On July 9, McCulloch moved out from Reynosa, as advance guard for the march to Camargo. The 7th Infantry and an artillery detachment made up the column. Supplies were already moving upriver to establish the depot at Camargo. After moving into the shed, the Rangers had enjoyed their time in Reynosa, but they were happy to move on. They were also happy to be on horseback. The poor infantrymen had a rough time, weighted down with all their gear and moving through sand while dressed for winter. When the march ended at night, they dropped down, almost in place, too tired to do anything.[8]

The army was on the move now, although advancing piecemeal. At least they were no longer fixed in the camps. Anything was better than the inaction and the sickness that afflicted hundreds. The movement was by brigades and divisions, and the two mounted Texas regiments and the infantry regiment did not move as a division or even a brigade. The 2nd advanced as a regiment, but the 1st, less two companies, was a considerable distance away. The Eastern Regiment, as they so considered themselves, was on the road to Camargo when they saw a large dust cloud and prepared for combat. After scouts had ridden out, they discovered the enemy was a large herd of mustangs. This "battle" was the cause of much laughter.[9] It came to typify what many were thinking: The fighting was over.

The only action they saw was when some of the "boys" collected some watermelons and the owner found Colonel Wood and protested about the loss. Evidently, he was afraid of arousing Taylor's anger, as Wood paid $20 out of his own pocket to calm the farmer.[10] It was a ridiculous price, as the man probably did not get $20 for his entire crop.

For the next week, Holland's notes show what life was like on the march, and how he saw the war. On July 13 he and another lieutenant became weary of the mess arrangement and hired a cook for $10 a month. They paid half and found some more mess mates to make up the differences.[11] Holland also made these notes:

"I am the dirtiest man in the regiment — but everyone else is dirty too . . ."[12]

". . . $500 for a good cool drink of water from the bottom of Ed Smiths well — the water we have is not fit for a hog to waller in — "[13]

"God save and bless the women until we all get back . . ."[14]

By the fifteenth, they were on the San Juan, near Camargo. Things were not going too well: "[On] account of the Texas infantry being about to be disbanded and old Taylors bad treatment to us as well as them — a great many of our regiment have manifested a desire to go home but the Col gave us a war talk and the furor has somewhat subsided tho there are still many going to return home."[15]

It is hard to determine what Holland meant by "Taylors bad

treatment." There is nothing in any official reports from this period to indicate any problems. Samuel Reid did not mention any bad treatment of any of the Texas units. It may have been the way Taylor struck the young volunteer lieutenant. Certainly, plenty of regular lieutenants felt the same way about the old man. On July 19, Holland noted another comment about his commanding general: "JBP and JKH called on his august presence this evening — found him a plain old farmer-looking man — no particular indications of smartness or intellect."[16]

JKH was probably Holland's uncle, who commanded the company. The fact that Taylor received a company commander shows his willingness to be on friendly terms with his subordinates. Other accounts show he would talk to any man in the ranks, even have a drink with them on occasion.[17]

Holland and the rest of the 2nd reached Reynosa on July 24 and began gathering pack mules. It was cold at night, and he described how he obtained a Mexican blanket to keep warm. The following day some of the Western Regiment arrived in town, ". . . now halted 75 miles away waiting for us . . . Their Regiment have enjoyed good health, etc."[18]

Despite all the printed forms and official designations, the Texans retained their fierce pride of place and called themselves what they chose. To them, they were the Western and Eastern regiments. Company A might be listed as such on the muster rolls, but the men referred to themselves as the Brazoria Company. The 2nd Regiment usually called companies by numbers, not letters. It really didn't matter to anyone but the clerks in Washington City. There, everything mattered — each and every comma in all the militia laws which governed volunteers and how muster rolls were to be filled in.

The question of volunteer service would plague Taylor as long as he commanded. The government wanted everyone for the duration of the war, at the very least for twelve months. Taylor had been signing them, especially the Texans, for six months, knowing he could hold them no longer than three, when he would have to discharge them. He explained this to the department on July 31, stating he wanted to keep the Texans: "All the Texas troops are anxious to go forward; they are hardy and can subsist on little." Taylor went on to state that it would be impossible for mounted regiments from other states to join him in time to be of service. Without the Texans he would be too weak in scouts. Also, the horses from other states were not accustomed to the country and would require a long period of time before they could be effective.[19]

As usual, the troops along the Rio Grande didn't know about all the correspondence affecting their fate. They were too busy in the day-to-day business of staying alive, keeping dry, avoiding hunger, and hoping they would not be the next to go lie in the hospital tents and await their turn to die.

McCulloch was worried that his time would be spent sitting by the Rio Grande. On July 20 he wrote Taylor a letter explaining they were still at Camargo and would probably stay there until their term of service was up. They were worthless where they were, he explained. He thought they could explore the country toward Monterey as far as the general thought proper, or perhaps just visit some of the *ranchos* "to conciliate the people." He went on to tell Taylor that the impressions made there had been so favorable that Canales had no following. Seguin had some forty men, and McCulloch could go after him. His horses were in fine shape, and he was ready and willing for anything.[20]

R. A. Gillespie's company arrived opposite Camargo about this time, having ridden down from San Antonio by way of Laredo, then to Mier and on to Camargo.[21] Finding the army moving upriver, Gillespie decided to keep his company in place while he went down to Matamoros to see what Taylor wanted to do with his Rangers. McCulloch made one more try for some action. On July 23 he wrote a letter to Captain Bliss, the general's adjutant and chief staff officer.

He began: "Capt Gillespie will hand you this he has just arrived from San Antonio with forty well mounted men. They are of the best material the country affords for scouts and he wishes to be employed in that kind of service." He was probably not sure where any of them would fit into the overall plan for the army. But they really didn't care, as long as they could follow their line of work.

McCulloch continued on in a long, two-page letter explaining that his horses, with a little shoeing, could take them on a scout all the way to Monterey and back without a scratch. He was extremely anxious to make another scout before the company was discharged. He was not certain of his position, and the regular officers who were in command were afraid to turn him loose without authority from General Taylor.

How he felt about the men they were chasing and his version of frontier justice is summed up in the final part of the letter:

> Seguin passed up San Juan a few days before we arrived. He had forty

thieves and murders from about San Antonio to kill which would be doing God a service it would be ridding the world of those that are not fit to live in it. They will never come to terms because they would be condemned by the Civil Laws and executed accordingly. They must do the frontier of Texas no little harm by robbing and stealing from its citizens.

Any orders the Genl may give will be thankfully received and obeyed to the letter.[22]

It may just be a coincidence that McCulloch made a point in both letters of assuring Taylor that any orders would be obeyed "to the letter" or "with pleasure." One wonders whether he had received any complaints about the Rangers *not* obeying orders.

There is nothing to indicate that the letters did any good. However, the Rangers did get a new mission — to chase Indians. Up on the High Plains, the Comanches were unconcerned about a war. They were raiding as they had always done, looking for horses and plunder and slaves. Now they were striking along both banks of the Rio Grande.

McCulloch reported to Gen. William J. Worth, the senior general at Camargo, and was told to run down the Comanches and talk to them. The Americans did not know much about Plains Indians at that time. McCulloch did not argue with him; he went back and selected thirty men and headed for the Rio Grande.[23] They had five days and nights of nonstop movement, crossing and recrossing the river several times. In those days the water was deeper and swifter, and a crossing was no simple fording, as it usually is today.

The first crossing, to the Texas side, was difficult. They managed to send their weapons and equipment over on one of the supply steamboats, but there was no room for their horses, and they had to swim. The river was in flood, with a current in excess of five miles, and the water was full of floating logs and trees. It took several attempts to get the horses across, as many of the animals refused to enter the muddy, swirling water. Then one of the younger Rangers, proud of his ability as a swimmer, started out by himself. Despite discouraging yells, he got well out into the center of the river before he started to slow. Suddenly, he was shouting for help and slipping under the water. The few Texans on the south bank had stripped naked to save their clothing from the waters and the horses that kept trying to return to land. Now they rushed to a small canoe and started paddling and pushing with a few poles, making a desperate effort to reach their drowning companion. He was calling faintly for help and was barely able to keep his head above the surface. The men in the canoe began yelling their encouragement and almost killing themselves trying to paddle with the poles. The canoe turned broadside in the swift current and started to break away. In a moment, they were becoming concerned for their own safety. Then the "drowning" man came up out of the water and started laughing; he turned and swam easily the rest of the way to the Texas bank. Eventually, the detachment was across and safe, though not dry, and the cursing at the swimmer went on for some time. In the end the men started laughing. Another legend was born.

They finally settled down and went a short distance to some high ground and a little settlement that would become Rio Grande City. They found a guide at about 4:00 in the afternoon and started following Indian tracks. This chaparral was no easier to cross than the country about Point Isabel. The Rangers wondered how the half-naked Comanches managed to move through the brush so swiftly, when they were being cut through boots and heavy trousers.

The guide was reluctant, fearing the Indians. Not even the generous wage was enough to make him enjoy his job. It is doubtful that he was much help, as they were able to follow the Comanche sign easily enough. The man did know where the ranches were located along the river, and the Rangers thought they could at least warn the people. However, most of the places they visited in the next few days were abandoned.

For the Rangers it was a relief to get away from town, even with such arduous and hazardous duty. They never did find the raiders. The first night a sentry fired on a prowler, but they never found a body. They did find tracks about their camp. After the shot, they moved the horses in closer, and each man slept near his mount, the animal tied down. This was the real danger: a few braves slipping through the line of sentries and cutting horses loose. The Rangers didn't bother about themselves. They slept with their weapons at hand. If the horses were secure, they had no reason to worry too much.

The detachment followed the trail for several days. Only once did they come across any people. At one large ranch, on the river, they saw people on the Mexican side. The Rangers shouted encouragement, but the Mexicans were afraid to cross. Finally, McMullen went over and a few came back with him. They unlocked the store rooms and sold the Rangers some food at inflated prices, as always, while expressing eternal gratitude for the Texans scaring away the raiders. The disgruntled Rangers had no choice. They had started on a short scout and carried nothing but dried meat and coffee. Even Rangers got hungry. After a good meal, they were in a mood to continue.

Finally, they came upon evidence of conflict — a raided ranch. Signs of battle were all about, including arrows and slain cattle, but the Comanches were well away. The Rangers rode on a few miles and camped on the river. Next morning some ranchers rode in and told them they thought the Indians had crossed to the Mexican side and were near Mier. Once again, the Rangers swam the river.

Near Mier, they had to cross a small stream, which was used as a bathing place by the local women. On the high banks, hidden from view, the sweaty, tired Rangers watched as the naked women and girls bathed and swam in the warm water. This might have gone on for some time, but someone evidently expressed his appreciation of the view in too loud a manner, and the startled women began screaming, grabbing for clothing, and running toward the nearby city. Giving them a decent start and time to dress, the Rangers followed, moving through the growing crowd in double file, rifles ready.

McCulloch led them to the *alcalde*'s residence and demanded meat and bread, an outright requisition. He didn't give them a chance to think or gather force; he didn't answer questions. The Mexicans must have assumed that such a small force, with such a belligerent manner, could only be the advance guard of the American army. Everything the Americans demanded and more was produced. The Rangers ate and left.

The last of the Comanche sign had led to the far north. There was no point in further pursuit.

While McCulloch was chasing Comanches, Gillespie boarded one of the supply steamers and rode downriver to Matamoros for orders.[24] He reached the city on July 25, with McCulloch's letter to Bliss. He must have been somewhat delayed in delivery of the letter, as he got roaring drunk in Matamoros and was arrested and finally turned over to the general. This didn't bother Taylor; probably by then he was getting accustomed to the behavior of his Texans.

Gillespie was released, apparently with no penalty, and told to return to Camargo and rest his horses. Taylor must have been turning over a plan for the use of the Rangers, as he made no effort to have the two companies join Hays. On August 3, Taylor wrote the adjutant general and mentioned the Comanche raids near Mier.[25] He reported that Gillespie's company had recently come down from San Antonio to Laredo, then down to Mier and Camargo, and found the country generally quiet. The idea of having two Ranger companies in the van of his forces appealed to Taylor; he could have one on scout and one available, a plan he put into immediate effect.

Already, by August 1, McCulloch's men had been alerted. They began moulding bullets, smoking food, and checking their mounts, reshoeing as many as possible since iron was in short supply. They departed on the third, a Monday, a perfect way to begin the week.[26]

Again, McCulloch split his company, though most went on this scout. Leaving ten men in camp, the others departed early. After a time, the others followed by another route, to confuse the spies that watched every movement. Samuel Reid said he had recovered from an illness and was on this reconnaissance, as was George Wilkins Kendall, the *Picayune* correspondent who had evidently tired of the joys of Matamoros and had rejoined his Texas companions. They started out and were soon drenched by a sudden downpour. Later, a guide overtook them and said he would show them the way to McCulloch's camp. The guide was an American named Baker, who had lived in Mexico for some time. After some twisting about, they reached the rest of the unit.

The first night out they camped near the San Juan, having covered about twenty-five miles. Fortunately, they found dry wood and dried out as much as possible by the small fires. They had hot food — coffee, fried bacon, and the hard biscuits they carried. Fresh water was at hand. Then they slept as best they could under the big trees, some shelter in case of another rain. Reid described how he went on guard from about 2:00 A.M. to daylight, giving some idea of routine. There were two watches a night.

General Taylor had sent them to check out the China route to Monterey. He may or may not have talked about capturing Juan Seguin. Certainly, McCulloch had added this as a secondary mission, which now became the main objective. The second day the Rangers advanced in a column of twos, moving at a fast walk. This pace continued until late in the afternoon, when they stopped under what vegetation could be found to rest the horses. They spread their blankets on the tops of bushes and led the hot animals under the scant shade. While men and animals rested, McCulloch checked his map. They drank sparingly and ate whatever they had and waited. Finally, the commander folded the map and told them to saddle. The command was on the road in minutes.

They could see mountains all about in the clear air. As the sun began to go down, the air cooled and the horses and men were revived. There were quiet orders, and the company stretched out in a single file, pack animals to the rear. No talking was allowed.

At 11:00 P.M. the column passed a large *rancho*. The place seemed deserted, though the Rangers could see a head now and then as someone opened the shutters to peer out. They passed around a large hill and went down into a deep ravine, where they found a stream and watered the horses. Coming up to level ground, they were a few hundred yards from China. It was almost midnight. McCulloch left Lt. James Allen and twenty men and the pack mules to guard the road and cut off anyone entering the town. They were to stay until daylight and join the others in the attack. McCulloch then went on, making a detour to enter the town from the Monterey side.

The pickets had barely settled in place some fifty yards off the road when they caught a man. He claimed that he was out looking for horses, an odd thing to do at midnight. While they were talking to him, they heard sabers rattling as horsemen approached. Two horsemen appeared in the dark and refused to stop and were fired upon; the Rangers thought they wounded one. The road pickets knew what was going on, but the rest of the party in the chaparral thought it might be a Mexican attack. In the confusion, the prisoner escaped. Allen decided to send a man to tell McCulloch what the shot had been and Sgt. Archibald Gibson volunteered to go. About this time, two more Mexican horsemen rode up and were captured. From these men, the pickets learned that Seguin had been alerted to the move of the Rangers and had ridden out of China about 9:00 P.M.

At daylight, the detachment under Allen secured the mules and their prisoners and rode into town, expecting to see the rest of the company. It was not the first time, or the last, a few Rangers entered a hostile town. And it was not the first or the last time the men advanced boldly along the narrow streets wondering if this was their last moment on earth. They found nothing save doors and shutters being barred. A few heads appeared and ducked back from the roof tops. Then they saw a few men peering at them from a street corner ahead, and decided they must be Rangers. In a few minutes the rest of the company rode into the plaza. McCulloch was disgusted, his hat brim turned up, and none of the men made any jokes about losing Seguin.

McCulloch told Allen to get the mules and join them outside town. They followed Seguin's trail for five or six miles and found he had split his command into many groups. They turned back and found where the *rancheros* had camped outside town. Some of the camp women had been left in the panic that followed the news of the Ranger advance. There was also considerable plunder left behind, but the Rangers did not bother anything. As they rode on, some of the women made fires and then threw wet brush on the flames. Several smoke signals marked the early morning sky as the Rangers reentered China.

They spent the night and part of the next day in the town. It was a touchy situation, for the *alcalde* had slipped out of town and ridden to the major ranch in the area and tried to arouse the people for an attack on the Texans. He had no luck, which saved a lot of lives. The townspeople were content to wait out the invaders. The Texans started back, moving by easy stages, lighting no fires at night. The return was uneventual, though cautious. At one stop McMullen recognized a man who had been the keeper of the names of the Mier prisoners. When the man recognized the lieutenant and saw that he in turn had been recognized, he knew he was a dead man. Hastily, the Mexican told his companions not to charge the Rangers for anything. It was the only time they had been given food as a gift.

Back in Camargo they found General Taylor had arrived, and started work on turning the town into a forward base. Gen. David E. Twiggs and the First Division had moved up and a large campsite had been cleared outside town. This was as far upriver as steamboats could operate, and the craft were constantly arriving, unloading and moving back downriver. Warehouses were filling. A sizable commercial operation was in full swing, with numerous civilian contractors making deals on everything from animals to flour.[27]

Taylor reported to the adjutant general on August 10 and mentioned McCulloch's scout to China, describing how he had gone up the Valley of the San Juan. He also mentioned that they had been after Seguin. According to him, the Ranger company consisted of about fifty and was checking on routes to Monterey. He concluded, "This expedition has given valuable information touching one of the routes to Monterrey." The information was that this way had water, unlike Linares, but the road was impassable for wagons and artillery.[28]

About a week later, he published Order No. 99, stating all troops were to be held ready to march on Monterey on the nineteenth if weather permitted. Supplies were to be moved forward to Cerralvo, with two companies of Wood's Texas Horse to accompany the command and bring back the pack mule train. Mention of the other units of the two Ranger regiments is infrequent during this period, but they were undoubtedly kept busy as escorts, scouts, express riders, and advance parties. Taylor had evidently developed an appreciation of McCulloch and kept his company busy. They got the good press. The commander must have felt the same way about R. A. Gillespie, for he kept his company at Camargo.

During this time in early August, the eight companies of the 1st Mounted Rifles had traveled on to Matamoros, reaching the town on August 2.[29] Order No. 118, the next day, directed the quartermaster to turn over to Hays necessary funds for supplies.[30] Their stay in the big city was brief. The following day, Order No. 185 directed the regiment to swing south and take San Fernando, then proceed up the San Lorenzo River to China.[31] The regiment departed Matamoros on the eighth. The next day the 2nd Texas, less the two companies, moved up the river road, heading for Camargo. The Texans were in the war now.

Sending the eight Ranger companies on this wide a sweep through enemy country was a gamble. Taylor must have had confidence in Hays to risk a force he valued and needed so far from any support. Maybe he thought they didn't need it. The regiment, less two companies, probably mustered 500 rifles, as the companies were still at higher strengths than they would be in a month. Taylor possibly wanted to overawe the Mexicans, keep them off balance. Whatever his reasons, the column moved through the countryside without trouble.

Kendall was not the only *Picayune* correspondent. A man named Lundsmen accompanied the Rangers on the march to San Fernando and sent back letters to the paper from time to time. He reported that the regiment reached the town, situated on the banks of a river by the same name, early in the morning of August 13. They were soon met by three messengers who informed Hays there were no troops in the town, the garrison having left when they heard of his approach. The *alcalde* informed him there would be no opposition and pleaded that neither the inhabitants nor their property would be harmed. Hays rode in and assured the man that they meant no harm. Through an interpreter, Hays told the *alcalde* and a gathering crowd that the Rangers had come to make war on soldiers, not civilians, and that the people and their property were safe.

There was no opposition to the brief occupation. The day before, a Mexican soldier had tested the alertness of the Rangers and paid for it. After two days in town, the Texans started for China.[32] Again, they found no formed opposition, only startled farmers. When they arrived in China, Hays turned the regiment over to Walker and rode on to Camargo for orders, arriving on August 26.[33]

Left in command of the regiment, Walker did not find matters to his liking. On August 27 he issued a regimental order. (There must not have been much correspondence or orders, as this document is unnumbered.)[34]

> The Lieut Col Comdg. finds himself under the disagreeable necessity of issuing the following orders for the better security and protection of the Camp also the reputation of the Regt and the State we represent in the field.
>
> Viz that hereafter any Soldier who shall be found sleeping on his post, or guilty of any pilfering or plundering or any disgraceful transaction while this Regt is on detached service shall forthwith be dishonourably discharged from the Regiment without any regard to their safety ordered forthwith to leave the camp and not make his appearance again in our lines under the penalty of being shot his name to be published in the *Picayune,* his place of Residence & place of nativity also. It is due to all good soldiers in the Regt that the above should be strictly enforced. It is expected that all officers and soldiers desirous of promoting the welfare and reputation of the Regt will cooperate with me in carrying out the above orders should it hereafter be found necessary.
>
> Yours Very Respectfully
> per order of
>
> S Walker Lieut Col
> Comdg the Regiment

The order indicates that the Rangers were not supermen; some must have gone to sleep on watch. Either there had been plundering, or Walker wanted to keep it from happening. The order also shows that Ranger commanders made every effort to control their men and provided stringent penalties for infractions that would disgrace the regiment and Texas.

In the meantime, the 2nd Texas had reached Camargo on August 15. They were put to work right away. General Taylor issued Order No. 99, August 17, sending two companies with Worth to Cerralvo as escorts and guards for the pack train on the return.[35] A and K Companies drew this assignment. On the twenty-fourth, Company H was escorting trains to Reynosa, and at the end of the month the first two companies were again on the road.

During these days, Taylor was still not certain what course the war would take. In a letter on August 19, from Camargo, he told a friend that he was marching on Monterey, but if there was no resistance he would continue on to Saltillo. There he would throw up strong fieldworks and, if there was sufficient corn, bring up a strong volunteer force and then "act as best judgment may warrant."[36] Interesting enough at this time, he wrote he did not dislike Scott, though he feared Scott had that impression. To the contrary, he admired him.

On August 25, again from Camargo, Taylor reported that the volunteers were duly reorganized. The Texas foot soldiers, under Col. Albert Sidney Johnston, not wishing to serve beyond term, were mustered out, but the colonel had stayed. Wood's mounted regiment was encamped in the vicinity of Camargo, rendering valuable service as escorts, among other things. Hays's regiment, also mounted, was on the way from Matamoros, going by way of San Fernando, checking new area of country.[37] The commanding general was getting a better feel for what his irregulars could do.

Naturally, his old favorite, Ben McCulloch, was active. Taylor began joining him with Gillespie's men. His next step was to check the road by way of Mier, as far as Cerralvo. About 8:00 in the morning of the twelfth, portions of Gillespie's and McCulloch's companies, with Capt. James Duncan of the 3rd Artillery and Lieutenant Wood of the engineers, as well as some bodyguards, started on a reconnaissance.[38]

It was another miserably hot day, especially hard on the horses. The column moved slowly to keep the animals from too much discomfort. They camped near a large lake and many of the men went swimming. About 7:30 in the evening, they started again. During the night they met a rider who refused to stop — and was shot. The Rangers discovered he was a celebrated horse thief and was riding an American mount. It was a good night's work, the column then being no more than twenty-six miles from Camargo. Three miles from Mier, McCulloch became sick and could not ride any longer. He turned the command over to Captain Duncan and headed for Mier.

This indicated Gillespie was not with them. The regular did a good job with his new command, evidently not pushing them and keeping in mind the men were better at this game than he was. They spent most of the next day resting their mounts and were saddling to make a night march when a horseman approached the camp. It was an American who had lived in Mexico for some time and knew everyone in the area. He told the party that Canales and a Colonel Ramírez were going to a dance in Punta Aguda. The man, Jack Everitt, rode on. Later he joined Company A and was present in the fighting at Monterey.[39]

Since the Rangers liked a *fandango* almost as much as a fight, they were pleased at the prospect of combining both. Duncan gave them permission to attend the ball, and they made a night march to Punta Aguda. At about 10:00 they reached the bridge giving the town its name and halted. They then posted a picket and scouted the small town. They could hear music from inside the place, as detachments rode around to block all exits. Sentries were posted at each avenue, with orders to shoot anyone leaving. By now, Reid stated, the town dogs were making so much noise they were sure their advance was known. Still the music kept blaring. When they got to the main plaza, the center of town, they found perhaps 200 people dancing and drinking and singing. It took the interpreter some time and numerous shouts of "*Silencio!*" to stop the festivities.

Once again, panic ensued as the women started screaming and running in every direction. The men tried to follow, but the Rangers had surrounded the small square. There was the usual search and the usual result. Canales and the colonel, if they had ever been there, had slipped away. The Rangers carried out their customary dancing with the ladies and a few toasts, while a surgeon with the scout set a broken arm on a rider they had captured earlier, his companion having been killed trying to escape. Then the Rangers rode away from town, dozing in their saddles; the excitement was gone, and fatigue had set in. They camped about 3:00 in the morning, but just for a few hours.

The command reached Cerralvo, about seventy-five miles from Camargo, on August 14. Duncan informed the *alcalde* that the army would establish an advanced depot in the town, but that neither people nor property would be disturbed. The man eagerly agreed to this and had food brought. The command moved on to finish the rest of the reconnaissance. They moved constantly, never resting long in one spot, so that any guerrillas or soldiers in the area would not have time to rally and attack. Once, having to cross a narrow but swift river, they had some of the locals bring axes to clear a path through the thorny brush and fell a large tree across the water. Several of the Rangers walked across to the opposite bank holding saddles, blankets, weapons, and anything else that would suffer from being in the water. Leaving a strong guard, the rest swam the horses across and clawed their way through the brush on the opposite side. They were able to ride on in some degree of comfort.

The scout was in the mountains near Cerralvo, and the route was confusing and difficult. Occasionally, they were able to find food at the isolated ranches, and corn for the horses. Most of the time they had their staple menu: coffee, boiled bacon, and bread. When they were about nine miles from Mier, Duncan left the detachment and rode on with his bodyguard to report to Taylor at Camargo. The Rangers rode on to Mier, where they found McCulloch just about recovered from his illness.

It was easier riding now, as Mier had an American garrison, and the road from that place back to Camargo was well traveled. Even so, the Texans captured two enemy soldiers on the way, the men having hidden their weapons in the brush and pretended to be civilians. The column reached Camargo on the afternoon of the seventeenth in time to see the grand parade.

Almost 4,000 troops had assembled in Camargo, and most of them paraded before Taylor in the late afternoon. It was an impressive sight, with soldiers and weapons as bright as could be, horses groomed, sunlight on the bayonets. Six regiments of infantry marched in review, with the artillery battalion as light infantry, plus the batteries of the "flying artillery." It is amusing to imagine this impressive, polished display, with rigid movements, shouted commands, and prompt execution, against the scraggly line of Rangers off to the side who watched in open-mouthed admiration. The review finished, Taylor and his staff galloped off and passed before the Texans.[40]

Now occurs one of the legends, heard ten years later by Frederick Law Olmsted as he made his celebrated tour through Texas.[41] As the story was told to him, the Rangers saw the general coming toward them and, having seen how the regulars saluted him, thought they should do *something.* One suggested they wave their hats and give him a cheer. No sooner said than agreed, and when Taylor rode by, they all waved their hats and gave him three cheers. Startled, but now expecting almost anything from the Rangers, the polite Taylor doffed his hat and gave them a bow. Never one to quit when ahead, some of the Rangers added a few distinctive yells and fired off a few rounds. The drill was unorthodox, but the spirit was clear.

The enlistment of McCulloch's company expired and the company was reorganized at the end of the month. It now became Company A, 1st Texas.[42] Not all the men chose to stay. Some twenty declined to reenlist. Fortunately, Samuel Reid reenlisted, so that his narrative continued throughout the campaign.

Early September was a busy period. The army was in constant movement, with troops advancing from Matamoros to Camargo, supplies moving by road and steamer. The advance was inland, always toward Monterey. Taylor had decided that he could not use all his troops, and he sent Butler's division, with the volunteers, to Cerralvo.[43] On September 1, Order No. 134 directed McCulloch and Gillespie to report to General Worth at Cerralvo.[44] In the same order, Col. Albert Sidney Johnston was directed to report to Butler as acting inspector general, in effect the next highest officer in the division. Johnston, a Texan, had stayed with the army when his infantry regiment voted by a narrow margin to go home when their enlistment was up. It was a fortunate choice by Taylor; later the Texan would perform admirably.[45]

Reid described how the companies went to work, expecting action. Once again, horses were shod, bullets moulded, equipment checked, food smoked. The two Ranger companies left as soon as they received their orders, marching for Mier, which they found almost deserted, all the males having left. There were rumors that men were riding to all the ranches trying to rouse the people to guerrilla warfare, or to join the regular Mexican forces. There was talk, too, that Monterey would be defended to the death — the next passer would assure them there would be no fighting anywhere.

The two companies were busy the next few days, as they scouted the country ahead of the advancing American forces. Lt. George Meade of the topographical engineers accompanied them to make technical reports on the road. They found enemy forces in some strength, but could not quite get close enough for a fight. Probably this was just as well, since the Mexican units outnumbered them considerably. They once again entered Punta Aguda, then on to Cerralvo. Units of the army were strung out on the way, with the 5th and 7th Infantry regiments at Punta Aguda.

During this scout Reid's horse went lame. Fortunately, they were on a road that had been traveled before, and there was no way to become lost. There was a danger of attack from *rancheros*. One of Reid's messmates dropped back and stayed with him, while the column rode on toward Cerralvo. He described the sinking feeling he had at being left out in the middle of Mexico, as well as the joyous satisfaction of finally walking into town and finding the rest of his company waiting for him. This was an ever present danger. The column could not stop for a man with a lame or dead horse, nor could any sizable detachment be left with him. At times like that the Rangers hoped they had memorized the map and could make their way undetected to the nearest friendly unit.[46]

The two companies reached Cerralvo on September 5 and camped; it would be the last quiet encampment they would have for many hard days.[47] The army was moving forward by brigades. On the next day, General Smith's brigade, the 5th and 7th Infantry Regiments, arrived in town from Punta Aguda, having been relieved by the Third Brigade of the First Division. Rumors were flying in every direction. Not a rumor was the proclamation issued by Gen. Pedro de Ampudia from Monterey, cutting off any trade with the Americans under pain of death and calling for an all-out war.[48] Of course, the local population continued selling whatever they could at the highest possible prices.

The Rangers probably didn't bother any more with this notice than they did with any from their own headquarters. They were concerned during early September about enlistments running out. Since no two companies had been mustered in at the same time, enlistments expired at various times. McCulloch's company had already been reorganized on September 1.[49] On the sixth, Company C dropped twenty-six men. This was the largest figure, but most units lost men who refused to reenlist. E, F, and G had considerable losses. It was a time of change. Not only were men returning home, but some rank changes were being made. Lt. Gabriel M. Armstrong of F Company resigned on September 14 and stayed in the company as a private. He would serve gallantly and be wounded at Monterey. Regimental headquarters was not exempt from turnovers. Charles W. Tait, regimental surgeon, resigned on September 6. The sergeant major, Francis L. Payne, resigned and returned to Company E on September 10.[50]

The 2nd Regiment went through a similar turnover.[51] If Holland can be believed, the Eastern Regiment was more disgusted with Taylor than their companion regiment, though he never gives any specifics. It may be that the 2nd was not as accustomed to living in the field as the others, and their company commanders not as experienced in handling complaints. The 2nd certainly suffered more from sickness and had a number of deaths from illness; they also had a considerable listing of discharges for medical reasons. Holland mentioned the large number that were sick.[52] Yet, this regiment had only one deserter during the campaign. The record of each regiment in this respect was probably the finest in the army. The desertion rate among the regulars was a source of chagrin to the officers.

The muster rolls for this early September period show activity that is not otherwise explained. The 1st was still at China and must have had some combat, for three men of Company H were shown killed on September 15. This was probably due to *ranchero* action. For all their indifference to administration, the men who kept the rolls were accurate about whether a soldier was *killed* or died. Six days earlier, a Ranger in Company G is listed as dying at China. Evidently, there was considerable activity in the vicinity, or Walker would not have been concerned about men sleeping on guard.

Of the twenty company rolls and two regimental headquarters returns, the easiest to read is Company K of the 1st. During the campaign, Eli Chandler lost three men killed and two wounded. Not one man deserted, refused to reenlist, or was lost to sickness. Chandler brought them down and took them back, a tribute to a commander in any army.[53]

The force that Taylor would use to attack Monterey was now moving by rapid stages south from the Rio Grande. It was a welcome advance. Not only did the chance for action bolster spirits, but the move away from the hot and dusty river valley led upward to cooler and healthier country. Every person who left memoirs of the northern campaign mentions the appalling sickness rates in the camps along the Rio Grande. Camargo was especially bad. Maj. Luther Giddings recalled that the hospital tents were cleared of dead morning and evening, so that new patients would have room to lie down. The death march never seemed to stop, as burial parties moved out into the chaparral on their sad mission. All suffered, but the volunteer units were hardest hit. Some of the commands never got into combat, yet they lost from one-third to a half of their men through sickness.[54]

Again, most of the eyewitness accounts mention the improvement when they began climbing into the hills. For one welcome change, there were numerous running streams and plenty of vegetation. Campsites were more like modern parks; food was plentiful, and if a lot of them were convinced there would be no resistance at Monterey, most knew a fight was ahead.

The final push would be from Cerralvo. On September 11, Taylor issued Order No. 115, stressing the need for security and outlining the order of march.[55] It was a detailed plan and tends to refute the modern-day concept of the general as a duffer who won despite himself. All the pioneers in the army would be in the advance to repair the road and make it passable for wagons and artillery. They would be proceeded and protected by a squadron of Dragoons and McCulloch's company. The 1st Division would advance on the thirteenth, to be followed on successive days by the 2nd Division. Gillespie's company would be divided — half under his command to report to Butler, the remainder under the first lieutenant to report to General Worth. They would serve as outposts, vedettes, and express riders between the various headquarters and Taylor's headquarters.

Next he ordered the Texans to parallel the main column, both regiments to join, and meet the army in Marin. This involved a sixty-mile ride by the 2nd. In three days they met the 1st and started together for Marin on September 15.[56] For the first time, Maj. Gen. J. Pinckney Henderson was in command of his Texas troops.

Once again, the two detached companies had been active. McCulloch's company led the advance, leaving on the twelfth.[57] They scouted well ahead, protecting the pioneers, who often had heavy going. From time to time it was necessary to widen the road, and the advance was slow. The Rangers took no chances, keeping a strong picket at least a mile or more in advance, moving or halted. McCulloch and a detachment sighted the first of regular enemy cavalry on the thirteenth, but the horsemen were a scouting party and refused to be drawn into a fight. The report on the Mexican force was sent back, and the advance was hastened. The Rangers had stopped at a large *rancho,* where they bought some chickens. Everyone had fled except for one man who sold them the poultry then vanished. They later suspected he was a spy.

Next day the company scouted toward Ramos and engaged the first of the enemy cavalry in open combat.[58] It was an inconclusive affair, with the Rangers playing cat-and-mouse in the mountains, taking care not to be cut off, as they were opposed to some 200 of Torrejón's regulars. There was a brief fire fight, with some wounded and a prisoner taken. They entered Ramos and drove the scattered horsemen into the hills. Coming back, they thought they were in for another fight with a large group on a hillside. It turned out to be some Dragoons.[59]

The prisoner told his captors that Torrejón had about 1,300 men at Marin, eight miles down the road from Ramos. There was great excitement in the camp, where most of the First Division had arrived by forced march. Everyone wanted to know about the fight. Eventually, some of the correspondents would give credit to Captain Graham and his Dragoons for chasing the enemy, much to the mixed disgust and amusement of the Rangers.[60] They had other business.

On the fifteenth the advance guard of the Rangers was in sight of Marin. Along the way several Mexican farmers had come up to the column and told them that Torrejón was stripping the countryside and forcing everyone to come with him to Monterey or flee into the brush. Several pointed out their homes and begged the Rangers not to burn them. McCulloch rode on to where he and a small advance party could see into the town square. The place was full of horsemen, in every stage of leaving. He had too few men to even scout closer and sent some of his people to watch the rear, in case the enemy horsemen tried to circle and cut them off. As usual he was miles ahead of the main force.

When the Mexicans formed, all in good order, and rode out of town, the Rangers followed and found the place almost deserted. Few people were left, as all the women had been carried off, and most of the men had fled or were with the column. They found one old woman who had been forced to prepare a lavish meal for some of the officers, who left before they could finish. Some of the Rangers finished the feast, paying well for the privilege.

They continued scouting as the rest of the army came up and camped about Marin. One group found a well-loaded mule abandoned in the retreat from Marin. They returned to camp with the orderly sergeant in a handsome Mexican uniform, the best-dressed man in the army. Several of the others had found skirts and draped them to advantage, parading about and scaring the horses — and possibly some of the men.

Several prisoners were taken, one who had been working on the fortifications in Monterey. This man described the works in some detail. Clearly, a major battle was ahead. When Taylor learned that Torrejón was nearby, off the main road to Monterey, he sent Charles May and the Dragoons and both Ranger companies to drive him off, fearing a raid on the pack and wagon train. They learned Torrejón and 500 men had passed near there but were gone, probably to Monterey.

On September 18, the bulk of the Texans arrived in camp. For the first time, all twenty companies were together.[61]

SIX

★ ★ ★ ★ ★ ★ ★ ★ ★

Monterey

"Texas went ahead Today — now that danger is expected old Taylor has put us in front . . ."[1] So James K. Holland describes what can be considered the opening of the battle for Monterey. He had earlier mentioned arriving in Marin and finding the lovely town almost deserted. The Texan thought it was the most beautiful place on earth; all the men who left any record of their visit agreed on the view from the town. They were up in the hills now, with the Sierra Madre in the distance. It was too beautiful for war.

Old Taylor probably wasn't too interested in the local scenery, at least it doesn't figure into his orders. No. 119, on September 17, details the order of march for the final advance. The pioneers were disbanded and returned to their units. The two Ranger companies and a Dragoon squadron would lead the advance.[2] Then the two Texas regiments reached Marin, and on the eighteenth he issued No. 120, which changed the order of advance. The Ranger regiments would lead, except for two companies to form the rear guard, with Gillespie's company to act as express. The advance would be on September 19.[3]

And that is why Holland made his sarcastic entry. It was quite an honor, though he didn't see it that way, and probably Old Rough and Ready, as Taylor was called, didn't see it that way either. He put the men best suited for the job where they could do the most good.

At daylight, on September 19, 1846, Gillespie's company started for Monterey, followed by the rest of the 1st Texas, then the 2nd Texas. The regulars came on in numerical order, First Division and Second Division, with the Third Division, the volunteer regiments, in the rear. Reid remembered how majestic it all was, how impressive: the steady tread of thousands of feet, the drums. There would be a few last orderly hours, a final drill-order sequence, before it all changed to chaos.[4]

By 8:00 a ground haze had blocked out the lowlands, with the mountain tops suspended above a white sea of mist. They moved steadily, Taylor and his staff well forward, watching the troops march by. As the sun began to dissolve the mist, they could see the distant city; by then they were passing a huge walnut grove, off to the left of the road, some three miles from the city. The march continued, the Rangers now scattered as foragers. They were soon no more than 1,500 yards from the outskirts of the city.[5]

Looking south to Monterey, the road divided in a Y. The right, or west, fork ran before a huge dark building that had stone walls some thirty feet high. Dirt had been piled against the stone to give additional protection against cannon fire. Fresh earth at ground level showed where a regular bastioned trace had been added outside the walls, turning the place into a fortress. This was the citadel; the Americans would call it the Black Fort, from the weathered stone walls.

Farther west, on the extreme right, outside the city, was a considerable hill mass, topped with another fort. Monterey stretched for a mile and three-quarters, east and west. The city proper was solidly built of stone and adobe, most of the houses being single-story, with a section of two-story buildings near the cathedral, somewhat off center in the town. The area between the city proper and the American scouts was broken, filled with houses in no order, cut with hedges and fences, overgrown with tall grass or crops. Even a casual look indicated this would be a difficult area to cross, as it would break formations, make communications difficult, and permit crossfire from all directions.

Tents could be seen atop many of the hills, but no other sign of enemy troops. All that the Rangers disturbed as they scouted through the fields were stray cattle. Then a bugle began sounding and a considerable lancer force formed on the slopes outside the city and began an advance. Hays's regiment was ordered to dismount and check their weapons (an unnecessary formality) and then they remounted and started out at a trot. One of the buglers sounded a charge, or what passed for a signal, and they started to rush, but the lancers wheeled and went back behind the shelter of the walls and houses.[6]

The advance had taken the Rangers close to the citadel, which was well away from the city. Suddenly, a twelve-pounder tore up the earth before the regiment, and Hays wheeled them and retreated a bit. Taylor and his staff and some engineers had come up to see what they could learn of the city's defenses. One round hit near them, but the old man, in his usual fashion, kept on with his work.

Moving back to a stream, the Texans watered their mounts and then came back for some games. Reid glosses over this, saying they marched and countermarched for a time, but others were more specific.[7] Giddings said they were like little boys testing the first ice, seeing how far they could go before falling through.[8] Circling the citadel, daring the gunners to hit them, they would deliberately wait until they saw the gun flash, then gallop on.

Holland made this note: "[I]t was cheering to see how the Texians greeted the Mexican Balls — Every fire was met with a hearty response of 3 cheers and such waving of hats and huzzaing Genl T says he never heart . . ."[9]

It was the frontier game they had learned from the Comanches: showing off, boasting by horseback, daring the enemy, shaming him. There was an element of risk, but not much. They had the range and knew when to run. They would even swing in under the elevation of the guns and then out as the gunners tried to depress the guns. Perhaps they thought they might entice the lancers out with the show. All they did was make the Mexican artillerymen burn a lot of powder.

The decision had been made to form the main American camp at the walnut grove, and a camp was being laid out while the Rangers were showing their skill as riders. The distant cannon fire and the steady yells convinced many of the marching soldiers that a battle was taking place. It was difficult to halt the advancing troops and get them to start pitching tents, laying out the kitchens and latrines, parking wagons, putting out sentries — all the duties of camp life.

Despite all their officers could do, in spite of sentries, many men wandered down the road or across the fields to see what the enemy city looked like. Some did not even bring their muskets. Fortunately, the Texans had gone back and selected a camp location, then returned to scouting the outskirts of the city. Foraging parties circled the area, seeing how close they could go to the walls. S. Compton Smith mentioned with some wonder that they seemed to go right to the guns and pluck out prisoners. This was more sport than riding the walls.[10]

While many of the Texans were scouting for prisoners, several units were sent out to protect engineers making a detailed reconnaissance of the city's defenses. This was a carefully coordinated effort which further refutes the modern opinion that Taylor bumbled his way through the campaign.[11]

Some of the Rangers escorted Maj. Joseph K. F. Mansfield within 200 yards of the Black Fort, where he made notes and examined the still uncompleted field works surrounding the older walls. This escort duty fell to Lt. Walter Lane of Acklin's company. Lane would be one of the few Rangers to write his memoirs.[12] He told how he was given twenty men and escorted the regular to examine the citadel (Black Fort). They were almost within musket range, and he scattered his men for safety while he and Mansfield dismounted to use their glasses. The engineer suggested that *all* the Rangers should be dismounted, so that the gunners could not tell the officers from the privates. Lane informed him haughtily they were paid a big sum to be officers and the risk came with it.

During the afternoon, R. A. Gillespie was detached to go with Mansfield and some Dragoons to check the Saltillo road and the fortifications guarding that route. They made this move without incident and returned to the growing camp in the trees. Meantime, Captain Williams examined the eastern side of the town and the defenses that had been constructed in one area. Elements of the 2nd Texas escorted him. There was not enough time to check the entire circuit during daylight hours. After sundown, Capt. James Duncan and a Ranger guard went to the west again to see if artillery could be moved through the brush to the Monclova road.

All in all, the Texans had a busy night. In addition to making a camp of sorts, they furnished escorts and aggressively patrolled the outer limits of the city, taking some thirty prisoners.[13]

When all the engineer reports were in, Taylor must have had a sobering view of his task. Capturing Monterey would be difficult. Approaching the city from the north would mean fighting through the maze of suburbs before even coming to the city proper. On the south, the Santa Catarina, a narrow but swift river, made an effective moat the entire length of the place. The eastern part of the city was guarded by a number of fresh earthworks and an old building that had been fortified. This would be called the "tannery" by the attackers.

The engineers had been able to make out a fort of some sort on top of a major elevation on the west of town. Now, with a closer look, the engineers could show that a large mountain, roughly in a T shape, dominated the western side of Monterey. The old bishop's palace was atop the mountain nearest the town. Also on the west, but across the river, was another high hill, also fortified. The first and largest elevation was Independence Hill; the smaller, Federation Hill. Both hills had steep slopes, and in some places sheer rock outcrops higher than a man. Climbing them would be an arduous task, even if not under fire.

Taylor decided to make a major thrust toward the western defenses, taking them from the rear. He assigned this mission to General Worth, giving him the 1st Texas. A division sounds impressive, but it was actually a small number of men for a big task. A battery of horse artillery supported the two brigades. One brigade consisted of all the artillery acting as infantry and the 8th Infantry. The other brigade had a battery of horse artillery, a separate infantry company from Louisiana, and the 5th and 7th Infantry Regiments. Hays's regiment could act as cavalry or dismounted infantry. Altogether the division mustered only 2,000 men.[14] Surprise would be their only ally.

Reid said that when they got orders about 9:00 in the morning, the Rangers thought it was another escort mission while Duncan emplaced his artillery. But soon they saw messengers running all over the large camp, now nicknamed Walnut Springs, and they knew it was more than another scout. The whole place was on the move, so they rode out, going west, and left the rest of the army to do whatever it was about.[15]

By noon the Second Division was on the march and had reached the Monclova road, where they were seen by Mexican observers. The command was moving across country, advancing through the chaparral. The pioneers were cutting paths where necessary for the artillery, and the advance was slow. It was easy to see that enemy infantry were running from the bishop's palace atop Independence Hill to take defensive positions to block the advance. Messengers were sent to Taylor, requesting a diversionary attack to distract attention from the Second. Taylor moved the other two divisions into an attack formation, threatening the northern approaches.

The Ranger advance found a road leading about the base of the hill mass, leading to the great Saltillo road. Here the head of the column halted, while the remainder of the division caught up.

Gen. Edward Burleson of Henderson's staff came up with twenty men and continued about the base of the hill. Hays, Walker, and

McCulloch, along with Lieutenant Colonel Duncan, climbed the hillside for a closer view of the enemy movements. Shortly afterward, General Worth rode up with an aide and climbed the hill. Worth checked the situation and rode off the brow of the hill to the right.

Burleson returned in a hurry, with the information that he had run into enemy pickets covering a large cavalry and infantry force, all coming to cut off the Americans. It was necessary to inform Worth of this development and get orders. George Kendall, who had come along, volunteered as a messenger and rode after Worth. While waiting for the division commander, all the officers except McCulloch descended the hill and waited.

Worth came up and sent part of McCulloch's company under Lt. William H. Kelley to join the bulk of Gillespie's men as advance. The officers rode out, followed by the remainder of Hays's Rangers and a body of infantry. They moved along the road, winding about the mountain, where the Mexican pickets had been spotted. There was a deep gorge on their right, with some huts and a well. The men took this opportunity to fill canteens and gourds, as Worth had halted the march while he and Persifer Smith climbed another hill to check the defenses of Independence Hill. With no sign of the enemy pickets or their main force, Worth decided to continue to the Saltillo road.

Hays left a picket on a commanding elevation with orders to signal if they spotted any movement. The division kept on, advancing another thousand yards along the road. There they found what had happened to the enemy force. The cavalry had dismounted and, with the infantry, had taken cover in a corn field. Another group was scattered along a series of fences. The Ranger advance was no more than seventy yards from the enemy when they came under fire. Fortunately, it was beyond effective range of the muskets and carbines. A real danger was the cannon on the hill, now in point-blank range. Round shot began tearing through the brush, cutting the chaparral. From time to time, the gunners lobbed shells into the field. As these exploded, the Ranger horses, accustomed only to small arms, reared and began running; several men were unhorsed.

Immediately the retreat was ordered, but some men had been left behind. The Ranger advance party was falling back, in considerable confusion, when Lieutenant McMullen saw a man on foot, with some mounted lancers a short distance away. This was no longer a show; this was life and death. McMullen wheeled back, got behind the man, then turned and came toward him at a gallop. He reached down, grabbed an arm, and swung the Ranger up behind him. They reached the shelter of the main body in safety. Reid said he was nearly unhorsed, but managed to cling to his horse's mane until he could get his feet back into the stirrups. The rest of the Rangers rode up and covered the retreat of the scouts. Despite the surprise, not a man was injured.

Lane mentioned another incident during the day, again involving Major Mansfield.[16] This time, the engineer was trying to learn more about the bishop's palace and was escorted by some of Acklin's men. They could not get a decent view of the fortification from the ground, without being hit by artillery fire, so the enterprising Rangers found a large mesquite tree and managed to get Mansfield up in the top. He had a good view with fieldglasses and began making notes. It will never be known if one of the Rangers saw, or thought he saw, enemy troops. There is a good chance that one of the Rangers had a fine sense of horseplay and came riding toward the tree, shouting that lancers were coming.

The escort began mounting and riding about. Poor Mansfield, thinking he was being abandoned, started climbing down and slipped and fell to the ground. He was not injured, other than to his dignity. Lane did not speculate about the validity of the alarm, other than to say they could not find any lancers.

It was close to sundown, and Hays brought up his command, some 250 men, and encamped near some more *jacales* near the road. The Rangers did not immediately unsaddle, since they were too busy grabbing the chickens and pigs running loose in the place. The laughing Rangers began attacking with stones and what swords they had. It was a scene of complete confusion as the yelling men chased cackling and squealing animals.

Hunger had displaced caution; there were no pickets to notice that an enemy cavalry force had ascended a nearby hill and was watching the collecting of supper. Suddenly they charged, opening fire at close range. Reid mentioned with some humor that now the chickens and pigs were not the ones running, but the Rangers.[17] Hays immediately brought order out of the confusion, forming the dismounted Acklin and Samuel L. S. Ballowe out in the road, the rest behind the chaparral fence. The wild yells began, with the rifles dropping the charging lancers. Closer in, the five-shooters began their work. It was over in a moment, with considerable loss to the attackers. It had been sundown when the first rush began, and it was almost dark when the fight was over. Reid suspected that at least 500 men attacked the camp. In his after action report, Hays said there were from 200 to 300. He reported that they attacked the camp and were driven back. His loss was one killed and one wounded.[18]

Everyone spent a miserable night. When they started out in the morning, the Rangers and the division thought they would be back in camp by nightfall; consequently, the troops had not brought food. The Rangers had left their pack mules behind, as well as blankets and jackets. Now they all took what shelter they could in the few huts and under trees, or behind fences. It was cool, and they could not light fires for heat, as the guns on the hills commanded the area. They did not unsaddle but merely eased the girths to rest the horses. A rain shower made those outside more miserable, but it at least provided some water. The people on the hill tops had control of the irrigation ditches running through the fields and cut off the water. The Rangers and the troops of the Second Division walked about in the dark, trying to find rain water in the ditches.

Worth was inside one of the corn sheds writing a dispatch to Taylor.[19] He used a pencil, trying to see by a torch made of dried corn stalks. He was going on with the plan to attack the city from the west, moving right at the enemy strength. The steep hills were so impassable, he gambled they might be lightly manned.

On the north of town, Taylor was emplacing a ten-inch mortar and two twenty-four-pounder howitzers. He left the 4th Infantry to guard them and pulled back the rest of his command to Walnut Creek. At least this part of the army had tents and some hot food.

On September 21 the 1st Texas, the division light infantry supporting, started off at dawn for the Saltillo road.[20] About a mile down the road they saw the advance pickets of a sizable force. The Mexican scouts approached, but the Rangers charged and scattered them, driving them back on the main body. This was a major force, estimated at 1,500, almost the size of the entire Second Division. Hays moved his companies forward, halting at a strong fence. His report says he saw the enemy in force and dismounted five companies, those of Acklin, Green, Herbert, Ballowe, and James Gillespie. He sent McCulloch to the right flank, keeping this company mounted. Later, there would be some confusion, with the idea that McCulloch did not receive the order in time and was caught out in the open. Hays evidently wanted a mounted unit to protect the exposed right flank.

The Rangers were not alone, as Smith's light infantry came up and took position, while Duncan's battery would enter the fight at a critical moment. For a time, though, they took the full brunt of the lancer charge. This was an elite unit, one of the best in the Mexican army, with a famous commander, Lt. Col. Juan N. Nájera. The lancers came full gallop at the fence line, green and red pennants fluttering in the wind.

The Rangers waited until close range and started firing with rifles and some shotguns. The lancers began falling, but others leaped the fence, reformed, and charged from the other direction. If any of the Americans doubted the bravery of the Mexican forces, this fight showed them the error of their ways.

Off on the flank, McCulloch's company was caught up in the melee as the lancers retreated. It was a whirling mass of screams, falling horses, wounded men crying in pain, the rapid firing of five-shooters.[21] The heavier horses of the Rangers saved many lives, as they bowled over the lancer mounts. This was a forerunner of the revolver battles of the Civil War, and the new weapons took a heavy toll.

Nájera fell after being shot, got up screaming for his men to stand, and was not seen again. Despite the revolvers, the Rangers with McCulloch had been carried along in the press of retreating lancers, when they were all caught in the fire of the light infantry and Duncan's artillery. Lieutenant Armstrong was wounded and unhorsed and was fighting on foot with a captured saber against two lancers. Killing one, the Ranger was being forced back when one of the dismounted artillerymen decided he was going to kill the Mexican — even if he killed the Ranger. Fortunately, he had loaded with ball and not buckshot, and spared Armstrong.

The Mexican infantry had not come up to support the lancers, falling back and climbing up the hills. The cavalry, now pretty well cut up, more and more falling to the advancing light infantry muskets, broke. As they fell back, the Texans along the fence brought them under rifle fire and further scattered them. The ground was littered with lances, sabers, colorful uniforms, and dead horses. The Rangers were impressed with the silver-decorated saddles, and probably a considerable amount of undocumented souvenir hunting took place.

Reid thought they inflicted 150 casualties on the lancers, but Hays's report mentions a hundred.[22] They both say that either thirty-two or thirty-three enemy dead were buried in one long pit. Hays mentions one lieutenant colonel and one captain killed and buried. It was not a one-sided affair. The Rangers had one man killed, probably by fire from the light infantry, and seven were wounded. There was a lot of damage to the mounts, including Walker's horse, which was badly cut by lance thrusts.

It is not clear where the other companies of the 1st Texas were during the fight at the fence, but they came up late and the entire regiment was ready for action.

Worth had sent reports to Taylor, asking for a demonstration, as he planned to take Federation Hill. The guns that had been emplaced during the night opened fire on the city and the other American divisions darted forward, as though they were attacking. The 2nd Texas rode out with this force.[23] Once again, the Eastern Regiment was doing a necessary task, but not one that gained fame. The demonstration did draw off considerable troops from the heights above Worth's small command.

Federation Hill lay across the river, commanding the Saltillo road. Of all the heights it was the one easiest to climb, as well as being isolated. Once taken, it would help command the road, blocking any reinforcements riding to the relief of the city. Until it was taken, no direct attack could be made on the southwestern part of the town.

At about 11:00, Worth ordered the attack. He told Hays to detail five companies for the assault — R. A. Gillespie, Ballowe, McCulloch, Chandler, Green, and McGowan, commanded by Maj. Michael Chevallie. Captain Smith and elements of the dismounted artillery made up the initial assault force, some 300 men. Well over half of the force were Rangers. There was some initial grumbling about Chevallie commanding the Rangers, as Smith was to be overall commander. The Texans said they didn't mind a captain leading a major, and the attack was on.

During this time, the batteries on the hill had been firing round shot and grape at the American forces along the road. Worth pulled his troops back out of range and sent the assault party forward. The Rangers and regulars advanced on the double through the brush, going single-file to avoid being seen, but they were discovered, and the shot began tearing the earth again. They were moving too fast for the gunners to change elevation. Reid recalled how Worth had ridden up as they left and told them they were to take the hill — and he knew they would. They yelled assent and started off.[24]

When they reached the banks of the river, they were suddenly exposed to the full view and fire of the troops atop the hill. The water was only waist deep, but the current slowed them, and the enemy shot was striking the water in a steady, hissing sound. To everyone's amazement, the force crossed the barrier without loss and sank down to rest a moment in the heavy chaparral that covered the base of the hill. Water was emptied from boots and shoes, and weapons checked for priming and caps.

Reinforcements could be seen on the hill, and swarms of skirmishers were descending the slope to open fire on the attackers. Worth was watching this action and sent forward the 7th Infantry as a reinforcement. The "Cotton Balers," only seven companies strong, started forward. The Rangers had become separated from the artillery acting as infantry, and the men of the 7th actually reached the Texans first. No longer trying to conceal their movements, all started up the slope. The rifles of the Rangers began their deadly crackling, far outranging the enemy muskets. Yelling, firing, reloading as they moved, the Rangers and the regulars moved up the slope.[25]

Back along the fence line, where the Ranger mounts were tied, Hays watched the fighting and gathered a hundred men and started for the hill. He did this on his own, seeing the descent of the Mexican skirmishers. In his report he says Worth ordered him to detach five companies for the initial assault, but of this movement he merely says he took a hundred men and went forward. As they were running forward, all could see the regimental flag move up the hill, and then the top was gained. Cheers could be heard, answered from the troops still along the road.

The infantry force on the hill did not give way easily, but the rifle fire and the steady advance was too much. Once started, they fell back toward a fort on the right of the hill. The Rangers found an overturned nine-pounder on the crest, evidently about to be rolled down the hill. They righted the gun, and soon it was placed in action by some of the artillerymen. Off to the right, about 400 yards away, was a major defense, Fort Soldada. The retreating defenders were streaming toward this shelter while the Americans were still climbing the slope. Worth had by then thrown most of his troops into the action. The 5th Infantry, made up of six companies, was on the move, with a company of Louisianians.

It was a mixed rush: part atop the hill, down toward Soldada, some still climbing, all heading for the fort before the enemy could get set and make another stand. R. A. Gillespie was the first man inside the walls, followed by the color sergeant of the 5th with the regimental colors. Sergeant Updegrass rammed the staff into the earth on some breastworks, while cheers echoed across the valley. In a moment, elements from all commands were inside, and the place was taken.

Lt. Thomas G. Pitcher of the 5th Infantry was one of the early ones in the fort. He walked up to a captured nine-pounder and turned to some of the Rangers. "Well, boys, we liked to have beaten you," he said. Then he took some chalk and wrote on the gun barrel: "Texas Rangers" and "5th Infantry."[26]

The Americans had a commanding view. This hill was not as high as the mass of Independence only 600 yards away, but for once they could look down into Monterey and the countryside. The city was half-covered in smoke, and the guns in the bishop's palace started firing; the Rangers returned fire with the captured guns on the hill. Considerable stores were taken, though most of the garrison got away. Losses were surprisingly light, all wounded. McCulloch's company had four wounded, including C. E. DeWitt of Reynosa chicken fame. He could fight as well as he could ride.

The assault lasted about an hour and a half, plus the time to move to the base of the hill. It was after 3:30 when parties began searching the slope and the chaparral for wounded and moving them back to the hospitals in the main camp. The Rangers were sent down to tend to their horses, while the bulk of the attacking force remained at the top of the hill in case of a counterattack.

It was another miserable night with heavy rain. For the second night the troops had little to eat, though Reid reported that a Mexican woman in one of the huts took pity on some of the Rangers who were trying to keep dry in her yard and fed them what little she and her family had.[27] Despite the rain, recon parties were out.

Monterey was a battle fought in two parts — east and west. The opening was in the west, with Worth's division and the 1st Texas. It is simpler to follow their actions to a conclusion, holding the account of the other divisions and the 2nd Texas as they attacked the eastern side of the city.

Worth next was going after Independence Hill and the bishop's palace. With this height in American hands, they could block any relief efforts from Saltillo, as well as control the western side of Monterey. It was an essential terrain feature in any further action, offensive or defensive. The main hill mass was 700 to 800 feet high, rising in stone ledges four to five feet high, with dense clumps of brush growing from the rock and earth. It was a difficult climb in daylight; Worth was going to take the place by night.

Walter Lane was picked again for special duty. Sam Walker came by Acklin's company and told Lane to pick twenty good men and get atop the hill and watch the bishop's palace.[28] Their mission was to put pickets as near the palace as possible to warn of a sortie. The rest were to guard the road and prevent a surprise from that direction. Lane recalled how honored he felt to be selected. Not being a complete fool, he also remembered that he would have given his last three dollars for some other officer to have been so honored.

They moved out in the darkness and managed to get about a half mile from the palace, with two men up close. The rest huddled in the darkness and cold and watched the road. They were half dozing when they heard noises about 3:00 in the morning. The attack force was on the move.

Seven companies of the 1st were in the assault, those of R. A. Gillespie, McCulloch, Green, Acklin, James Gillespie, Herbert, and Ballowe. The remaining three companies were returned to guard duties and keeping the horses. Three companies of the artillery battalion and three companies of the 7th made up the party, all under the command of Lieutenant Colonel Childs. Hays said he had 250 Rangers in the force, well over half. He and Walker went along, the force being divided into two units: Hays and Childs on the right, Walker on the left. They moved out in silence, led by Lt. George Meade and a Mexican guide. The command was undetected in the darkness and divided at the foot of the slope, each team starting to climb.

The Mexicans had not placed pickets on the slope, nor did they appear to have sentries on the top of the hill on the side away from town. Given the nature of the ground and the darkness, it seemed ridiculous for anyone to attempt an assault up the almost vertical surface of the reverse slope. But the Rangers and their comrades were steadily but slowly crawling hand over hand up the ledges. The climb took quite a long time, as the men had to reach about in the darkness to find a firm hand or foot hold and then inch laterally to another ledge. The regulars had a somewhat easier time, as they could sling their arms, but the Rangers had no slings and each was forced to secure his rifle and use one hand to climb. Nevertheless, they managed to get within a hundred feet of the summit before they were discovered. One regular's tin canteen clanked against the rocks and the alarm was given.[29] Numerous skirmishers rushed from the Mexican defenses to the rim of the hill and opened fire into the darkness. Still the men kept climbing, not returning the fire or answering the cries of defiance. About twenty feet from the top, some of the Texans began using their rifles. They could probably see the Mexicans outlined against the sky as they leaned over to fire down the hill. Up close, the flash from the enemy muskets helped locate them.

Now the fight began.[30] R. A. Gillespie was the first to reach the top and was upon some earthworks when he was hit. Lieutenant Nelson shot the enemy sniper. Some of his company started to assist him, but he waved them on. The brow of the hill was quickly cleared, the defenders running toward the bishop's palace on the T end of the hill, down the slope toward the city. Some had the forethought to haul away a cannon. The attackers were too exhausted to chase them. It was just getting daylight, and the Texans were yelling, joined by the regulars. Part of the job was done.

There might have been a counterattack, but Worth had ordered the 7th to make a diversionary attack at daylight. Across the river, the companies of infantry came down from Federation and started toward the bishop's palace, yelling as they came. They began to draw grape from the guns in the palace, but they took shelter behind a fence and suffered no loss. The diversion was enough; the enemy infantry continued their retreat. The companies of the 7th went back to their positions on Federation.

Having command of the hilltop meant nothing until the palace was captured. The 8th was sent forward; the other three companies of the 8th, still in camp, were brought up and a diversionary force was sent toward the palace. A strong Ranger group was in this unit, and they began sniping at the defenders of the palace with considerable effect. The defenders threw out a strong sortie to drive back the snipers but were repulsed with some loss.

Worth next brought down the 5th from Federation and they crossed the open ground and forded the river under heavy artillery fire. Again the hail of grape whipped the water but caused no casualties. A twelve-pounder had been brought around from the main camp, disassembled, and carried up 700 feet of hill. Again assembled, it began firing on the palace at a 400-yard range. The shells tore apart the walls. This, with the constant sniping, forced the Mexican commander to make a last effort to clear the hill.

Mexican cavalry and large infantry formations could be seen coming up from the city, massing before the palace. The American plan was simple — if it worked. There was a pile of rocks, almost a fence, across the middle of the hilltop, sloping slightly toward the palace. The regulars were slipped forward, reinforcing the Rangers who had been using this for cover. Around the crest, out of sight, were other troops, largely Rangers. Blanchard's company from Louisiana was to be bait, falling back as if retreating, drawing the enemy into the trap. If they could break the attack and follow close on the retreat, they might get into the palace with the Mexicans.

It all worked for these lucky men, who had led a charmed existence. Blanchard fell back as the enemy bugles sounded the charge. Lancers and massed infantry rushed after the retreating Americans, yelling defiance.

They were twenty yards from the hidden men when the command was given. The regulars stood and presented bayonets, a long line of steel across the hilltop. The front rank of the charging force was almost on the bayonet tips before they saw what had happened. Then the regulars fired. At that range even the muskets were accurate. The advance stopped, those in the rear shoving the ranks ahead. They tripped over the dead and wounded, tried to turn, but those behind could not give way. The attack had been almost a column, blocked by the line of infantry. Now the Rangers along the crest stood and began firing into the flanks of the column, yelling and reloading, firing again.

A cry of "Charge!" came forth and the Texans rushed from the flanks; the bayoneted line rushed forward too. The shattered Mexicans ran, streaming on either side of the palace, running down the slope toward the shelter of the city. The Mexicans were followed into the palace before they could barricade the entrances, and the place was taken without opposition. About thirty prisoners were captured inside the fort, including an officer who was trying to fire the magazine. The four artillery pieces were shifted to bear on the city and were soon bombarding the western edge of town and the fleeing enemy.

Lt. G. W. Ayers of the 3rd Artillery hauled down the enemy colors, but Walker upheld the honor of Texas by cutting down the signal flags before the place. More artillery was being brought up and a brisk fire opened on the troops trying to reorganize in the western part of Monterey. This shelling was so intense and accurate that the Mexicans retreated beyond the cemetery. The rest of the division came up to the area near the palace, while the Rangers went back to the old camp near the road intersection to water and feed their horses. It was about 4:00 in the afternoon, and the rest of daylight was spent looking for wounded and taking them to shelter.

Gillespie was carried down the hill and placed inside one of the huts, along with a Private Thomas from McCulloch's company. There was little they could do for Thomas. He died the next day and was buried atop Independence Hill, near where he was shot.

The two days of success and low casualties enjoyed by the 1st Texas and Worth's Division were in marked contrast to the heavy losses suffered by the other two divisions attacking the eastern side of Monterey. Those two days went like the Mexican defenders had probably hoped and expected for all the defenses. In addition to the outer houses being loopholed, making strong defense against infantry attacks, there were numerous field works and fortified buildings of exceptional strength. The field works, unfortunately, were low-profile defenses and could not be seen from a distance. The heavy fire from the citadel had prevented recon parties from plotting them.

Taylor evidently intended to make a strong diversion in favor of Worth's attack of September 21.[31] He told Col. John Garland "to take any of them little forts with the bayonet if you can." They started out with this as a guide. Wood and the 2nd Texas went with May and the Dragoons to the west, while the infantry and artillery marched to attack the east. As the troops closed on the city they came under fire from the citadel, then again as they approached the houses and field works. Garland's command became heavily involved, and reinforcements were hurried forward. Once begun, the fight became a slugging contest; the intended diversion turned into a bloody struggle.

Any battle, in any age, is confusion, but fighting in towns is especially difficult. Some of the troops had to cross the river, where they were completely open and exposed to heavy musketry. Some regiments had to fall back before the enemy fire — something no unit in the army had experienced before. Giddings watched his wounded of the Ohio Regiment being butchered by the Mexican lancers. Companies of the 4th Infantry, leading a charge, lost a third of their ranks in one terrible volley. Regulars and volunteers alike were caught in crossfire and frontal fire. Men saw their officers fall, and the surviving officers came to lead squads.

Somehow, in all the chaos, some units held, crept forward, and found themselves overlooking the enemy. The Mississippi Rifles charged the tannery *(el teneria)* without bayonets, their new rifles having no bayonet lugs. They got a firm foothold on the eastern edge of the city. Leaving a strong force to hold the captured buildings, Taylor pulled back the rest to camp. It had been a terrible day, with most of the losses for the battle concentrated among the participants fighting in the eastern outskirts of Monterey.

There was little activity on the eastern side on the twenty-second. Most of the morning was spent bringing in any wounded not killed by the lancers and further consolidating the captured area. Troops were relieved and rested. A considerable force of lancers was massed before the citadel, but demonstrations failed to bring them into fighting range. Shelling came from both sides. There was a rumor of lancers coming up the Caderits road, and Wood's Texans were sent to stop them. After a five- or six-mile scout, no enemy were found and the Rangers returned to camp.

Holland had a single note for the day: "[O]n this day our Company was ordered to guard Bragg's Batteries — and to keep off the Ranchers and Lancers."[32] Bragg had been a key player the day before. But now, on the west side, most ot the activity was carried on by the American artillery.

Many of the troops on the eastern plain had a good view of the fighting that took the bishop's palace in the afternoon, and they cheered their comrades in the west.[33]

On September 23 the 2nd Texas got into the fight. They had been busy before, but it was not the action that got in Kendall's dispatches to the home papers. The mundane trivia of bringing up food and supplies required large escorts, and one company of the 2nd was on detached duty protecting trains coming up from Camargo. Some of Henderson's staff had been placed in charge of the huge mule trains, doing commendable service. Maj. H. L. Kinney would be specifically mentioned in Taylor's report for this service.

At 8:00 in the morning, Wood was ordered to take his regiment and investigate reports of enemy advances on the eastern side of the city. His report says the unit was mounted and the nine companies in the saddle within ten minutes.[34] They scouted and found that the enemy cavalry had retreated back inside the city. Wood left Capt. O. M. Wheeler's company to observe any further move and returned to a covered position north of a battery captured the preceding day. About 10:00, Wood received an order from Taylor to report for further orders.

When he reached the general, he was told to dismount his regiment and assist the Mississippi Rifles and the Tennessee Regiment, which had taken some houses on the outskirts of town. He went back and sheltered his horses as well as he could, leaving the necessary horse holders and security, and turned toward the city with a force slightly below 300. He divided his men into two battalions; Lt. Col. John

Myrick took one side, Maj. W. R. Scurry headed the other.

They started out at a run, crossing 200 yards of open ground under fire. Wood went where he thought he could do the most good. In a short time they were joined by Henderson and his staff. Captain Truett and Captain Thompson started up Matamoros Street, two other companies paralleling them. The rest spread out, and all began a new form of combat.

The Texans soon caught up with the mixed force of volunteers and regulars who had moved some distance into town. They added a new dimension — noise. Holland wrote for the day: "[S]uch shooting and huzzering and hallowing seemed by instinct to let the enemy know that Texas had come to Town . . ."[35]

T. B. Thorpe, inside the city with Quitman's brigade, watched as the Texans came up. Until then, he said, the 2nd had not fired a shot, but they rushed to battle. Mirabeau Lamar remained mounted, but the other senior officers were more sensible and were on foot. Wood was running about yelling about Mier and Goliad, and the Texas yells took on a wild note. "It was a terrible sight, even compared to all those exhibited in the two days of sanguinary battle of Monterey, to witness the Texans; adopting their own mode of fighting, they soon broke into the shut up houses, scaled walls, and appeared on the housetops. Wherever a Mexican displayed himself, the deadly fire of the rifle brought him down."[36]

Thorpe described how the Rangers would select a house for attack, rush across the street under covering fire from their rifles, and batter in the door with axes or sledges. Once inside, they cleared the rooms and then fought up the roofs and across to the next house by the roof. They avoided the streets and the barricades at street intersections.

It would be expected that the Rangers of the 1st would be the ones who developed this form of street fighting, but Wood's men had evidently listened to the stories of fighting in San Antonio and Mier. The Texans were the only ones in the army who had experience fighting in towns.[37] Everyone who took part in the fight and left any record mentions their method of fighting.

About 10:00 in the morning in the west, McCulloch and some of the regulars made a reconnaissance and found the garrison had pulled back from the western edge of town, at least as far as the cemeteries. Worth could hear firing from the opposite side of Monterey, but he was so far from Taylor's headquarters and the route was so hazardous that there was almost no communication between the two forces. He was shifting troops and moving artillery during the morning and started in some of the regulars about midday. Early in the afternoon, hearing the continued fighting and thinking a major attack was taking place — which was true — Worth sent his entire division into the fight.[38]

He ordered in the 1st, and Hays took every man he could muster, some 400. Because of the necessary horse guards and some men on scout, sixty Rangers were absent from the main fight. The figures are from his after action report and show that the regiment was still in good shape, even after the heavy losses during the recent reorganization. A number of men in the regiment had been at Mier and were familiar with street fighting. As they started for the city they picked up axes, sledges, and picks from the abandoned Mexican earthworks, tools they soon put to good advantage, as had their fellow Texans on the eastern side of town. Some of them, assisted by the artillery, carried mortar shells. Instructed by the gunners in setting fuses, they would introduce a new dimension to house-to-house fighting.[39]

The main avenue in Monterey, Calle de Monterey, started up near the bishop's palace and ran through the central part of town, finally forming the southwestern side of the main plaza. On the western end of this street was a ruined church and a cemetery. Farther in was Plaza de Carne, where the main business section began. The plaza had a lovely fountain. Hays and his men came along this axis, while Walker attacked along Iturbide Street.

Although largely uncoordinated, the two American forces were moving from west to center and east to center, compressing the defended toward the main plaza and the great cathedral.

The Rangers fought inside the houses and across the roofs, using their rifles to clear the opposite rooftops and to drop enemy snipers. There is no doubt that in the close fighting, after entering a room, their Colts would have been deadly weapons. Some Mexican accounts support this, as they claimed the bullets could fly up stairs and around corners.[40] The walls between rooms and houses were largely adobe and could be hacked through. Ladders were found or manufactured to gain the rooftops. At times the men would cut a small hole and stuff in one of the mortar shells to blow out a large section of rock and adobe. There was constant yelling, which kept them elated and worried the defenders.

This was different from the days before, when the troops under Twiggs and Butler suffered so terribly. The regulars and volunteers in the east seemed to be having a somewhat easy time. Holland noted in his diary for the day that they advanced so fast, Taylor thought they were retreating Mexicans and opened fire: ". . . fired on us — well nigh ruined us — but it was stopped in time."[41]

In all the fighting and confusion the usual strange things happened. Smith described a certain Señor Gehar who had resigned himself to the inevitable and knew he would be robbed and slain. Hoping to get some degree of mercy, he put all his silverplate on a great table to save the invaders the trouble of destroying his house and also set a banquet with all the food he had. To his terror, the first Americans who broke in his door were the bearded Rangers. He and his family offered the men food, which was accepted with gratitude. As that group went their way, several others came in. At nightfall all the food was gone, and not so much as a fork had been taken from the table.[42]

It would be untrue to suggest that the fighting on the twenty-third was simple, or that the Rangers carried the entire fight. One participant said he thought the Texas rifles made the difference, but Hays said half jokingly that if the Mexicans had been better shots none of them would have survived. The Rangers did have a feel for this form of combat and the weapons and training to carry it off. It was frontier cat-and-mouse played among the rooms and halls and across the rooftops. Regular and volunteer troopers saw and adapted and followed their example, though most of them had to fight along the streets, where they were subject to heavy fire. The artillery crews, as always, performed gallantly, suffering terribly as they could find little shelter while trying to blow away the street barricades.

Both Ranger regiments were closing in on the main plaza as the day was ending. Wood's men were at Santa Rita and Morelo, a block from the cathedral, with others up on Santa Rita leading south to the cathedral. Hays's men were at about the same relative location on the west side of the plaza.

Commanders in both areas agreed that they were within a square of the main plaza when Taylor decided to call a halt for the night. Holland said they were almost in control when ordered to withdraw so that the city could be bombarded. He says they withdrew only after the third order. Hays in his report diplomatically skirts the issue. According to him, Walker stayed in place, while he pulled his Rangers back under Worth's orders. Part of this was probably to care for the mounts.

According to all sources, getting the Rangers on either side to fall back was difficult. W. S. Henry, probably talking about the 2nd

Texas, said: "General Taylor, finding the field-pieces of little use, ordered us to retire as soon as the volunteers had withdrawn . . . It was a difficult matter to get the volunteers out; they were having their own fun."[43] The Americans did not have the experience of Mier, nor the recollection that the Texans had almost won that town when they agreed to parley and lost the battle.

On the west, word went back to Worth that they had taken the lower city by themselves and would hold it by themselves.[44] And they did. After the rest of the troops had withdrawn, shelling began, but the Rangers took what shelter they could and suffered no damage.

They were active during the night. Walker occupied the post office and governor's house and scouted enemy positions. Somehow, he managed to get a little rest. Walter Lane said that he and the lieutenant colonel got a few winks in General Ampudia's bed, spurs and all. It must have been a brief nap.

McCulloch's company was on picket duty when they heard the fighting start again and came into the outskirts at a gallop. Hays had them dismount and tie their horses and started them down the streets on foot. On the way they helped some artillerymen clear barricades so they could haul up their guns. By then, more of the regulars were entering the area. Mexican women were offering them oranges and telling them the lancers had slipped away during the night. Before they could get fully involved, Mexican buglers were sounding the calls for a parley.

The Texans were on a rooftop when an officer and a flag bearer suddenly appeared. The two were immediately shot by the Rangers. Walker cautioned them about firing on a white flag — unless there was some reason. Despite their better instincts, the Rangers held their fire. Eventually, another truce team appeared, with understandable reluctance. They were not shot and were taken to headquarters.

It was early morning, September 24, 1846. The battle for Monterey was over. The Rangers just didn't know it yet.

SEVEN

★ ★ ★ ★ ★ ★ ★ ★ ★

Armistice

The Texans didn't pay too much attention to the bugles calling for a parley. They supposed the Mexicans were trying to bargain for a little time, and they continued with preparations for the fighting that could start up at any moment. The Rangers on the western side of the plaza were in a very advantageous position, overlooking Mexican positions below them, with the enemy troops protected only by sandbagged barricades. As the Rangers went on chipping loopholes in the roof parapets, they picked out their targets. Below, Mexican women were still in the occupied houses, cooking meals which the hungry Texans bought for a picayune — the best food buy of the campaign.

The houses showed every sign of hasty flight. Cartridges, weapons, maps, chests, and uniforms littered the floors and tables. The Rangers enjoyed a large supply of tobacco and waited. At noon, orders came to hold positions and not to fire unless a cannon shot was heard, which would mean the fight was on again. There had been no firing since early morning, when they shot the messengers. The last shelling had been several mortar rounds. Unknown to the Texans, these rounds had stopped the fighting. One round had been short, but the American gunners changed the charge, and the next shell exploded near the cathedral, causing great damage. General Ampudia was afraid that following rounds would detonate the magazine in the cathedral; it was then that he signaled he wanted to parley.[1]

All afternoon the Texans and the rest of the army waited, for once in a hot sun. About 5:00 in the afternoon word came that both sides had signed a truce. The fighting was over. There were strict orders not to cheer, but the Rangers were in no mood to celebrate. They were bitter. For three days they had battled to get the garrison in a position to really cause damage, and now they were to be stopped. They did not understand this type of combat. Diplomacy was not their forte.

Not only the Texans but his own government would castigate Taylor. In retrospect, engrossed as we are now in total war concepts, his decision to allow the garrison to withdraw with their weapons was unthinkable. Eventually, his superiors felt the same way, but at the time there may have been reason on his side. First, diplomatically speaking, he still thought the northern provinces might be broken off from the central Mexican government. If he gave generous terms, this would show the Americans were fighting not Mexico, but the government.[2] Throughout history this very plausible reasoning has not worked. On a purely military basis, he was still facing a force at least double his own army. He did not have the confidence of the Texans that another day would lead to a slaughter of the garrison. There were several thousand civilians cooped in the center of the city with the garrison. Shelling and close combat would take a heavy toll of innocent people.

Whatever his reasons, Taylor selected three commissioners to talk with the Mexican representatives. General Worth, Governor Henderson, and Col. Jefferson Davis drew up and signed the document that ended the fight. Taylor's letter on September 25, explaining his action and his reasons, indicates he was not too certain what reception his decision would have in Washington City. In the meantime, they were there and he was here and a lot of weeks were between them. Some of the commanders on the ground agreed with Taylor. Jeff Davis, one who had negotiated the truce, which extended into an armistice, wrote to a newspaper a few months later and vigorously defended the action, listing excellent reasons why they had acted as they did.[3]

None of this made any difference to the Texans. They knew what would have happened — and nothing ever changed their opinion. They were told not to cheer, which they would not have done under any circumstance, but no one said not to curse — and there was probably considerable profanity along the rooftops that September afternoon.

Formal surrender took place on the twenty-fifth, with the Mexican flag atop the citadel being replaced by the Stars and Stripes. It was a glorious ceremony. Officers on both sides embraced as though they had attended a social event and not a bloody street fight. The same day the first large contingent of the garrison marched out with full military honors, flags flying, bugles blowing, much as a conquering force.[4] This further disgusted the Rangers, and the irony was not lost on others in the army who gathered to watch. Throughout the week, other detachments left the city, and it was this phased withdrawal and the blowing of trumpets that proved too much for some of the Rangers.

On September 26, Holland had the following entry: "Col Woods brot in the news that we were no longer needed — and that Genl T was well pleased — and that we might go home when we pleased, but if the war continued he wanted Texians. So now as soon as we get our little might we will be off — our departure seems to be very much regreted."[5]

The discharging of the Texans has been treated in various ways by modern writers, and even many of the contemporary observers did not know about the peculiar enlistments of the various companies. McCulloch's time was already up; the rest of the companies would have to be discharged in a few days, or weeks at most. Without knowing this, some have said the Texans went home because they wanted to.[6] Even Giddings, who had a better understanding of these wild men than did his contemporaries, said it was a shame they did not stay and devote their attention to fighting guerrillas.[7] As far as the Texans were concerned, the war was over. The signing of the truce when they were about to begin serious killing had undoubtedly soured them on army life. Besides, they felt needed at home. The men of the 1st had left their homes and families along a frontier that was being raided by Comanches.

During the week following the surrender, the Texans wandered about Monterey, saw the sights, and prepared for the long ride home. The various commanders wrote reports. In Taylor's initial report, he stated that he was describing only the events he had personally witnessed or taken part in; this initial account mentions the 2nd Texas.

General Worth issued Order No. 39 on September 28, reporting on the troops under his command. As might be expected, he gave high praise to the 1st Texas, devoting a paragraph to the Rangers: "The general feels assured that every individual in the command unites with him in admiration of the distinguished gallantry and conduct of Col. Hays, and the noble band of Texian volunteers — hereafter they and we are brothers, and we can desire no better guarantee of success than by their association."

Worth, a fair man and a fine commander, followed with a long list of individuals who distinguished themselves in the three days of fighting. In another report the same day, he mentioned Hays, Walker, Chevallie, McCulloch, and R. A. Gillespie, with appreciation for the work they had done in taking the city.[8]

Major General Henderson, the titular commander of the Texans, filed a report on October 1.[9] He correctly mentioned that the 2nd did not have the opportunities of the other regiment but had fought bravely when finally committed, fighting house to house and then being pulled back, to their great disgust.

Col. George T. Wood wrote his report the day the fighting ended.[10] He followed the actions of his regiment from their alert the morning of September 23 through the next day, outlining their progress by the streets in Monterey. He mentioned the "gallant bearing and lofty courage displayed by the Inspector General Mirebeau *[sic]* Lamar."

In fairness to one of his commanders, he made a special point of explaining why Captain Wheeler had not joined in the street fighting. Being detached by Wood to protect against an attack, the Ranger had been kept on this duty by Taylor. Wood explained that despite repeated requests, Wheeler was not allowed to enter the city. Wheeler and his men spent the day under fire from enemy batteries, listening to their comrades fighting inside town. Captain Goodloe had been dispatched on the twenty-second to go to Camargo. Wood said that these two detached companies, plus necessary details, reduced his strength to slightly under 300 men.

Hays wrote his report slightly later. Because he was with Worth, his report begins on September 19. It is a rather full accounting, though restricted to basic facts.[11] Hays had an intense pride in his men, but he expected them to perform to a high standard. When he mentioned names, it was to tell who was at a certain place at a specific time. The only man mentioned in the form of a commendation is R. A. Gillespie.

The last paragraph is of special interest. "In the various conflicts in which my Regiment has been engaged the officers and men under my command has been so completely satisfactory to me, and I hope the Commanding General that to undertake to designate the conduct of individuals might have the appearance of calling the roll of my command and pronouncing an eulogy upon each."

This sentence tells much about Hays and the reputation he had developed.

The days following the capture of Monterey evidently were not entirely peaceful. Occupying forces have never gotten on with a conquered city, and this was no exception. The Texans were still bitter; most wanted to go home. On September 28, Taylor reported on munitions and stores captured in the city and now catalogued. He continued: "The Texas troops have expressed a desire to return home, and I shall soon give the necessary orders for their discharge and payment."[12] This rather bald and not completely true statement was the basis for later historians to think the Texans left on a whim. Actually, their time was up. Company I had already been discharged; Company A would be out two days later.[13]

Samuel Reid described the days following the fall of the city, as the Americans were examining at leisure the places they had fought so hard to capture. When off duty, Reid visited a school in the city and several wealthy families. On Sunday he and friends attended services in the cathedral. He mentioned that everyone felt certain the truce would lead to a permanent peace.[14] On September 30 they rode to General Taylor's camp to be mustered out, and the two regiments were disbanded, according to Reid.[15] Actually, it was his company, McCulloch's Company A, that was mustered out on that day. Reid described how the Rangers laughed and told jokes as they saddled up for the final ride. The following day a large quantity of captured cigars and tobacco was distributed to the men.

Now out of service, the Texans waited for several days to assemble a party to start the march to Camargo and the long trip home. The company had scattered, as Reid was not going back with them to Texas but to his home in New Orleans. Not being a fool, he wanted the security of a large train and so waited until October 5, when a group of men and some captured artillery were to leave. Captain Shiver's company and a small party of Rangers acted as escort.[16]

The night before he left, Reid visited with General Taylor, as did others. "We called upon Gen. Taylor to take our leave of the gallant veteran, who received us very cordially, and with his characteristic kindness."[17]

Reid was certainly a Ranger supporter, but once before he had mentioned what he considered punitive measures by the Texans. Nowhere in his chapter on the week following the capture of Monterey does he mention anything that suggests the Rangers ran wild, or even behaved in a manner other than curious soldiers examining a city they had fought hard to capture.

When the volunteers were mustered out of service in Mexico, as most were, they were generally on their own as far as returning home. When Company A was discharged, some of the men stayed in Monterey for a time, as Reid describes, while a group of sixteen under McCulloch started overland for San Antonio. This was a large enough — and tough enough — group to risk the trip through enemy country. They had no trouble until well into Texas. Near the Nueces, while camping, two Comanches sneaked into the camp and stampeded all the horses except McCulloch's mount and one other. The angry and likely chagrined captain took out after the Indians, and was followed soon after by the other mounted man.

When he caught up with the two Indians, they all started playing a cat-and-mouse game. The Ranger had a Colt but could not get a clear shot as they dodged about in the brush. One of the Indians had a rifle, and McCulloch had to do considerable ducking to avoid being a target. At length the other Texan rode up and tried bringing down one of the Indians, but missed. McCulloch managed to get off several rounds, without damage, but the Indians decided it was not worth the risk and ran, leaving the horses. McCulloch could not find his five-shooter, but he was happy enough to recover the horses, and they rode on for San Antonio, reaching the town without further trouble.[18]

Back in Monterey, the other Texans were waiting. Taylor had a special order published on October 1.[19]

Orders) Head-Quarters, Army of Occupation.
No. 124.) Camp near Monterey, October 1, 1846

1. The mounted troops from Texas having expressed a desire to return home during the present cessation of active services, will be mustered out of service and discharged to-morrow. The pay department is prepared to pay the regiments on presentation of proper rolls. The 1st regiment quartered in town will be mustered by Major Thomas, assistant adjutant general, with the exception of McCulloch's and Gillespie's companies, already discharged. The 2nd regiment will be mustered by Colonel Belknapp, and both regiments at such hours as may be appointed by the colonels and mustering officers.

2. The commanding general takes this occasion to express his satisfaction with the efficient service rendered by the Texas volun-

teers during the campaign, and particularly in the operations around Monterey; and he would especially acknowledge his obligations to General Henderson, Generals Lamar and Burleson, and Colonels Hay and Wood, for the valuable assistance they have rendered. He wishes all the Texas volunteers a happy return to their families and homes.

3. Colonel A. S. Johnston, who has served in the campaign as inspector general of the volunteer division, is hereby honorably discharged from the service. He will receive the thanks of the commanding general for the important services rendered by him in that capacity.

By order of Major General Taylor:

W. W. S. Bliss
Assistant Adjutant General

If other such orders for volunteer regiments were issued, they are lost in the archives. It is interesting to note that this order listed the 1st as being quartered in town, which was a mistake. Also, Colonel Johnston, not a Ranger but a Texan, was being thanked for services with the Volunteer Division — services some said included really commanding the division at a critical period.

The war was winding down for Lt. James K. Holland and his diary. On October 2 he noted they were mustered out. On the third: "all is dull — nothing going on in camp rumor say's several Mexicans killed — Texians done it of course — we are all extremely anxious to get off — but they won't pay off — Western Regt is being paid off and going home — "[20]

In a few following sections he noted how they finally were paid and broke into small groups for the journey home, much as Reid described in his account.[21] Some stayed, finding work as teamsters.

Reconstructing a history is more difficult than plotting a novel. In fiction, events can be placed in decent and proper order. In fact, happenings have a life of their own, with scant regard for chronology or geography. While the Texans were being mustered out in early October, Samuel Walker was out and reverted to his rank of captain in the new Mounted Rifles. Special Order No. 148, October 1, 1846, directed Captain Walker, mounted rifleman, to report to Washington for duty.[22] He evidently left right away, though many of the Texans in the 1st were in Monterey for some time, not always to Taylor's liking. At least one, Harrison Beal, stayed and opened a saloon.[23]

It was not always easy to figure the old general. He had signed a very effusive general order. Yet, a few days later, on the sixth, he wrote the adjutant general that the entire force of Texas volunteers was mustered out of service and returning home by companies. "With their departure we may look for a restoration of quiet and order in Monterey, for I regret to report that some shameful atrocities have been perpetrated by them since the capitulation of the town." He mentioned in passing that a company of Texas foot, who had rendered good service in the campaign, were on their way to Camargo to be mustered out of service.[24]

In a following section he stated that it was necessary to provide protection for the Laredo area. He had been in discussion with Governor Henderson and had authorized General Lamar to raise an eighty-man company to be based in the town. So, the ex-president/general, Mirabeau Lamar, became Captain Lamar and served on the Rio for the duration.[25]

"Atrocity" was a favorite word with Taylor. He was never known as a scholar and certainly benefited from his son-in-law, W. Bliss, who edited and wrote the final drafts of his dispatches and reports. Several of his remarks have given later historians full excuse to blame the Texans for outrageous conduct. In all fairness it is time a closer look was had of the wild men of Texas, "the human blood hounds, the *Sangrito Texanos*."[26]

Consider Taylor's dispatches of November 27 and December 2, wherein he mentions "many outrages in Monterey" — as well as near Marin and Ramos.[27] He was determined the good name of the U.S. would not be sullied by plundering and marauding. Obviously, the Rangers were not responsible for these atrocities. This was no excuse for actions that were outside the law, but the Texans were later pictured as the only troops who crossed the line.

A lot of this was due to the high profile of the Rangers. Everyone who left any form of memoir or personal experience of the war, in whatever theater, has some mention of the Rangers. Some of these are probably larger than life; some are definitely biased. Often overlooked are the various Ranger commands.

Dr. S. Compton Smith, a contract surgeon with Taylor's army, mentioned the differences in the Texas units: "The first Rangers from Texas, of whom I have already spoken, were genuine, brave and hardy pioneers of the young and rising State. They were the men of Goliad and San Jacinto — men whose greatest sport was an open prairie-fight with the untamable Comanches. They had measured arms with the Mexicans and had a just appreciation of them. They knew their weakness and how to take advantage of it. But some of the so-called Texas Rangers who came into the country at a later period were mostly made up of adventurers and vagabonds whose sole object was plunder."[28]

There is no doubt that the most skilled of the Rangers took part in the Monterey campaign, but classing as brigands all the ones who served later is not only unfair but inaccurate. Even Smith would contradict himself in praising later Rangers, and his remarks were directed against one company, all to be described. Again, interestingly enough, there are broad and general statements about the conduct of the Rangers, but there are few specific examples. Taylor had stated that he was glad to get the Rangers out of Monterey because of their conduct, but we have only one documented example.

Taylor wrote the adjutant general asking instructions on how to handle a case, as he had no authority for trials. The case involved a man named Fitzsimmons, held in confinement. Attached was a report, dated October 5, 1846, signed by a Lieutenant Gaines of the Brazoria Company and endorsed by Colonel Hays.[29]

As Gaines reconstructed the incident, a Mexican lancer, uniformed and armed with lance and gun, rode before the quarters of Captain McCowan. Several Texans saw this and started talking about stopping the man. Nothing much actually happened, and the Mexican continued to ride down the street. At least one of the men walked across the street and entered another house. A few moments later, a shot was heard. The lancer rode on for ten or fifteen paces and fell dead into the street.

Hays ran up at almost the time of the shot and entered the house. Inside he found Fitzsimmons sitting down, with a rifle nearby. Hays took the weapon and opened the pan; smoke curled out. Fitzsimmons refused to make any statement, even when Hays accused him of the killing. The Ranger was then placed in confinement. Hays endorsed the report, saying it was true from the point where he was mentioned.

William B. P. Gaines had been a private in Company D until August 19, 1846, when he was promoted to lieutenant.[30] "Captain McCowan" was J. B. McCowan, commanding Company H, and the man in confinement was a member of his company, Pvt. John Fitzsimmons, who had transferred from Company G on July 12.[31] For reasons not stated on the rolls, a number of men had transferred from Company G on July 2 and 12. He might have been better off staying in his original outfit. The roll does not show any information on Fitzsimmons' fate, nothing to indicate arrest or punishment. Nor is there anything about actions *against* Rangers in the city following the surrender. Evidently, it was not all one-sided. Again, muster rolls show events that never made it to official reports. On September 28 a member of Company K was killed in Monterey.[32] Fitzsimmons could have been aroused over *that* "atrocity."

Whatever opinions they may have had, the men who served with the Rangers knew they had been in the fight. Of all the writers who mentioned the men from Texas, Luther Giddings, major in the Ohio Regiment, probably had the best understanding and most objective evaluation:

> Their knowledge of the character of the enemy and of the military frontier, acquired in their long border struggle, rendered them valuable auxiliaries in the invasion.
>
> As a mounted soldier he has had no counterpart in any age or country. Neither Cavalier or Cossack, Mamluke nor Morstrooper are like him; and yet, in some respect he resembles them all.
>
> Chivalrous, bold and impetious in action, he is yet wary and calculating, always impatient of restraint, and sometimes unscrupulos and unmerciful. He is ununiformed, and undrilled, and performs his active duties thoroughly, but with little regard to order to system. He is an excellent rider and a *dead shot.* His arms are a rifle, Colt's revolving pistols and a knife. Unaccustomed to the saber or to move in mass, the Rangers are of course unable to make a charge upon, or to receive one from well-armed or well-disciplined troops. But when an enemy's line is broken by the rapid vollies of their rifles, they then pitch in promiscusly, and finish the work with the "five-shooter," delivering their fire right and left as they dash along at full speed. And it must be confessed that for a chaparral skirmish, or an "up and down" and cross over fight upon house tops, such as the third day at Monterey, the Rangers have few superiors. Centaur-like, they seemed to live upon their horses; and, under firm and prudent leaders, were efficient soldiers, especially for scouts and advanced post-service, where the necessity for uninterrupted vigilance left them no opportunity for indulging in the mad-cap revels and maurading expeditions for which they are somewhat celebrated.[33]

There is one final after action report of interest — that of the Mexican commander, Gen. Pedro de Ampudia.[34] This general was second only to Santa Anna on the Texans' wanted list. Having him escape was a bitter blow. His description of the fighting around Monterey is a classic example of a defeated leader explaining his loss. Ampudia said the Americans came to the city on September 19 and spent the day in scouting and going into camp. He stated that two days later an assault was made in great force on Diablo and Teneria and the bridge across the Purisima, but that his valiant veterans threw them back with great loss, at least 1,500 casualties.

Next day, General Taylor threw his forces against the bishop's hill, resulting in their repulse. A full brigade then returned to the attack, but a mortar and two cannon would not function and the Americans gained the hill. Ampudia declared that as soon as he saw what was happening, he hurled reinforcements to the aid of the garrison — too late. These incidents forced him to concentrate his troops in the plaza, where they repulsed the enemy, but he was short of ammunition and decided on a parley.

Ampudia assured his countrymen that the affair at Monterey was of no importance and they would shortly drive the invaders out. And, in closing, he promised them that their favorite general, Señor Don Antonio López de Santa Anna, would soon take charge. This was the only factual thing in the report, written September 29 in Saltillo.

He did not know, of course, that accepting the truce would put Taylor in deep disfavor with the American government. President James K. Polk's diary is full of his anger over this development and how the cabinet directed Taylor to resume the fighting. At the same time he was trying to decide whether or not to appoint Winfield Scott to command an expedition against central Mexico. The problem was, poor President Polk hated both of his senior generals.

EIGHT

The Walker Colt

The Mexican War, as in most conflicts, has to be examined in terms of time and various geographical areas. The simplest way is to follow one campaign to a conclusion, but it is helpful now to digress for a time and follow Samuel Walker as he changes from lieutenant colonel, 1st Texas Mounted Rifles, to captain, United States Mounted Rifles, Regular Army. He had been directed to proceed to Washington for orders by Special Order No. 148, October 1, 1846.[1] While no longer a Ranger, Walker would still have an impact on Ranger history.

Evidently he wasted little time around Monterey, leaving for San Antonio. A letter in his papers, dated October 20, from a Henry P. Casey, was addressed to Casey's brother in Washington, saying Walker was leaving for the capital the next day. He asked his brother to show Walker "any attention in your power . . . and by introducing him to the heads of the departments."[2]

There is a slight conflict in dates here, as the *Texas Democrat* says Walker was in Austin on October 19, where he stated he hoped to arm his Company C with Colt revolvers.[3]

Hays was with Walker; they traveled to Houston together. Hays went on to Mississippi, while Walker turned north to Washington, as reported by *The Telegraph and Texas Register* on November 9. It is believed that Walker carried a letter from Hays asking information on an expected call for a new mounted regiment from Texas.

Walker was sent to his old state of Maryland to recruit fifty men for his company in the Mounted Rifles. It was probably believed that his fame would make this an easy matter, and so it turned out. How well this mission was performed can be seen from various letters in Walker's files. He mentions advertising in the Baltimore paper for men for a new corps to be armed with an improved rifle and a new six-barreled revolver.

Several letters remain from young men requesting details about the new regiment. Also, there are various letters from parents and friends of potential recruits, vouching for their character, patriotism, and desirability. Walker soon wrote his brother that he had his fifty men and could get more — and might even be asked to raise as many as 250!

The former Ranger was a national figure, and his arrival in the East made him a social figure as well. His papers contain invitations or his replies to invitations from Washington, New York, and Maryland. The fighting man was also a skilled politician. On December 29, 1846, he regretfully declined an invitation to a major affair that had decidedly political overtones. Walker tactfully explained that because of the division into two major political parties, he did not think it wise to accept any invitation that was clearly in favor of one party and not national in nature.[4]

Walker was involved in another activity that would be of far more importance than recruiting or being the social lion of the moment. During his stay in the East, he played a major part in Samuel Colt's reentry into the firearms business.

Most of the details of this fascinating story are known — only the beginning is missing. There is no documentary evidence showing who, if anyone, sent Walker north to contact Colt and see about getting new revolvers for the army.[5] Nor do we know the who and when of his authority to speak for the Ordnance Department. The story simply begins in the middle.

First it might be well to digress a moment and put to rest one of the legends surrounding Walker and Colt: the myth that Walker came up to Colt in 1839 and told him how to redesign his pistol for effective frontier use. This tale has been around so long that even reputable historians picked it up.

The beginning of this bit of fiction began in 1865.[6] In that year Mrs. Colt financed and published a memorial volume, which outlined the history of Colt arms as she and the writers knew it. Unfortunately, both Colt and Walker were dead. Many early factory records, drawings, and models had been destroyed in a major fire. And it had been close to twenty years since the events of the Mexican War, so memories were dim.

There is a large illustration in Mrs. Colt's book of a revolver identified as a Walker Model 1839. The weapon is clearly the 1847 Model. This was the kind of mistake that has happened before. The revolver *is* a Walker; Colt used the name as a popular designation. Someone may have found a tag on the arm with this name. Whatever the reason for the mistake in year and the inevitable connection with a trip by Walker in 1839, the damage was done.

The most obvious fallacy in the story is the fact that Walker was busy in various adventurous activities, including the Seminole War, and did not get to Texas until 1842! His activities for the next years, until his death, are well known. Also, it is doubtful whether any of the Ranger brethren could have financed a trip to the East, even for such a worthy mission as designing an improved handgun.

One thing that may have helped early writers adopt this fable had to do with a loading lever, supposedly suggested by Walker in 1839. Colt *did* design and patent such a device in 1839, and some of his Patersons have this feature.[7] However, when Colt wrote Walker in November 1846, he was obviously writing a man he knew only through newspaper accounts.

Legends often outlast history.

Sam Walker was a busy man. On November 26, 1846, President Polk made the following entry in his diary: "Capt Walker of the Texan Rangers, whom I had appointed a captain in the mounted Rifle Regiment, called to pay his respects. He had been in the City several days and made an apology for not having called earlier."[8]

It seems a little unusual for a very junior captain to call on the president, but Polk was evidently pleased. The entry has another importance, as it has been suggested that Polk had something to do with getting a contract approved for the manufacture of new revolvers. If so, there is no mention in Polk's diary, and he went into detail about all aspects of the war. Something as new, as important, and as costly as a contract for revolvers would certainly have been discussed.

In New York, Samuel Colt had read about Walker's arrival in Washington and wrote him sometime late in November, introducing himself and asking Walker's opinion of his revolvers. He offered to equip Hays's new regiment and Walker's company with revolvers. He mentioned he had written Hays in Monterey, but doubted the letter had reached there.[9]

Walker replied on November 30. In this letter he stated the Rangers had been using the Colts for three years, got them from the Texas Navy, and felt enough confidence in the pistols to tackle heavy odds.[10]

Walker went to New York, where he and Colt must have immediately started a rather remarkable series of talks on producing new revolvers. On December 1, Colt put an answer in writing concerning prices for quantities of weapons — 1,000, 2,000, as many as 5,000.[11] Colt did not have the facilities to repair a pocket watch at this time. Two days later, Colt was still worried and wrote Walker more on price and urged Walker to talk to the president. He mentioned an interview Walker was supposed to have with Polk.[12] There is no record of any such meeting.

Returning to Washington, Walker must have enjoyed some busy days. From outright opposition, the Ordnance Department changed to approval, though the people in authority there never accepted the new contract and would do all they could to make life difficult for Colt. Colt and Walker did not know this at the time. On December 1, 1846, Colt wrote Col. John Mason to introduce Walker, requesting that the colonel give him a pistol he had for purposes of experiment.[13] The same day he wrote John Homes Offey, a clerk in the office of the secretary of war, with the same request.[14] In a postscript, Colt hoped Offey would do all he could to aid Walker in carrying out the purpose of his visit and "greatly oblige your old friend."

On December 7, Walker wrote Colt that the Ordnance Department had agreed to a contract for a thousand new model revolvers, but they were very skeptical about a three-month completion date.[15]

The same day, Lt. Col. G. Talcott, chief of ordnance, wrote Colt:[16]

> Sir:
>
> At the instance of Capt. Walker, the Secretary of War desires you to furnish one thousand revolving pistols — bore 50 to the pound (round ball) with elongated moulds in addition, at twenty five Dollars each, in accordance with your letter to the Captain, the whole to be delivered in three months. Please inform this Office whether or not you will engage to furnish the pistols as above.
>
> G. Talcott
> Lt. Col. Ordnance

This must have seemed like something in a dream to Colt. When his firm went bankrupt, Colt had engaged in various other technical and scientific efforts. He worked on telegraph projects and had been granted $50,000 to develop mines for harbor defense before he was invited to once again manufacture firearms, his first love. He lost no time in informing the War Department that he would accept the challenge.

Over the next few months, correspondence generated by the proposed new revolvers filled a book. The original letter to Colt ended up with several endorsements and notations: Did the $25 include any extras? Was a delivery time a necessity? The project was in motion, and so was the bureaucratic infighting. This correspondence has been reproduced in various degrees of completeness in several publications.[17] It is of interest mainly to gun collectors and historians. Only the key features are germane to this story.

First, Walker emerged as the representative of the government. There must have been some preliminary work before this happened. A new captain simply did not walk into the War Department and walk out as the agent to sign a major contract for a new weapon. It is easy to understand why Walker would be selected as an authority on revolvers and capable of making suggested improvements. His fame was nationwide, and he knew more about mounted combat with revolvers than anyone in the service. But this is of importance after the War Department had decided to buy an improved revolver. It is stretching belief to think the ex-Ranger walked into the red tape of the War Department and changed the old beliefs without a lot of help from powerful friends.

On January 4, 1847, Colt and Walker signed a memorandum of agreement, describing the new revolver in detail, the time of delivery, the kind and number of spares to be delivered with each weapon, each ten weapons and each fifty.[18] Walker signed as the representative of the secretary of war. The secretary, W. L. Marcy, signed the contract on January 9, but four days earlier Colt had signed an agreement with Eli Whitney to manufacture the 1,000 revolvers.[19]

The new revolver was the largest handgun ever made in the United States. It was a .44-caliber arm, as it was agreed the smaller calibers of the Paterson Colts were not entirely adequate for combat. This weapon did not disassemble to load; instead, an improved loading lever was developed to seat the bullets in the chambers. With the increase in caliber, the chamber size was enlarged and the new Colts held six charges. The era of the "six-shooter" was at hand. The chamber held a hefty powder charge, so that the handguns could outshoot the common musket at any range and hold their own with a rifle at a hundred yards. The heavy bullet and the standard powder charge provided tremendous shocking power. The weapon would outshoot present-day revolvers, other than magnums. It was officially the Colt Patent Arm, 1847, U.S.M.R. Colt himself early called it the Walker, and it is known by that honored name today.

All in all it was a fine arm. The only fault was that it was too much of a gun. Unless carefully loaded, the powder charge was enough to burst a cylinder. Unfortunately, in the haste of meeting production deadlines, some of the metal used was inferior. A high percentage of these revolvers would be lost by mechanical failure.[20]

When he began a project, Colt did not slow for anything, and he was a fine organizer. On January 4 he sent a wooden model of the improved Colt so that holsters could be made.[21] In a letter to Walker he mentions "the pistols for your regiment." (Clearly, the contract was to arm the Mounted Rifles, or part of the command.) Always the businessman, Colt suggested the contract should be increased so that each officer and man in the Rifles would have a new Colt. He assured Walker the additional arms could be added without any problem. Then he set out to find workmen for the new assembly line at Whitney's plant. Colt was not only designing new arms, he was laying out new and improved manufacturing techniques, paying overtime to meet schedules. A new age was dawning.

If Colt was pushing his workers to meet the deadline, trying to increase orders, the Ordnance Office was in no hurry. No one seemed the least concerned that a war was being fought and that these new weapons could make a difference in the outcome. The matter of inspecting the arms was presented, and this feature of negotiations and the demands for changes in the original agreement to include extra tools and flasks became a major haggling point. Colt was a better engineer than speller, but he managed to make his meaning clear in a letter to Walker on January 10, 1847: "I am satisfied that it is the determination of that department to through [throw] every obstical in the way of my making these arms they can and but for your letter I would have at once abandoned the undertaking."[22]

The factory of Whitney was manufacturing the new pistols at a decent rate, but the weapons were not going anywhere. The detailed story of Colt's fight with the Ordnance Department is not pertinent to this story, but a few brief incidents will give an idea of how this battle progressed. On February 19, 1847, more changes were suggested.[23] It took *six weeks* to get the first 220 revolvers inspected.

Some of the delays were due to changes in design or materials, suggestions that arose after the original design was approved. Walker had some suggested changes for the front sight, for example. Colt made changes in the loading lever to take care of conical bullets. He also wanted a change to brass from iron for the trigger guard and strap assembly, saying this would cut down on delivery time.[24] This has led to some dispute as to how much Walker contributed. Undoubtedly, the basic weapon was Colt's design. It was, after all, a modification of the earlier Paterson — stronger, simpler, suited to combat use. Even the trigger guard had been considered by Colt originally and tested on experimental models. From Walker's letters to Colt it is clear he did make suggestions for extending the grip and he mentioned the trigger pull. He was not too sure about using brass for the trigger guard.[25]

Walker had completed his basic mission of recruiting men for the Mounted Rifles, and he was finished with his other task of starting production of a new revolver. The war might be of secondary importance to ordnance clerks, but not to fighters. Walker and his recruits had been moving south. They were at New Port, Kentucky, in early March of 1847, and he was still trying to get the new revolvers for his company.[26] On February 19 he had instructed Colt to letter the first 220 arms to indicate Company C, provided that a new law passed which would authorize increased strength for the regiment. If not, then Colt would number the first 76. Another matter complicating the distribution and numbering was whether each soldier would be issued one or two revolvers, which naturally complicated the question of spares, flasks, molds, wrenches, and so on.[27]

As far as Walker was concerned, this was all settled for him on March 20, when Lieutenant Colonel Talcott wrote, telling him he and his recruits would be on orders to Mexico in a short time. Since the riflemen would go without horses, there was no need for any arms other than rifles. He also stated that Lieutenant McLane had already drawn weapons for the company.[28]

This was really the end of the matter of Colts for Walker, at least officially. Back in Texas, the governor was concerned about raising more troops and sent Jack Hays to Washington to talk with everyone from President Polk on down about length of service, as the Texans had no more inclination to sign up for the duration now than they had evidenced earlier. Hays left with a letter from Henderson to Polk dated February 18, 1847. His trip to the capital was a success; he returned home with at least a verbal agreement to a twelve-month enlistment for a Texas regiment.[29]

Colt read the papers and noticed that Jack Hays was in Washington trying to get approval for a new Ranger regiment. On March 21 he wrote the Texan and offered to show him the new revolver.[30] It is clear from this letter that this was an initial contact. He solicited Hays's support and thanked him for proving the worth of the original Colt five-shooters. In this letter Colt mentioned the opposition of the colonel and officers of the Ordnance Department to his revolvers and that the only way to get orders was to approach the president and have him instruct the secretary of war. He had written Sam Houston, now a U.S. senator from Texas, much the same letter.[31] Colt naturally offered to outfit Hays's regiment with revolvers, if orders could be obtained.

Walker kept asking for Colts. On April 2, Talcott wrote him again telling him that the Mounted Rifles had already been issued 1,008 sabers and 608 *flintlock pistols*. His terse letter of two short paragraphs tells the captain he may pick up other arms along the way from whatever depots had them.[32] As far as the army was concerned, that was it. No one was changing procedures for contracts for Walker, or anyone else.

The Mounted Rifles assembled in stages in Vera Cruz, without horses. In late April, Walker was still crying for the new arms.[33] A man accustomed to cap-lock revolvers was not too happy with a single-shot flintlock, but he started training his new men. The war went on, with or without Colt revolvers.

On July 6, 1847, Colt finished the first 1,000 Model 1847 pistols and asked the government if they wanted more.[34] At this time not one Colt had been issued! Walker, now in Mexico, was informed in a letter dated July 8 that the initial 220 revolvers would be shipped to him, in care of the ordnance officer in Vera Cruz.[35] They were shipped —and remained in storage in Vera Cruz. There was little Colt could do to help Walker, but he was doing what he could.

How many revolvers were made is unknown, but there were spares. On June 3, Colt sent a pair to Hays, with a covering letter explaining that the cylinder engraving was inspired by his celebrated fight with the Comanches at Walker Creek.[36] His correspondence shows a pair sent to his old friend from Seminole War days, David E. Twiggs, now a brigadier general.[37] While Colt papers do not show a gift, Taylor's records include a letter of August 17, 1847, thanking Colt for two Walkers and praising the weapons.[38] Taylor must have shown the weapons to his officers, as Colt had at least one request for pistols from an officer in Monterey the same month.

It would be easy to say the pistols represented a thank you for Taylor's help in getting the contract, but that is just speculation. By then, Taylor's influence was so low in Washington that endorsement would have been more of a kiss of death. More likely, Colt was just demonstrating his penchant for public relations and salesmanship.

Thus everyone went back to his own war: Colt against the War Department in Washington, Taylor in northern Mexico (now that the truce was out), Scott in central Mexico, the Rangers wherever they were. They had, in fact, already done their most important and lasting work. There was much hard fighting ahead, but their use of revolvers and the demonstrated effectiveness of the new weapon would have a marked impact on warfare and a most remarkable influence on civilian life. The legendary men were creating a new legend.

NINE

★ ★ ★ ★ ★ ★ ★ ★ ★

Buena Vista

The armistice General Taylor had thought might end the war didn't hold. The administration was furious with him for allowing the Mexican force to escape.[1] The Mexicans had not really been hurt and saw no reason to sign a peace treaty. Trying to bring a political end to the war, President Polk hatched a secret plan to return Santa Anna, who would overthrow the central government and make peace. It didn't quite work as planned. The old fox came back from exile, assumed control, and turned the full force of Mexican arms against the invaders. The armistice was terminated on orders from Washington, though it was obvious that the present course of fighting in northern Mexico could go on for decades without any military solution.[2]

As early as July 2, 1846, Taylor had stated his view that an invasion into Mexico from the north was impossible.[3] It was over a thousand miles to Mexico City, even if there were roads all the way. To supply even a small force, much less move artillery and wagons, would be difficult. Gen. Winfield Scott, who was the senior general and in effect the chief of staff of the army, had suggested to move inland from Vera Cruz, capture the enemy capital, and end the war. President Polk could not stand either of his generals, but he was forced to agree to this plan.

On November 25, 1846, Secretary Marcy informed Taylor that

the president had decided to send Scott to the seat of war.[4] Scott had been informed on the eighteenth. The secretary stressed the need for caution and security and mentioned the difficulties of communicating. He noted that a dispatch of September 2 had been intercepted. Taylor had previously complained about the department communicating directly with his subordinate commanders, and Marcy made every effort to soothe his feelings; however, he ordered the resuming of hostilities.

It was clear to everyone in Washington that the war in the north was over. Scott had been working on his plan for some time and had a clear idea of his order of battle. The small, battle-tested American regular army was largely in Taylor's force, and Scott wisely decided to use these veteran regiments as the main component of his invasion force.

On the same day that Marcy sent his letter, Scott wrote Taylor a confidential note, explaining that he was coming south — not to relieve him, but to prepare for a campaign in a different area. However, he continued, it would be necessary to reduce his command to a purely defensive role. The letter was a very flattering one, carefully worded to enable Taylor to keep his pride, though he would lose most of his army.[5]

While the truce was over, it was assumed — even directed — that Taylor would remain in a static defense, concentrating in the Monterey area. He had his headquarters there, but not his forces. On November 24, before he got the above letters, he reported his troops had occupied Saltillo.[6] Shortly after the new year began, he wrote that he had occupied Victoria. He asked when Scott would arrive and what he would want.[7]

It was rumored that Santa Anna had raised a large force and was training the men as he moved north. His army was known to be near San Luis Potosi. Taylor had what was left of his command scattered over a wide area. Whether by spite, or the difficulties of travel, Taylor never met with General Scott as ordered. He stayed so far west that Scott gave up trying to meet him and stayed at Camargo. On January 3, 1847, Scott took the bulk of Taylor's seasoned troops — 4,000 regular infantry under Worth, and the same number of volunteers, plus a thousand mounted troops and some artillery. This was conveyed to Taylor in a secret dispatch sent with Lt. John A. Richey.

Scott turned back to Point Isabel to organize his invasion, a mission he performed with the skill of a master professional. He had his problems with weather, lack of transport, landing boats, and wagons, but let none of this stop him.

Far west, Taylor was having a few problems of his own. Lieutenant Richey had stopped for supplies in a small town and wandered away from his escort. He was surrounded, butchered, and stripped. Someone in the group of robbers probably recognized the value of the dispatches he carried and took them south.[8]

Taylor wrote the department on January 26, announcing Richey's death and the recovery of his body.[9] Taylor said that he had made every effort to find the secret papers, but to no avail. He was well aware of the importance of the loss and what it could mean to him. The Mexicans were now aware of how many troops he had lost, as well as Scott's plan to invade central Mexico.

The same day he wrote a second dispatch, asking for some regular artillerymen to bring his batteries to fighting level. Other than some Dragoons, about all he had left of the regulars were General Bragg's few cannoneers. He had just lost 9,000 men; it probably did not seem unreasonable to ask for "one hundred good men, enlisted especially for the field artillery . . ."[10]

Taylor never got the artillery reinforcements. He began concentrating his scattered forces, now almost completely volunteer regiments. John Wool's force, about 2,400 strong, was called in. The Americans were in mountainous country beyond Saltillo. Taylor set up headquarters at a large *rancho,* Agua Nueva, with about 6,000 troops. There were rumors that Santa Anna was coming with a huge force.

Taylor was in a ticklish situation and a vulnerable location. His present position was relatively open. Retreat to the north was through narrow passes. If he stayed too long, he could be cut off and overwhelmed in the open. He didn't want to run too soon and give up ground.

Taylor had two regiments of cavalry, one from Arkansas and one from Tennessee, and he made efforts to locate the advancing enemy. Both units lost considerable troops in scouting, without gaining any intelligence of the enemy. All the old man knew was that he had a list of known missing. His problem was solved in an almost Hollywood fashion.

Benjamin McCulloch and twenty-six Rangers rode into camp. It is sometimes assumed that the Texan and the general had an agreement that McCulloch would come back if hostilities broke out again. Samuel Reid stated this in his book, though this was after he left the company and was safely back in New Orleans.[11] No other written evidence supports an understanding, certainly nothing in Taylor's dispatches, and

McCulloch never said anything. It is entirely possible. Taylor had a special feeling for McCulloch and Walker; they had each rendered special services. Or there may have been nothing more than a natural desire on McCulloch's part to return to a fight unfinished.

Whatever the circumstances, McCulloch had been planning to return for some time. He was sick during most of December, but recruited as much as possible. Much of his time was spent in and around Gonzales, with most of his recruits from this area.[12] By January 12, 1847, he had moved on to San Antonio, with less than thirty men (from twenty to twenty-seven, depending on which records are used). These were good men, with his former lieutenant, William H. Kelley, as first lieutenant. Fielding Alston, from his old company, was along as second lieutenant. He didn't have enough men for a company, certainly not enough for two lieutenants, but McCulloch started south with what he had.

Amazingly, as they passed the site of the Comanche brush, someone found McCulloch's Colt five-shooter. The weapon was recharged and worked perfectly. Later, Samuel Colt would use this as another example of the durability of his pistols.[13] It was an ad man's dream, and he made the most of it.

The party of Rangers arrived in Monterey on January 31. McCulloch found much confusion in the town; Taylor and most of the army were gone. The Rangers headed for Saltillo, where the commander was supposed to have his headquarters. On February 4 the Texans rode into Saltillo and reported to Taylor.[14]

Two years later, McCulloch wrote a letter to a friend, describing the events leading to Buena Vista.[15] It is a pity he did not write more, as his letter is an interesting account with a good narrative style and sense of humor. Unfortunately, he does not clear up the matter of *why* they came back to fight. If he had any understanding with Taylor, it certainly isn't mentioned in this letter. McCulloch says he came down with twenty-seven men, including officers, all paying their own expenses.

As usual, there was an argument over time of service. The Rangers would have nothing of any twelve-month contract, much less for the war. As McCulloch said: "We held on, knowing the Old General was in a tight place."[16]

They gave him a choice. They had really come down for a fight, so they would stay for the upcoming battle, if there was one, for subsistence for men and horses. Or they would sign on for six months at soldiers' wages. After sitting about for a few days, Major Bliss, Taylor's adjutant, came in and told them they were to be signed on for six months. On February 16, 1847, Taylor had them mustered in, dating from their arrival in Monterey. They went on the rolls as McCulloch's Company, Texas Mounted Volunteers (Spies).[17] They were too small for a company, with a completely illegal service period, but it was the best bargain Taylor ever made, even if he would be explaining why for months to come.

Eleven days later, Taylor sent for the detachment, ordering them to report to his camp at Agua Fria. He was increasingly worried about the lack of information on Santa Anna's army. Taylor wanted the Rangers to scout south along the road through the mountains as far as Encarnacion, some thirty miles to the south. This was a very large *rancho* and a likely site for a staging area for the Mexican army.

McCulloch took sixteen men, including a civilian, a lieutenant from the Kentucky infantry, and a Captain Howard. The party kept to the road, doing much of their travel after dark. About 11:00 they encountered some pickets, who fired and fled. The Texans continued, very carefully taking advantage of the darkness. Later, they slowed, thinking the Mexicans had built a barricade across the road. Feeling their way, the scouts found the barrier was actually a party of enemy horsemen.

"Quien vive?"

Before the Rangers could reply, the horsemen opened fire. McCulloch then acted in Comanche fashion, rushing them before they could reload or draw other weapons. He gave a wild yell and the Texans charged through the dark. The enemy picket split in half and fled, as the Rangers rushed down the road and almost into the camp at Encarnacion.

McCulloch was daring, but not foolish. Taking advantage of the surprise rush, he pushed his luck for a moment, riding about among the disorganized and startled Mexicans. It was a sizable cavalry encampment, with possibly as many as 1,500 men. The Texans gathered what information they could in the darkness, but the risks of being cut off were too great. McCulloch signaled them out. They rode through the night and arrived back inside the American lines the next day.

This was the first firm intelligence on the location of enemy forces. It indicated that the main Mexican army was still south, but Taylor doubted that a large mounted force would be operating without the main army supporting them. This was too large a force for a raiding party.

Taylor's basic problem was still the same. If he tried to fight a large force on the open plains at Agua Fria, he could be cut off and surrounded. If he left too soon and ran too far, he would abandon a fine defensive position to the north where the road to Saltillo ran through a series of defiles. He must have been considering his options for some time, as he could not have developed plans and a defensive position on the spur of the moment. Intelligence was the key.

On February 20, Taylor ordered that McCulloch return to Encarnacion to see if the main enemy force had arrived. McCulloch started out about 4:00 P.M. There was no water on the way to the *rancho,* and night travel would keep down thirst. Also, he wanted the concealment of the long winter night. Everyone knew the importance of the mission. He took four of his best men, plus Lt. Fielding Alston. The only outsider was a Lieutenant Clark of the Kentucky infantry.

McCulloch was not a man to grant favors and play at war. If he took the others on his first scout, it was because he was certain they would not be a burden and would not risk losing his men. If he took Clark along a second time, it was because he had confidence in the man. Whatever the reason, the small party rode south and passed the American pickets about six miles down the road.

A short time later they captured a Mexican who said he was a deserter and offered all kinds of information on the strength and location of Santa Anna's forces. According to him, the army was at least 20,000 strong. McCulloch had been hearing this kind of bragging for days. He went back to the pickets and turned the captive over to them, with instructions to get him to Taylor.

On this scout they knew a little more of the road and the countryside. At sundown McCulloch left the open road and took to the thick brush. It was late February and the night was cold, which made for miserable travel but helped them remain undetected. During the long ride they crossed the road only twice, using it as a general guide as they stayed well into the thick chaparral. They easily located the enemy pickets and passed between them, as the Mexicans were guarding the road and never considered a small party would ride cross-country.

McCulloch was relatively safe between the outer pickets and the stationary camp guards, for by now it was a major camp. It was clear Santa Anna had come up with his army. For some time they rode up and down and around the sprawling tents and fires, pacing off the extent of the camp. The moon had set some time before, and they moved silently in the darkness. Soon McCulloch had a reasonably accurate idea of the enemy force; the deserter had not been too far off his count.

Next, McCulloch pulled his detachment back to a safer position and fed the horses from the grain bags. Reviewing everything with Alston and the patrol, he said he wanted more detailed information but did not want to lose what they already knew. He kept Pvt. William Phillips with him and sent Lieutenant Alston back to Taylor with what they knew. Although he wanted to learn more, Taylor had enough information to act, and he was not going to jeopardize that. Quietly, Alston took his few and the precious information and slipped away.

Fielding Alston was then about twenty-six years old. He had been with McCulloch in the old Company A and had been wounded at Monterey. It was one more example of how good men kept returning to the Ranger service. McCulloch undoubtedly felt safe in entrusting the news of Santa Anna's camp to the young lieutenant. His confidence was not misplaced.

Daring as it had been, the preceding scouting was nothing compared to what McCulloch now planned. He and Phillips rode *inside* the lines, into the scattered camp. A picket saw them, challenged, and started chasing them. The two could not risk a close examination and rode even closer to the campfires, losing the Mexicans in the brush. McCulloch fell back now to a hill a mile or so away and hid on the slope until daylight. With his fieldglasses McCulloch planned to make a minute inspection of the camps. It was an excellent plan, but it did not develop as he had hoped. A great blasting of trumpets signaled reveille and almost stampeded their horses. By the time they calmed the startled animals and got back under cover, the Mexicans had started huge cook fires all over the camp. Before McCulloch could make any accurate daylight count, smoke from the green wood hung over the entire area.

In the early morning stillness, the smoke hung along the ground, and McCulloch was afraid to waste more time waiting for a clear view. He and Phillips mounted and started back. The main road forked north of the *rancho,* with pickets guarding each branch of the way. It was bitterly cold, despite the early morning sun, and the sleepy and half-frozen Mexicans had started fires for warmth. Slowly the two Rangers rode along, keeping their distinctive rifles along the sides of the horses. It was no more than a quarter mile between two of the pickets, but they were coming *out* of the camp area and the Mexicans must have thought they were their own *rancheros* looking for horses. The two Texans kept on with their deliberate pace and passed through the main picket lines.

On the way in, McCulloch had found a likely spot for another picket. About four miles north they spotted the last of the enemy outposts, atop a hill, guarding a defile. He saw the picket from a far distance and waited for it to be relieved. By 9:00 McCulloch was afraid to wait any longer. He and Phillips rode carefully through the brush, made it to the base of the hill, skirted the mountain, and finally got back on the road out of sight of the enemy.

That was the last sight of enemy forces. McCulloch started out at a gallop; the poor horses got little rest until Agua Nueva was sighted. Where there had been long rows of tents, picket lines, all the equipment and wagons of a major camp, now was an empty plain. In the distance was a dust cloud, the rear guard of the American army. It was late in the afternoon of February 22, 1847, and history was in the making, but the weary Rangers could not have known that.

The only American troops in sight were a small party of horsemen. As they rode closer, McCulloch saw it was the general, staff officers, and aides. He rode up and gave Taylor a final report of the enemy numbers and the clear indication that the enemy was advancing.

This scouting expedition, along with his exploits in the Monterey campaign, made McCulloch nationally known. It took some time for the story to get back to the States, but eventually the part the Rangers played was common knowledge. One newspaper account in the *Democratic Telegraph and Texas Register* for August 2, 1847, has a long account of the activities. It must have been from an eyewitness. Unlike other versions, including McCulloch's letter, it has one anecdote that shows the easy camaraderie of the Rangers. McCulloch and William Phillips were almost caught several times as they slipped out of the Mexican camp. Once on a hillside, they were seen, and McCulloch turned to the private and said calmly, "Billy, we better slope again." They got away. It was a first-name basis with McCulloch, and many of his men, old friends, called him Ben.

It is doubtful that he and Phillips were concerned about fame as he finished his report. They were probably too tired to care much about anything other than food and rest.

There are several versions of his talk with Taylor. McCulloch himself said: "He seemed right glad to see me, saying, Maj. I feared the Mexicans had caught you. I gave him an account of what had detained me, which appeared to satisfy him, saying you must be tired Maj., you had better repair to camp and take some rest and sleep. He and his staff mounted and rode off for Buena Vista."[18]

McCulloch and his men spent the night in the field. Next morning, Lieutenant Kelley and fifteen men scouted toward Agua Nueva. About two miles down the road they ran into the enemy advance, opened fire and fell back, shooting. McCulloch galloped into Saltillo and informed Taylor of the advance. There was little action the rest of the day. That night some of the Rangers were on picket duty.

In telling the Ranger story, many combat actions of other units have to be compressed or omitted. While the Rangers performed a major scouting feat in finding and locating Santa Anna and his army, it is only fair to mention the actions of the Dragoons on this same mission. When McCulloch and his Rangers left, they were with Lieutenant Colonel May and the entire Dragoon force, as well as Lieutenant O'Brien and two six-pounders — well over 400 troops. The two groups split very soon.

The Dragoons were going away from Encarnacion, heading for a large *rancho,* La Hedionda, out on the desert. They reached the place about 3:00 in the afternoon, tired and thirsty. They began to observe dust clouds many miles away in the desert, as well as signal fires on the mountains. May sent a patrol out in the desert and put a two-man patrol up a nearby mountain. The men in the patrol were captured. He could hear firing and began barricading the buildings.

Some of May's troops captured a Mexican and learned that there was a force at Encarnacion. May began to worry about his exposed position. He had too many to run and not enough to fight if a major force came after them. He wisely decided to return to the main American base before he was discovered.

The Dragoons returned without incident and gave Taylor some indication that the enemy was near.[19] The information would supplement what the Rangers discovered. It also shows the difference in techniques and operations of the regulars and the Rangers.

As it happened, all the news reached Taylor. He did not wait for McCulloch to return to start moving the army back to a position he could defend. What Lieutenant Alston told him reinforced the tales of the Mexican deserter. Taylor had instructed General Wool to prepare defensive positions in a defile about three miles south of another ranch, called Buena Vista. Knowing what he was facing, Taylor had selected a spot where he could only be hit from the front and where the three-to-one advantage of the enemy would be somewhat nullified.

Next morning, around 8:00, long drum rolls in both armies signaled the start of the battle of Buena Vista. The Rangers served along the line until May came up with the Dragoons, then the Texans fell in with them for the fight.

Twenty-seven men could not make a major impact on the fight, not even Rangers. Their job had been done. Without them, there probably would not have been a battle — more of a Cannae out on the open ground. In his account of the fighting, McCulloch made no great claims. He described matter of factly wounding and capturing an enemy captain of cavalry. Later, while scouting, he captured a lancer lieutenant, who was German. He and his Rangers spotted a number of stragglers along a hill and rode to pick them off, but were driven away by heavy fire from the slopes.[20]

McCulloch was riding with a Major Coffee when he began to see a slight break in the Mexican attack. He declared the fight was won, and Coffee reached down in his pistol holsters and pulled out a bottle of champagne. They toasted the victory. McCulloch says they scouted the rest of the day, keeping the Mexican cavalry in check.

In his memoirs, George Washington Trahern states he was with McCulloch during this time. His account does not match known battle actions by the Rangers, though he was undoubtedly in the fight. Trahern was back to his old trade of cattle contractor, but he was willing to work as a courier as needed. He and a friend made one daring ride during the fight to carry dispatches ordering the American heavy artillery to move forward. The ride was through enemy cavalry that had slipped around the flanks and cut off the main American force at Buena Vista from the base to the north. His recollections of leaders and units is amazingly good, and he evidently was well known to most of the senior commanders, both as a ready source of cattle and a teller of tall tales. The men also had a keen appreciation for his ability to cross enemy-controlled terrain.[21]

The full account of Buena Vista is not a part of this story.[22] The battle was a defensive struggle by the Americans, beginning at dawn on February 23 and halting at darkness. It was fought by volunteer regiments, reinforced by the regular artillery batteries. These red legs played key roles in turning back enemy assaults, even though they lost two guns. It has been the fashion to sneer at the conduct of many of the volunteer regiments, while overlooking the fact that Taylor won with volunteers. Several units fought bravely and finally gave way before overpowering assaults. An order to retire in one sector, while immediately countermanded, caused confusion and led to further retirements.

As the battle was fought in stages, over extremely rugged country, neither side could bring all units into combat at one time. The Americans were forced to stand fast and turn back the separate Mexican attacks, which were pushed with determination and a good eye for ground and position. It has also been the custom to write off Taylor's part in this battle with the usual bow to his personal bravery while stating he won despite himself, or because of subordinate actions. It may be time for an impartial review of this general's actions. He did use his best men to obtain enemy intelligence, acted on this, and fell back to a defensive position. During the battle he moved over a considerable area, advising and encouraging artillery under Bragg, and moving the Mississippi Rifles to a key spot, having gone back to Saltillo to bring them up to the battle.

At last, battered, with heavy casualties, but holding the field, the Americans saw night come. They stayed in position in the cold darkness, not even unhitching the exhausted artillery horses. They did what they could to prepare for fighting to resume at dawn, but when the sun finally rose over the mountains the enemy was gone. Old Rough and Ready had won his greatest victory, one that would make him president.

Now began the sad task of searching through the gullies and ravines, along the road, up the mountainsides, and atop the plateau where so much fighting had taken place, trying to find dead and wounded. There were no wounded Americans. All they found were stripped and mutilated bodies. There were some wounded Mexicans in the cold morning air, and they were moved back for treatment.

Pursuit was not ordered. Taylor was in no condition to follow. His mounted units had been severely mauled and unable to mount any form of chase, even to locate the enemy. It is possible that the few Rangers may have been used to scout after the rapidly retreating Mexican force. They had come through the various actions in remarkable shape. William H. Anderson was the lone casualty.

The other Texas unit in the battle, the Texas Foot Volunteers, was commanded by Capt. Charles A. Seefeld. Formed at Camargo on September 1, 1846, this unit has been virtually forgotten. They were not overlooked during the battle; their casualty list is the longest of any Texas company, foot or mounted.[23]

Buena Vista was the last battle in the north. It would be enough to make Taylor president, but he probably didn't worry too much about his growing political ambitions at the time. The general set up headquarters again in Monterey and began to conduct an occupation. American troops took several key cities, and they all settled in to see what would happen. Everyone was aware that the main war was now in the south with Gen. Winfield Scott.

During this period the Rangers were probably used in their old role of couriers and escorts. The detachment was too small for major duties, and Taylor desperately needed men who could combat the guerrillas. He sent McCulloch north on detached service March 7, 1847, both to recruit, bringing the detachment to company strength, and to buy horses.[24] McCulloch left and reached Camargo on March 27. Crossing the river, he would be gone for many long weeks. Meantime, Fielding Alston died on March 22 from natural causes, and the little force had a leadership shakeup. George H. Tobin, another old 1st Texas man, was advanced from first sergeant to lieutenant, and William S. Phillips, who had served so well on the scout to Encarnacion, was made first sergeant.[25]

McCulloch evidently had trouble buying horses; finding recruits seemed easier. The first of May he started south again with 150 horses and over forty men, largely from La Grange. It was slow herding the animals, and they had to come the long way, by the coast. Late in June they were at Brazos Santiago, then to Matamoros. Men and animals left for Camargo on June 29, 1847.[26]

In a way it was fortunate that there was no communication between the army and the detachment of new Rangers. There was communication of a sort between Taylor's headquarters and the War Department, but the Ranger detachment, the celebrated Spies, weren't aware that they had been ordered discharged on May 14.[27] McCulloch and his new men had been marching cross-country for over a month to join a company that no longer existed.

Taylor, naturally, knew about all this. He had just finished another explanation to the War Department on enlisting the Rangers. On June 8, 1847, he was telling the clerks and adjutants in Washington that he *did* know that volunteers were to be accepted for the war, but he still took the Texans for six months.[28] He explained:

> Major McCulloch joined me with some twenty picked men, a very short time before the battle of Buena Vista, and when his valuable services as a partisan spy, were greatly needed. His men, however, were unwilling to engage even for twelve months, and, after much

> hesitation, I determined to accept them for the period of six; trusting that the peculiar necessities of their services would justify this departure from the prescriptions of the law. The services rendered by Major McCulloch and his men, particularly in reconnoitering the enemy camp at Encarnacion, and advising us certainly of his presence there, were of the highest importance.

The general further explained the excess of officers and McCulloch's rank of major, stating the Texan was mustered as a captain and expected his detachment to be filled to a full company. Besides, he continued, McCulloch was detached and the unit commanded by a lieutenant.

No one cared about the old man winning a battle. All they could see was that he had unlawfully enlisted twenty Texans. To his credit, Taylor didn't slow when there was a battle to be fought. He had a need and there was a possible solution, and he signed on the Rangers — and won his greatest victory. And he would continue to bend the rules when justified or necessary.

There was still more paperwork. McCulloch and forty-two Rangers were in Monterey. It was July 31, 1847, and they would not sign on for the war. Subsequently, there was some discussion and the Rangers were mustered in — and mustered out. In the adjutant general records there are two copies of the muster roll for these men.

The mustering officer, Colonel Croghan, wanted no more problems with the War Department. In the space marked "notes" he explained how McCulloch went home to raise another company: ". . . he learned of critical situation and . . . he hastened off with what men he had and was fortunate enough to find him [General Taylor] and be accepted on the 31st of Jan 1847, in full time to render most valuable service both before and during the battle of Buena Vista. Almost immediately thereafter he returned to Texas to recruit. The men whose names are here inserted are now discharged as the co to which because of disapproval of Gvt of the act of maj Gen Taylor in accepting services of volunteers for short period."

There are a lot of blanks on the copies. The space traveled is filled in with 700 miles, but there is no mention of pay or clothing.

Fortunately, there is a little more to the story. In a report on August 3, 1847, the general felt it necessary to explain about this seemingly absurd situation of the one-day service. Taylor described how he ordered McCulloch to return to Texas in March to recruit for a full company, not the detachment he had brought to Buena Vista. Also, he wanted the Texan to buy horses. McCulloch was not aware that the men he left behind under a lieutenant were soon discharged. Taylor mentioned that the Texans acted in good faith, bringing a large number of horses from Texas to the army at Monterey and even escorted a supply train from Camargo. They had done a good piece of work before they even showed up for duty. He then concluded: "I have deemed it no more than just to allow them pay and travelling allowances they have actually served and gave instructions to Colonel Croghan to muster them into and out of service on the 31st of July."[29]

This sometimes bumbling general could also show compassion and fairness. He was certainly not the aimless clod pictured by many later historians. True, he had blown hot and cold with the Texans — and would again — but he was also capable of doing the right thing, even if it meant breaking the law again. Paying the Rangers on July 31 was one of his finer moments.

McCulloch rode back to Texas for the third time. He would not return to Mexico again, or serve as a Ranger. In the listing of Rangers, his name is far to the top. He was an exceptional company commander and would have made a fine colonel, had the opportunity arisen. Still, for all his leadership abilities, his most outstanding talent was in scouting, even lone reconnaissance. His work before Buena Vista made him famous, a scout that even today serves as a model for combat intelligence.

This was a textbook case on how to conduct a reconnaissance. McCulloch had gone in with some force at first, when he was doubtful about enemy location and intentions. When opposed by small forces, he had replied with fire and movement, scattering them. Later, with more knowledge, he scouted with minimum numbers and stealth. Every bit of information was immediately sent to the rear, whether it was a prisoner's doubtful story or a carefully measured description of the enemy camp. This was critical intelligence, not guesswork, and McCulloch sent it to Taylor with a trusted lieutenant and several trained scouts, allowing more chance for the news to get through than with a single messenger. He stayed for a final check and kept a man with him so that, again, there would be a better chance of any new information being relayed to the rear.

McCulloch's role was ended, but the war went on.

TEN

★ ★ ★ ★ ★ ★ ★ ★ ★

Chevallie's Battalion

The war in the north, after Buena Vista, entered a new phase. Supposedly, it was a defensive-occupation period; the reality was far different. The main Mexican forces withdrew to fight against General Scott, leaving the battle against Taylor to the *rancheros* and guerrillas. The Americans found this to be no easier than any other army before or since. Seldom was there any enemy force to engage, but there seemed to be hundreds of horsemen hanging onto the flanks of every wagon or pack train, shadowing every courier or small detachment.

In late February 1847, a large train was attacked some nine miles from Marin. There were 200 wagons and about the same number of pack mules, escorted by two infantry companies. The long line was suddenly jumped by a large guerrilla force. The infantry made no defense and withdrew to one side, but the teamsters knew what was in store and made a gallant effort to get the wagons together for some form of defense. They were all civilians but tough men, and they put up the best fight they could. Even so, they were heavily outnumbered and outgunned. Over a hundred teamsters were caught and killed, though some got away in the brush. They were not only killed but horribly mutilated. The wagons were looted and burned. The attackers suffered their heaviest casualties when some of the ammunition in the burning wagons exploded.[1]

This was probably the worst loss of the campaign, in money and equipment. The ghastly nature of the killings brought about countermeasures by some of the Americans. Samuel Chamberlain, a young Dragoon serving with Taylor, wrote a rather biased account in later years, saying Taylor turned loose on the country packs of human bloodhounds called Texas Rangers.[2]

Taylor didn't have "packs" to turn loose. For all his talk, he probably wished he did have Ranger companies to protect his trains and serve as couriers. Ben McCulloch was still with him, with his detachment. In a few days he would send McCulloch north after horses and to recruit, so *that* Ranger wasn't turned loose.

Chamberlain loathed anything Southern and he had a special hatred for the Texans, for whatever reason. He said the names "Old Reid," Captain Bayley, Henry Love, Ben McCulloch, and Mustang Gray became feared and hated across the land. Some of the other names are difficult to identify, but Mustang Gray was well known.

Mabry B. Gray, nicknamed "Mustang," organized a company in July 17, 1846, based in Matamoros.[3] The Texas Mounted Volunteers were not exactly noble representatives for the state. They served in various capacities during the campaign in the north, taking no direct part in the capture of Monterey. They began to play a more active, if not noble, role when the *rancheros* started their campaign following Buena Vista.

In early March the commander of the Camargo garrison became alarmed at the attacks on his forces and the growing guerrilla movement in the countryside. Col. S. R. Curtiss of the Indiana Volunteers issued a call for help.[4] This was on the second of the month, and the colonel thought 2,000 Texans would be enough. All he received was Gray's company, which was put to work patrolling the road between Camargo and Monterey. They did some good work at times, but Mabry Gray's nickname gives an idea of the man. He was arrested in Monterey for being drunk and acting in a disorderly manner. Eventually, the members of his command were not allowed into town unless accompanied by a noncommissioned officer.[5]

There is no doubt that some of the later criticism of the Rangers was caused by Gray's company. S. Compton Smith, a surgeon with Taylor's headquarters during the entire campaign, gave good marks to the Rangers, but he said the later ones were brigands: "The gang of miscreants under the leadership of Mustang Gray were of this description. This party, in cold blood, murdered almost the entire male population of the rancho of Guadalupe — where not a single weapon, offensive or defensive could be found! Their only objective being plunder."[6]

Smith's account shows the danger of taking any one reference as a source for blanket condemnation — or praise. He said the early Rangers were good men, of the breed of the Alamo and Goliad, but the later ones, such as Gray, were brigands. It is true he did not see Gray, or at least hear of him, until after Buena Vista, long after the 1st and 2nd Texas had gone home. Gray had been one of the early ones, being in Walker's company from the first, before the others had shown up. Evidently, then, he did not come for plunder. He came, as did most of the others, to fight. There was a war going on, and both sides fought as best they could.

Chamberlain has an account of Gray's men attacking a *rancho* on the Camargo road near Agua Fria. He identifies this as *rancho* San Francisco. In this massacre, the Rangers allegedly tied thirty-six men to stakes and shot them. Neither Chamberlain nor Smith was a witness to the event or events, and the accounts do not match; or, there *could* have been two ranches destroyed. Chamberlain at least says there was some excuse for Gray, as his entire family had been murdered in 1840, when outlaws under Canales raided Texas.[7]

Gray may have been seeking revenge for the teamster massacre. One version of the *rancho* raid has the men hanged, a form of death the Mexicans loathed and one suitable for payment for butchering the teamsters.[8] It is all speculation. What is not speculation is the way the guerrilla attacks increased; what is not in dispute is the hatred each side had for the other, after years of border raids. There seems little doubt Gray overstepped the line, even given the circumstances. Nothing specific is mentioned in the official reports, but his actions probably had much to do with Taylor's feelings about the Rangers.

There is very little to indicate what McCulloch and his men were doing in this period. S. Compton Smith made the only reference to the spies after Buena Vista.

Following Buena Vista, the troops were invited to numerous *fandangos.* Smith wryly noted that some of the *alcaldes* and *ranchero* leaders got rich on what the Americans paid at the dances. Unlike some, Smith was very flattering about the looks and dress of the Mexican ladies, and he fully enjoyed these dances. Both officers and enlisted men took part.[9]

Smith and a few Rangers went to one *fandango,* which must have been held in late February or early March, as McCulloch is mentioned.[10] A friendly guide had led them to the location and everyone was having a wonderful time when some of the people began showing signs of nervousness and started slipping away. Someone said a large party of guerrillas was coming, and the Mexicans vanished. Staying and fighting seemed the best bet, and the Ranger lieutenant sent the guide to find McCulloch and the rest of the Rangers. It was a very long shot in the dark, but it was all they could offer. They got their horses into the largest building and began cutting loop holes in the adobe walls. The roof had a four-foot-high parapet, and the doors were stout with wooden shutters.

Soon a large number of guerrillas rode up and surrounded the *rancho*. A man came near, waving a white flag and demanding surrender. The terms were very generous: surrender, give up their arms, and the Rangers would be allowed to go free. The lieutenant told the messenger they would need to discuss this for fifteen minutes. The man waved and rode off in the dark.

Since Mier, no Texan would ever surrender. They just needed a little more time to cut firing ports and get ready. The best shots were with rifles on the roof, while those with side arms were on the ground floor to defend the doors and windows. In fifteen minutes the messenger was back, again demanding surrender. One of the riflemen shot him through the head. Smith was bothered by this, but he rationalized later that they were fighting guerrillas, who cared little about rules.

There was a great cry from the darkness, as the guerrillas rushed the building. Well protected, the Rangers shot the attacking party to pieces. The guerrillas fell back and began scattering, trying to outflank the house, firing at the men on the roof. The riflemen, despite the poor light, kept any rush from gaining the building. Throughout the rest of the night, there was firing from both sides, but no more attacks.

About daylight, McCulloch and his men rode up. They spread out and trapped the guerrillas between their rifles and the defenders. Despite the disparity in numbers, the guerrillas promptly surrendered. The Rangers rode back with 212 horses and some 200 prisoners. They kept the prisoners' knives, pistols, and belts, and destroyed their muskets. Taylor turned the prisoners free, after they promised never again to take up arms. Most of them were probably back attacking wagon trains within a week. At least the Rangers kept the horses, selling them and gambling them away. Even Surgeon Smith remembered he took one to replace his mount.

If this version is factual (and Smith is indeed reliable in his other accounts), this was McCulloch's last service before returning to Texas in March.

The other Ranger company in the army was Lamar's unit, based in Laredo. The original company had eighty-two men, with fifty-three from the old 2nd Texas and fifteen from the 1st, which gave it a large number of experienced Rangers.[11] They were on station and patrolling by early November of 1846. In January 1847 Lamar lost one man killed by Comanches.[12] At the end of the year, Texas had raised six mounted companies and one foot company to combat Indian raids, but there was the growing threat of increased guerrilla activity in northern Mexico.[13]

Lamar, who was under Taylor's command, not that of the state, wrote the general on March 1 that the Mexican government was regaining control of the north, expelling Americans who had lived and traded in the region. His district was calm because of his company, but in the interior all trade had been suspended. Not only were marauders after trains, they were cowing the local populace. His report goes on to mention they needed to be paid and their horses were having trouble, but his command was generally healthy, despite an epidemic in the area. He concluded with the first of many suggestions that he be given 300 men, so that he could hold the frontier from San Fernando to Mier.[14]

To cover all bets, he sent much the same letter to his friend Governor J. Pinckney Henderson, now back from the wars and once again governor of Texas.[15]

In the following months, Hays was again in the Ranger business, in Texas, though in an unsatisfactory manner. He organized a new command, the First Regiment Texas Mounted Volunteers. This was a six-month outfit, organized in May 1847. It did not meet anyone's idea of what was needed and was mustered out in early June.[16] There was a commitment to Texas for a twelve-month mounted regiment, and Hays started work on this unit. This is listed officially as Texas Mounted Volunteers (twelve months) with Hays as colonel, P. Hansborough Bell as lieutenant colonel, and A. Parker as surgeon. Governor Henderson also had an understanding with the federal government to keep at least five mounted companies on the frontier as a barrier against Indian attacks.[17] This arrangement was helpful to Texas civilians, but did nothing to aid Taylor in his fight with guerrillas in northern Mexico.

A good deal of politics played into the forming of companies and bargaining for rank during this period. The federal government wanted to keep Governor Henderson happy and still not have half of Texas mustered into service. They were trying to fight a war in Mexico and still look out for the frontier defense of the newest state. Comanche raiders were extremely active during this time, and many Texans felt their first obligation was to defend their own homes, not fight Mexicans hundreds of miles distant. Hays was working to organize a twelve-month regiment, working with his old companion, Michael Chevallie. He instructed Chevallie to use his own judgment and act as though Hays were present.[18]

A number of companies were being formed in and around San Antonio during February of 1847, and this activity went on through the next weeks. Three of these groups gained enough recruits to become companies and were inducted into Federal service, remaining in San Antonio. The call for help from the Camargo garrison put them on edge, but they stayed in Texas until Antonio Canales declared all-out guerrilla war on April 4, 1847, and the situation in northern Mexico became even worse.

Chevallie decided somewhere in this period that he had authority to march, or else just acted on his own. He gathered up the three companies in San Antonio and started for the fighting. The usual election was held and he became major, commanding.[19] They reached Camargo on April 23 and went on to Monterey, being mustered in as a battalion on April 25, 1847.[20] The arrival was noted by Taylor. On April 21, 1847, the general wrote that since his dispatch of the eleventh, Major Chevallie had reached Monterey with part of his command, the remainder being on the way by the China road, escorting a wagon train. They had explored between China and Montemoreles and found Gen. José Urrea had fled beyond the mountains. The countryside was infested with bandits.[21]

For the time being, Taylor sent the three companies to General Wool at Saltillo, where a fourth company joined and was mustered in as part of Wool's command. There is no official record of a conflict between Wool and Mike Chevallie, but it must have begun at this time.[22] The general delighted in timing the Ranger alerts with a watch. They never took more than thirty minutes to collect equipment, saddle, mount, and be on the road. This delighted Wool.[23]

The companies were evidently active, though we have no extensive accounts of their activities. The *Democratic Texas and Telegraph Register* for August 2, much delayed, carried a story on guerrilla activities, mentioning that Chevallie was near Saltillo and "that no guerilla band dares show its face."

The Texans do not figure in dispatches for a few weeks. On June 21, Taylor said a company of mounted men from Texas had been mustered for service, commanded by Capt. H. W. Baylor. This brought the number of Texas units to the authorized five companies and completed Chevallie's Battalion. Taylor included a section on the atrocities committed by discharge volunteers as they marched home. He rightly saw this as inciting further unrest among the Mexican population.

Something must have happened in the roughly two months the Texas battalion had been in his command. He continued: "Of the infantry I have little or no complaint, but the mounted men of Texas have scarcely made one expedition without unwarrantedly killing a Mexican. I have in consequence ordered Major Chevallie's command to Saltillo, where it can do less mischief than here, and where its services, moreover, are wanted."

After more on atrocities, he finished, "requesting no more troops be sent to this column from the State of Texas."[24]

Taylor has to be read as carefully as all other sources. Taking one dispatch, as many have used this one, and making blanket statements is misleading. One must read *all* of Taylor. When he had the chance, he later took every Ranger he thought he could get and refused to release any he had, even under what came close to an order.

The men in the battalion had no way of knowing what Taylor was saying; they were busy. This largely overlooked command was operating in the worst possible military environment of all-out guerrilla warfare. Once again, they were the ones to carry the load of dirty fighting in the brush and mountains, a job the few Dragoons with Taylor did not do too well. If some of them were guilty of atrocities, most were not. By now, the war in the north was more treachery than tactics, more butchery than battle. If they had faults, the Rangers saw to it there were no more large-scale attacks on wagon trains.

Chevallie's Battalion, for so it became known, deserves a closer look after nearly a century and a half of neglect. The companies were larger than the earlier units in the 1st and 2nd Regiments. Most had over a hundred men, and it was a fortunate thing, as they would have considerable losses, largely noncombat.

The companies were as follows:[25]

Company A was commanded by Walter P. Lane, age twenty-eight, and was inducted on February 19, 1847.

Company B was inducted into service February 24, commanded by Capt. Robert H. Taylor. Most of the men came from Fannin County. Taylor was twenty-three at the time inducted.

George Williams Adams, age thirty-three, commanded Company C, recruited from Navarro and Limestone counties and Clarksville. This unit was not mustered in until March 6.

Much later, on May 24, Company D was mustered in at San Antonio. The commander was Capt. James B. Reed, at fifty-two well over the age limit, but no one seemed to care. He was usually called Reid, perhaps the "Old Reid" mentioned by Chamberlain.

Company E, also from San Antonio, was commanded by Henry W. Baylor, twenty-four; mentioned in Taylor's dispatch, it did not arrive and be accepted until June 17, 1847.

The battalion was complete and saw immediate service, though it was not the full-scale campaigning of earlier months, and it certainly brought the battalion no glory. In honesty, many men came south because they thought it their duty, not for plunder, and some examination should be made of what they faced and what they did.

The battalion never fought as a unit. It was intended to fight robbers and keep the roads open or serve as train escorts, and this was the way it was used. Looking at muster rolls gives some idea of what they did.[26] There are few other accounts to go on. Companies A and B were evidently based for some time at LaEncantada. The number of desertions from this place is astounding. Company A had fourteen men go over the hill — literally — from this place. B Company was almost as bad; even a lieutenant deserted, as well as numerous privates and noncommissioned officers. Some of these took off as early as July, just as they were settling in, but the larger numbers came later. Considerable desertions occurred in winter (December and January) when weather must have been a factor. The listing of dates suggests the men talked it over and left in groups. This was sensible, as a single man stood little chance of finding his way home.

Two privates left the battalion under unusual circumstances. On April 24, 1847, John M. Perkins and John P. Wallace resigned to accept commissions in the new 13th Infantry of the regular army. This was a rare event with the Rangers.

There are few written accounts of the battalion; muster rolls suggest a lot, tell a lot.[27] This was a fierce struggle, and the losses were not all on one side. Any Ranger who was careless was likely a dead Ranger. Company A showed a man wounded in December 1847, with two others killed the same day in Parras. Another was murdered in Concepcion, May 25, 1848. Company D listed men killed in Papagallos on July 29, in Camargo in September, another in Monterey in October, all in 1847. Company E lost a man to assassins in Monterey in February and again in August 1847. Parras and Monterey were bad towns for the Rangers.

The Rangers were involved in several Indian fights, again with little or no official mention, but the rolls show casualties. Company A had a Ranger killed at Agua Noche on November 21, 1847, with other casualties on December 15. Company C was in on this fight, with men wounded. C also had casualties in April at Lake Parras, and a year later had two more men wounded in Indian fighting. Company E had the heaviest loss in a fight at Los Tablas, August 5, 1847, when one man was wounded and four killed. The ironic thing about the Indian fights is that they were engaged in to protect the Mexicans from Comanche or Apache raids.

The Texans show up now and then in Taylor's dispatches. On June 30, 1847, he wrote the adjutant general from his headquarters near Monterey that all the twelve-month volunteers had been mustered out, or would be shortly. He mentioned they included a company of Texas foot and Captain Gray's company of Texas horse. This was Seefeld's company, the same group that had fought so well and had "Mustang" Gray and his Rangers. Strangely enough, Taylor did not have anything to say about them; considering all the trouble they supposedly caused, a few words of relief or thanks at their departure might have been in order. He merely noted the country was calm and people were returning to their homes.[28]

By August 10, Taylor was reporting a different picture. The countryside was definitely not calm. Peace offers had been rejected, and the guerrillas were again active, attacking small parties; robbers were active as well. He reported that Captain Baylor (Company E) had engaged *rancheros* in a sharp fight at Rancho Sablas on the middle route to Camargo and a report would follow.[29] Baylor evidently never made the report. According to Compton Smith, the Rangers were caught off guard at the ranch and driven back.[30] Taylor seemed to treat it as a victory. Company E rolls show losses on August 5 from Indian fighting at Las Tablas. This does not seem to be the fight Taylor — or Smith — described. Yet, if Baylor was cut up as Smith indicated, no losses show on the company roll.[31]

At the end of July 1847, Taylor received a letter from Jack Hays, saying he had been directed to join the general with his new regiment. This authority had been dated June 2, 1847, giving some idea of the time lag in directing the war from Washington. For a man who had requested no more Texas troops, Taylor seemed remarkably receptive to the offer. He wrote Hays to leave part of his command to protect the Texas frontier and to come south with at least five companies. They were to march to Mier and await orders.[32]

Hays started south with five companies, leaving the others under the command of Lieutenant Colonel Bell (though this was never too definite a command). Events in central Mexico were changing matters even before Hays started to join Taylor.

On August 17, 1847, Henderson wrote his friend and political ally, Lamar: "Hays will receive orders to move on and report to Genl Scott for duty about the time he arrives at Genl Taylors Head Quarter — this got from Washington City last night."[33]

He wrote Lamar again, on August 21, saying orders to have Hays join Scott had come from the secretary of war in the previous night's mail. Hays was to go to the mouth of the Rio Grande and then to Vera Cruz. Henderson continued, "They seem to have forgotten in Washington City that Coln Hays has been previously ordered to report to Genl Taylor." He mentioned he would send the orders by express. There was no word from Washington on the three companies Lamar wanted to form. He thought he had better send Taylor a copy of the orders, in case the department neglected to inform him that Hays was going to Scott, not his command. Henderson was going to keep six or seven companies on the frontier, a command that would justify a lieutenant colonel, and he would be happy to have Lamar for the job. Unfortunately, Lamar would have to be elected, as Henderson could not appoint officers.[34]

The War Department was a little more careful than Henderson thought. Taylor received a copy of the orders diverting Hays to Scott, dated July 17.[35] The order specifically said Hays was to go to fight guerrillas that infested the routes to the interior. It also directed Taylor to issue orders to any member of the Texas horse he could spare. The old man did not release a single Ranger. He may not have liked them, but he wouldn't spare them either.

Chevallie's Rangers had been kept busy, though not too much of their activities is documented. Evidently, the disagreement or personality clash between Chevallie and Wool had not improved, and the Ranger resigned on August 31, 1847.[36] The records show just that — resigned. After about a month, Walter Lane, the senior captain, was appointed major and commanded the battalion until the end of the war.[37]

Most of the details of their operations are known because Lane wrote his memoirs many years later. The first major scout was directed by Taylor when he called them from Saltillo to Monterey and then to Cerralvo to keep the road open and to find a Juan Flores, chief *ranchero* in the district. This expedition started on August 19 and was commanded by Lane.[38] Whether Chevallie was no longer commanding before his resignation or stayed behind is unknown.

Like most guerrillas, Flores made a specialty of attacking wagon trains. Any teamster caught was killed and his heart cut out and placed on his chest. Considerable booty could be had with little risk, losses mounted, and Taylor wanted the *rancheros* broken up. Flores didn't have too large a gang, and the Rangers managed to track them through the brush and surprise their camp. Eight or ten were killed, maybe more lost in the brush, but Flores got away, at least for a time.

Lane found some informers who led him to Flores's home. The Rangers captured him and held him for trial. The cut-and-dried case ended with a guilty verdict, and Flores was sentenced to die before a firing squad. Lane said the man died bravely; he refused a blindfold and would not turn his back on the firing squad. Juan Flores smoked a cigar and stared them in the eye as he went to whatever world awaited.[39]

Lane said Taylor was "right pleased."

Pleased or not, Taylor believed in keeping the Texans occupied. Next, he ordered them to Medelina, some 150 miles from Monterey, supposedly to confirm rumors that 110,000 Mexican troops were gathering in the town.[40] Lane, with some logic, wondered why Taylor would send a battalion to check on an army, but "he had a queer opinion of Texas troops." Lane figured if the rumor were true, not many of the Rangers would get back to tell about it. But orders were orders.

Fortunately, the report was false. The battalion made the trip in three days, close to forced march conditions, but had to rest their horses and purchase food and forage. One of the regular lieutenants had accompanied the Rangers and acted as commissary officer.

It was a welcome break in the campaigning, marred by only one incident. One day a Mexican rider refused to obey the guards and would not stop when repeatedly warned. Lane had given strict orders, and the man was shot. Returning by easier stages to spare their horses, the Rangers went back to camp near Taylor's headquarters, while Lane rode on to report. He recounted how Taylor met him in a rage outside his tent and started berating him for a murdering scoundrel. When the Texan managed to ask what the general was talking about, Taylor informed him that he knew all about the murder of the innocent Mexican and how the Rangers had seized forage and property in Medelina. He had a long letter from the *alcalde* describing in detail the misdeeds of the Rangers. An express rider had beaten the column back to Monterey.

Lane tried to explain to Taylor that it was all a lie, but the general refused to listen. Lane told him to talk to his own officer, if he didn't believe the Rangers, who would tell him how they had paid for the supplies. Taylor demanded that the Ranger who had fired the shot be arrested and brought to him in irons. Lane, who had a short temper, began losing control. He shouted back that he had given the order to shoot the Mexican; Taylor could arrest *him.* Taylor started screaming that the Ranger was relieved, but Lane turned and left, galloping back to his camp.

He dismounted and searched for the private who had been on sentry duty. John Glanton was the unlucky man. Lane told him to get his equipment and horse and head for San Antonio. Glanton didn't waste time; when Bliss and some guards rode up a short time later to arrest Lane, the man was far from camp, too distant for the Dragoons to consider following. Lane was relieved of his command for a time, but Taylor finally had the good sense to ask the regular officer who was with the command what had happened. Lane described with relish the half-hearted and embarrassed apology he received.

The incident shows how ready Taylor was to believe the worst about the Texans, yet how willing he was to use them. As to what happened to Glanton, some Rangers were hard to kill. He would join again.[41]

At least one major Indian fight is mentioned by Lane.[42] This took place near Encontalla, where Lane was camped. Several of the pickets barely managed to escape the Indian rush, riding back to the main force bareback, losing their saddles. Lane gathered his men and started out after the Indians, who turned out to be a large Comanche war party, loaded down with horses, mules, and some prisoners. Lane must have had several companies, as he described how they chased the party and caught up with them, and how the Comanches stopped and formed a long line, awaiting battle.

Lane gave the command of right front into line, which suggests some degree of training, and ordered a charge. There was a brisk fight, but the Comanches broke and scattered, with the Rangers rounding up a large number of animals, plus much camp booty left on the ground. It was not an easy victory. Four Rangers were killed and fourteen wounded. It is difficult to fit this action into the known losses of the battalion. The fight at Las Tablas resulted in four deaths, but there are not fourteen wounded in all the Indian fights listed on the rolls. Perhaps the clerks or orderly sergeants showed only real wounds.

An interesting aftermath followed the fight. Several days later, Mexican ranchers in the vicinity began coming to Wool's headquarters to claim horses stolen by the Comanches. These were returned to them. Lane began to suspect that some of the men selling them supplies were checking the horses and mules, marking color and brand, then going to headquarters and claiming them. He became sure when one claimant and his friends showed up and claimed a paint horse that belonged to one of the Rangers; he had been riding the animal for over two years. This was too much. Lane told some of his men to take the ranchers down into a ravine and reason with them. As he reported, they gave them a hundred apiece — and there were no further claims for lost horses.[43]

Little of this activity shows in official reports. On August 24, 1847, Taylor reported some troop movements to the south were under way. Dragoons and Texas cavalry were scouring the region between Monterey and Camargo to clean up robbers and guerrillas.[44] After a long gap, he reported on October 19, 1847, it was generally calm, but there was always a danger of guerrillas, or more likely just robbers. Getting mail through was a problem. He had dispatched a company of mounted Texans to Cerralvo to keep the road open.[45]

About the last official combat report, dated November 3, 1847, is from 1st Lt. R. B. Campbell of the 2nd Dragoons. In this fight between a large party of guerrillas and some twenty dragoons, we find a few Texans. It was probably the custom to include some of the Rangers, though these men, a lieutenant and two privates, may have come along for the fight. Lieutenant Campbell says: "Lt. Clark, Texas Rangers, was of much assistance to and behaved in a commendable manner throughout the affair." He goes on to mention that when the fight started one of his men and one of the Texans lit out for camp. They were not all heroes, whether volunteer or regular.[46]

Taylor also mentioned a fight in a letter written November 2, one of his last from the war zone. He said about twenty 2nd Dragoons and a few Rangers were attacked by 150 guerrillas no more than fifteen miles from Monterey. Taylor was prophetic: "This is a description of the warfare which will be carried on for the time to come in Mexico . . ."[47]

Writing from Camargo on November 14, Taylor acknowledged receipt of approval for his request for a six-month leave.[48] He mentioned an attack on guerrillas by some Dragoons. Taylor reported that on the seventh of the month a command of Reid (Captain Reed, Company D) surprised a guerrilla camp between Ramos and Capadero. Patrols were keeping the roads open. It was the old man's last mention of the Rangers. He returned home on leave and never came back. From then on, his interests were political. The command passed to Wool.

Operating conditions under Wool were not much different from Taylor days. He was, by all accounts, a difficult man to have as a commander, but he seemed to get along with the Texans. However, like Taylor, he had no hesitation about sending them on impossible missions. In the waning months of the war he ordered Lane to take the battalion and scout to San Luis Potosi.[49] There were rumors about a large enemy force in the city.

Lane knew this mission was dangerous, if not impossible. The battalion was too large to hide or run and not large enough to fight an army. He suggested that he take forty men to make the reconnaissance, a force which could roll over smaller guerrilla bands and hide from major cavalry units. After some discussion, Wool agreed.

The Ranger party left, accompanied by Lt. John Pope of the Topographical Engineers, who would map and make notes on the route and the country they covered. It started as just another scout, normal for the Rangers. Then it changed into something spectacular.

Off the route, but nearby, was Salado. The place was infamous to the Texans, as it was here that the Mier prisoners had been quartered for a time. It was here, too, that they had been forced to draw beans from a jar. If a Texan drew a white bean, he lived. Those drawing a black bean — every tenth man — would be shot. The unlucky men had been seated on a bench and shot in the back. Just when Lane got the idea to find the remains of these men and take them back to Texas is unclear, but somewhere along the route he began making plans for the attempt.

In a remarkable march, even for the Rangers, Lane's detachment twisted about in the hills and kept the guerrillas guessing. He moved with boldness when necessary, or hid, moving by night much of the time, until he arrived at Salado. Then he acted swiftly, asking questions, probing, keeping officials off guard. All he knew was that the bodies had been buried somewhere in the vicinity. By a stroke of good luck he found guides who knew the spot and agreed to lead the Rangers to the location. Working at night, the Rangers dug up the remains, carefully wrapping the sixteen skeletons, keeping them together as much as possible. Then they started back to their main camp.[50]

Wool agreed to let an escort take the remains back to Texas. Today, outside La Grange, overlooking the Colorado River, a monument marks the resting place of the Mier prisoners. It is a tribute to that unlucky and unnecessary expedition, and, in a way, to the Rangers who brought them back.

Smith recalled in some detail one of the last fights of the war in the north, this in December 1848.[51] A group of Rangers and Dragoons, some forty men, set out to break up a guerrilla band. They were particularly interested in this unit, as it was led by El Mocho, a one-handed brigand who had terrorized the countryside. Carefully slipping from camp, the Rangers caught the guerrilla pickets off guard and captured them. As the pickets had been posted to warn if the Rangers left camp, the Texans and the Dragoons were able to get away unnoticed and select a site for an ambush.

Scattering on both sides of the road, the party waited for the bandits to ride by. Smith mentioned there were an estimated 300 in the guerrilla column, but he said the Rangers and Dragoons had 500 shots between them. This has to be a gross exaggeration. If every man in the party had two Colts, an impossibility, they could not have thrown 500 rounds without reloading. Whatever they had, it was enough for them to chance a fight. As the column rode by, they opened fire, achieving a complete surprise.

The rear of the column broke and fled back down the road, but the middle group ran into a field, hiding behind some hedges and fences. A considerable number of guerrillas had fallen in the first volley, but the Americans still had heavy work as they started across the field. Two Dragoons were killed immediately, with three Rangers wounded. Regrouping, they charged again, firing as they rushed. Once the Rangers got through the hedges, their revolvers came into play, dropping the guerrillas at close range. Smith said El Mocho had several Colts, which he fired and then threw at the Rangers, clutching a saber under his handless arm.

One of the shots wounded the lieutenant commanding the Rangers, as Smith delicately expressed it, forcing him to ride side-saddle. With his last bullet gone, the guerrilla grabbed his saber and rushed the lieutenant. Carefully, the Ranger waited and shot him through the head. What fight was in the remaining bandits evaporated as their leader fell. They scattered in the brush. The event had not been cheap: Besides the two Dragoons, the Rangers lost four killed and fourteen wounded, out of twenty. There were fifty of the enemy on the ground, plus those along the road. Once again, these losses are not shown on company rolls.

The war was over, except for both sides signing papers and getting the word to the scattered troops. Wool began gathering his units and started marching north to the Rio Grande. There was still some danger of guerrilla attacks, and the Rangers were the rear guard. In this capacity they performed the dual function of keeping *rancheros* off the column and picking up deserters and stragglers. Lane remembered they had a wagon in their train, which they filled each day with anything from foot-sore troops to those trying to desert. He had no wish to cause trouble for anyone at this stage. Each day, they drove the wagon close to the camp and turned the soldiers loose.[52]

Finally, again, most of the army was concentrated around Camargo, with streams of soldiers going downriver to meet the ships that would take them home. Wool held a final officers' meeting in the mess. Lane was there, along with some forty officers of all ranks and commands. There were many toasts offered, and finally, to Lane's surprise, Wool rose and offered a toast to the Rangers! He mentioned Lane by name and thanked him and his men for all they had done for Taylor and himself.[53] This gesture made up for a lot.

It was over for Chevallie's Battalion, long since Lane's Battalion. This forgotten command may not have brought fame to the state, but they served in trying times and generally did good work. Some died in battle; others were murdered. They had more than their share of deserters, a few thieves, and others who ran off for various misdeeds and crimes. Many perished from disease. Yet, when it was finished, the battalion, shrunken, battered, occasionally villified, was still an intact combat unit that was bringing up the rear, the position of danger and honor. Company D was mustered out on June 29, 1848. The other four companies left Federal service the following day.[54]

The ex-Rangers crossed the Rio Grande as best they could and rode home. They left, as they came, without flags or standards, no beat of drum, no trumpet fanfare — just their ragged clothing, their weapons and horses, and their pride.

ELEVEN

Central Mexico

The Mexican War was fought on widely separated fronts and over a considerable period of time. In highlighting the actions of the Rangers, many interesting and commendable events.must be slighted or completely omitted. For example, the expedition to conquer California involved truly heroic marches across half the country, with regular and irregular civilian forces from California fighting a largely native Mexican army in the region. The 2,000-mile march by the Missourians under Colonel Donavan, a minor epic in its own right, must at least be mentioned. The campaign by Gen. Winfield Scott in central Mexico was largely over before the Rangers arrived there to fight guerrillas.

Some brief account must be made of this latter campaign, so that the work of the Texans is placed in proper perspective.

Scott landed his invasion force near Vera Cruz and invested the city from the landward side. He knew a seaborn assault would be a disaster and wisely took the place from the rear. Despite some pressure to assault the fortifications, Scott called for a surrender on March 22, 1847. Refused, he began shelling the city. In four days, the city capitulated. His loss was less than twenty killed — Scott's first and only cheap victory.[1]

Then sixty, Scott had spent half his service time as a general officer. Many consider him without doubt the finest military mind the young country had so far produced. It was largely his plan to strike at the center of Mexican power and end the war. He had to contend with an administration that considered him a political danger and would have done anything not to have him command or win, but could find no alternative. It was one of the ironies of the war that Polk could not stand either Scott or Taylor — who, in the end, could not stand each other.

Scott was on a swampy seacoast, soon to be within seasonal time for yellow fever epidemics. He needed wagons, mules, and supplies, for there was at least an 8,000-foot mountain range to cross with one long mountain road into Mexico City. He gathered his army and started inland. On April 8 he marched toward Jalapa. Ten days later, at Cerro Gordo, the army fought the first of several major engagements. The battle was preceded by Scott's use of engineers for thorough reconnaissance. The officer who performed this mission was Capt. Robert E. Lee, seeing his first combat service. Winning, but with losses and some criticism by his generals, Scott went on to Jalapa.

On April 24, Scott wrote Taylor from Jalapa complaining about the "exasperated *rancheros*."[2] He did not think the Mexicans any longer had an effective army, but sand, disease, and the guerrillas constituted "difficulties," as he expressed it. Actually, they were more than difficulties. The single road was an easy target, and there were no mounted troops to combat the guerrillas. Infantry, regular or volunteer, did not have the training to cope with the hit-and-run tactics employed by the raiders, certainly not the mobility. Any wagon train, unless heavily guarded, was in danger. Even a force of a thousand men lost a hundred moving from the coast inland. Smaller bodies were cut up. Stragglers or individuals wandering from guarded camps were cut off and killed, usually by galloping horsemen who lassoed them and drug them to death.[3]

It was almost impossible for couriers to get from Vera Cruz to Mexico City. Scott had few mounted units; the few companies of cavalry had no luck in scouting and antiguerrilla actions. Finally, in desperation, his inspector general, Ethan Allen Hitchcock, tried an original remedy: He hired some Mexican robbers to serve as couriers![4] This solution seems incredible, but it was not so unlikely, given the conditions in Mexico at the time. A few years before, Manuel Dominguez had been a prosperous young man engaged in trade. One day his caravan was stopped and robbed by an army officer. From then on, Dominguez was a bitter foe of the government and became a bandit. When

Hitchcock approached him, the man was quite receptive and brought his band to work for the invaders.

The Americans did not trust him at first, gradually increasing the documents and the level of secrecy they entrusted to his care. Dominguez took the money and served well. In a short time he became known, but the few men who actually handled papers were carefully protected. The bulk of his company, perhaps a hundred, were not involved in anything of a clandestine nature, acting as soldiers and guards. Later, Santa Anna made a special effort to get Dominguez back, offering rewards and a pardon, but he stayed with the Americans. His hatred for the Mexican government and army officers must have been intense, as he was never completely accepted by most Americans.[5]

Hiring Dominguez was a stop-gap solution which did help get dispatches along the road. However, it had no impact on the overall guerrilla situation.

There was some relief when Sam Walker reached Perote on May 25. The Mounted Rifles had lost their horses on the way down, but Walker's Company C and Company I were given mounts and assigned the duty of keeping the road open between Jalapa and Perote. A number of the soldiers who left memoirs of this campaign mentioned his arrival. Walker was well known for his service in northern Mexico, and most of the Americans still thought of him as a Ranger. One, J. J. Oswandel, serving with a Pennsylvania regiment, noted his arrival, warning the guerrillas to beware, as the Rangers didn't take prisoners.[6] Later, he was surprised when Walker brought in some captives.

Walker was active during June. He and his commander, Colonel Wyncoop, had several fights with *rancheros.* These engagements led to some bitterness on Walker's part, as he accused his superior of running. As a result, Walker was placed in confinement in Perote Castle during September.[7]

Scott began to have other problems, this time with his own troops. The question of short enlistments plagued his army, as well as Taylor's.

Seven regiments and some companies' enlistments ran out and they had to be discharged. The troops had not been paid, and supplies were low. When he started for Puebla, Scott had about 4,000 privates for the move, no more than 7,000 men altogether. He stayed at Puebla for some months, drilling, making maps, getting ready for the thrust inland. Fortunately, reinforcements and some money began to arrive.

By early August, he mustered over 10,000 men, largely well trained and disciplined. Other than the 1st Infantry holding Vera Cruz, he had the rest of the regular army, plus some very good volunteer regiments.

Scott's decision to break free and march to Mexico City was considered military suicide, and his army was given up for lost. Old Fuss and Feather pulled it off, leading the Duke of Wellington to call him the premier military commander of the day. The army started for Mexico City on August 6, 1847. Jack Hays and five companies of his new regiment would start south from San Antonio on August 12.[8]

The Americans had engagements on August 19–20 outside Churubusco, a battle with numerous smaller engagements. It was a bloody, heavily contested series of fights. While the losses ran about ten-to-one against the Mexicans, they fought with bravery, and the thousand or so casualties the Americans suffered constituted a great number of their total force.

These engagements outside Mexico City put the capital at the mercy of the invaders, and Scott, unfortunately, was merciful. Historians and partisan writers have taken both sides of argument about the armistice he offered and the Mexicans accepted. There was no doubt how Scott's officers felt; they rightly thought they would have to shed the same blood again to finally take the city. One of the stipulations of the armistice was that each side would stay in place and do nothing to improve its position. Scott kept his men in place, while Santa Anna had his forces improve their defenses in clear view of the Americans.

Two weeks were wasted, and finally Scott ordered the attack on the city. An assault was begun September 8 on Molino del Rey, supposedly full of ammunition and weapons. The place was taken after heavy loss and proved to be empty. After a day of planning, the assault on the city, from the west, was started. By the fourteenth, the American forces were firmly in command of Mexico City and made a triumphant march through the streets, though most of them looked as if they had been in a savage fight.

Within a few days, snipers and discharged troops were firing on the Americans from the rooftops. It took artillery and a firm show of force to clear the city. Santa Anna had long since fled to safety, and the war was pretty well over — again.

The only Texan to play any role in the fighting thus far in central Mexico was Sam Walker, as a captain in the Mounted Rifles. Hays and his new command were on the road, but a long march and sail away. Today we think of Hays as a legend, but then he was still a young man, newly married and off to war again. This time he did not have a regiment but more of an oversized battalion, companies gathered out of a new twelve-month regiment. Governor Henderson was still playing games and keeping as many Rangers on the frontier as he could. So Hays, following Taylor's orders[9] and those of the War Department, started south with five companies, leaving the rest to fight Comanches.

The company letters were not even in sequence. Company E had been recruited in Shelby County and was commanded by Capt. Alfred M. Truett, age thirty-one.

Capt. Jacob Roberts, thirty, led Company F from La Grange.

Company G came from Washington County and was commanded by Capt. G. M. Armstrong, twenty-seven.

Company I was commanded by Capt. Isaac Ferguson, listed on the rolls as forty-four.

K Company was from Dallas and Fannin counties, with Stephen Kinsey as commander.[10]

This new command was from a broader area than his old 1st Texas, but the men were generally good, if inexperienced. There were a few old hands from northern Mexico along to add combat experience. The major difference was in the size of the companies. The smallest company had 110 men, the largest 130. While he had only five companies, Hays had as many men as he had before with ten companies.

Because of the small number of companies, Hays had no regular staff. As they did with most things, the Rangers did the best they could, improvising as they marched. There was no lieutenant colonel; he had stayed behind to command the rest of the regiment. There was no major, as Chevallie had taken his three companies and gone. Hays seems to have been picking up some of the army system and did need an adjutant. One of the privates in Company D, John Salmon Ford, twenty-seven, was selected as his adjutant and rode south with the five companies. It was a wise choice. Not only was he a good administrator, Ford turned out to have a natural talent as a soldier. Originally a doctor, he had turned to the newspaper business before the war and developed a keen interest in writing. In later years he would amass a vast amount of historical material and add his own memoirs to form an invaluable account of Texas history from the 1830s through the 1880s. Ford is the major eyewitness of Ranger actions in central Mexico.[11]

The command rode to Laredo, visiting for a time with Lamar's men, before moving on toward Mier.[12] Ford recalled that they had some sore backsides and trouble getting the new men accustomed to the countryside. At Mier they created considerable commotion. The sudden appearance of over 500 Texans scared the townspeople. However, they all settled down for the usual *fandangos* and parties, to the delight of the ladies and the disgust of the *caballeros*.[13] Hays by now had received orders sending him to Scott's command; he did not pause long at Mier.[14]

There were no troubles as they rode downriver to Matamoros, but the fleshpots of the big city were too much for some of the Rangers. Hays moved his camp twenty miles south to Ranchita.[15] During the time in Matamoros, Pvt. Thomas McLaughlin killed one Mexican and wounded another, "wantonly," as the town newspaper expressed it.[16] The man was sentenced to three years in solitary confinement. Hays approved the sentence, stating it would last for three years, or until peace was made, whichever came first.

The only enemy the Texans could not fight was idleness. Boredom was a problem in the camp as they awaited transportation to Vera Cruz. Griping about food and housing became common. This was not the usual griping of soldiers, but a more serious, pervasive grumbling that began to erode morale. There were some desertions, something that had not happened in the two earlier Ranger regiments.

Ford mentioned this discontent in his memoirs, saying some of the men did not like the army rations.[17] This regiment apparently was fed differently from the first Rangers, who bought their own food. Complaining about army chow would almost put the Rangers in the category of regular troops, a comparison they would not have relished.

At any rate, the grumbling got to the point where Captain Truett assembled the men and spoke to them. His talk was a pretty straightforward message about discipline; then one of the men got up and gave his own speech. It was John Glanton, who had rejoined the Rangers.[18] He had evidently been drinking and proceeded to tell his comrades how things really were. He reminded those who missed their families that their families, from what he could see of *the men,* were better off without them. How could some of them complain about the food when they were not accustomed to anything but scraps? He went on and made most of the Rangers stop grumbling. By now, the ringleaders had been identified. Ford said a few were sent home.

It is probably during this time that Chevallie rejoined his old friend and commander.[19] Ford's memoirs are not too accurate as to dates in all cases, but the mentioning of Chevallie comes while the Rangers were still at Ranchita, and the timing would be about right for him to come across after resigning on August 31. Chevallie would play a role with the Rangers, but he never had a specific position with the regiment. Ford praised him, saying he could do anything in an administrative capacity and eventually served as a contract buyer and commissary officer with the command.[20] How he managed to fit all this in with the fighting he did is a mystery. He figures into several official combat reports as Major Chevallie, as though he were a regular member of Hays's command, but he was definitely not in the chain of command. It became necessary in Mexico to elect a major, as Hays was the only field-grade officer.

The Rangers did not go to Vera Cruz in one unit. Hays sent Ford and two companies, those of Truett and Ferguson, ahead. They were able to take their horses with them and landed at Vera Cruz. Their mission was to establish a camp, which they did about two miles inland on the Jalapa road. Vergara was not much of a place, consisting of a few houses, but it was better than some camps the old ones had been in. At least they had tents and lived more like soldiers than had the earlier Rangers. They were billeted near the Massachusetts Regiment, which had been semiexiled to Vera Cruz. The Irishmen of Massachusetts and the wild Texans made an explosive combination. Surprisingly enough, little happened, at least not mortally.[21]

With the bulk of the American army on the way to Mexico City, guerrilla bands had become exceedingly active around Vera Cruz. The Rangers had come down to fight this enemy. There were plenty of them, and they wanted an opportunity to see action. The camp life was fine, for a few days, but they were getting bored. Maj. Gen. Robert Patterson was the senior officer in the area, commanding a volunteer division. The Texans had been temporarily assigned to his command. One day the two company commanders, Truett and Ferguson, with Adjutant Ford, called on the general to pay their respects and see if they could find some work. During the conversation Patterson mentioned there was an outlaw band some thirty miles away, but he doubted if the Texans could penetrate the country. They assured him they could, but would like a guide.

Patterson had a guide brought in, and the man explained the location of the *ranchero* hideout. There were distinctive landmarks, fortunately, as the guide did not show up the next morning. The Rangers had all the information they needed. Ford remembered detachments from three companies took part in this mission, so Patterson's company must have been landed by this time. The expedition left at 4:00 A.M., moving rapidly along the Jalapa road until they came to a designated turn-off trail.

The country was mostly jungle, vines, and trees almost choking the narrow path. Ford, in the advance, saw a horseman ahead and drew his revolver and spurred hard. At this moment, Old Higgings, his horse, stepped in a hole, sending horse and rider sprawling into the mud. Ford fired a shot as he fell, which alarmed the rest of the command, and the Rangers crowded ahead, thinking the adjutant was killed. A disgruntled Ford got to his feet, muddy, with weapons soaked, then remounted. A short distance down the path, as the country opened into more of a forest area, they came upon a series of buildings.

All the commotion had alerted the guerrillas, who showed good judgment and fled. A few stayed and put up a fight and were shot. Ford saw one, tried to shoot him, but the caps had been soaked or had fallen off in his fall. The revolver snapped, and he began chasing the man with his drawn sword. Somehow the bandit vanished. They went on to the *hacienda* and had a brief fire fight, with the usual results. The house belonged to a Colonel Zenobia, who was the local guerrilla chief. It was a fine building, full of captured American supplies, bloodied American clothing, and uniform parts. After a short discussion, they burned the place, giving the women time to leave.

Coming back by another route, they ran onto some small groups and cut up the guerrillas some more. They thought one officer they killed was a general, and they took his uniform for a trophy. When they rode back and reported to General Patterson, they had covered some sixty miles. It was their introduction to central Mexico — and the guerrillas' introduction to them.

Hays and the remainder of the regiment landed sometime after the scout to find Zenobia.[22] This group had encountered heavy weather, as was often the case, and some horses had to be thrown overboard. This would be cause for some scouting in the future, finding new horses, but for the time being, the Rangers were busy getting established in the new camp.

The Rangers lived a pretty Spartan life, even though they were in better circumstances at Vergara than at any place before or after. Hays had a Ranger named John Buchanan as general handyman. In the regulars, he would have been classed as an orderly. Being an active commander, Hays was out scouting most of the time, leaving Buchanan in charge of his personal effects, such as they were.

Ford described a time when Hays was given a half barrel of good whiskey by one of his fellow colonels. In his absence, Buchanan held open house, with a considerable portion of the Massachusetts boys as his guests. A volunteer sergeant was looking about Hays's tent and saw something that he fancied and picked it up to leave. The Rangers crowded in the tent and outside and began to sense what was happening. Hays had been sitting to one side and saw the man leaving with his property. As Ford recalled the scene, a slight man, who was Hays, told the sergeant to put it down, and the sergeant drew himself up and asked if the man knew who he was. In short order a file of Rangers had the sergeant confined, where he stayed for two days. He did not return.[23]

It was just one of many times when anyone in the command would have been taken for the celebrated Ranger. Hays was about five feet eight inches, as most accounts agree. All say he was slightly built and wiry. The only guess as to weight was about 150 pounds. Descriptions during the Monterey campaign and later in central Mexico are generally in agreement.[24]

His appearance was a source of amusement to some of the practical-joking Rangers. One big fellow, who looked like he was a colonel, took to playing the part, when people asked which one was Hays. It was funny for a time, but the man overdid it, and Mike Chevallie took him aside and beat him into some degree of respect. The Ranger stopped his impersonations and probably lost out on a lot of free drinks.[25]

The Rangers kept busy scouting the region inland, trying to cut down on the guerrilla activity that was costing a steady loss of life and property. Most of this activity was unreported; general references by Ford and others are the only source. The main activity at Vergara, as far as eventual results, was the drawing of the new Colts.[26] Ford passed this off in a casual manner. Fortunately, some correspondence in the Ordnance Department concerning the turn-in of the weapons gives an idea of how many revolvers were issued. Two hundred and eighty of the Model 1847 were drawn by the Rangers.[27]

Some of the men had their old Patersons. Ford mentioned using a revolver in their first scout; others must have had them. One observer, describing the Texans, mentioned five-shooters.[28] However, it is safe to assume most of the Rangers arrived without revolvers. This is clear from Ford's half-disgusted accounts of the men having to learn how to load and fire the new weapons. They had plenty of ammunition and time to become acquainted with their new weapons. From later actions, they did learn — and well.

Hays's second so-called regiment was an odd command. He was a full colonel commanding a large battalion, but there was a clear need for another field-grade officer so that the command could be divided or have an acting commander when he was absent. Permission was granted for a major and an election held. Capt. Gabriel Armstrong and Capt. A. M. Truett were officer candidates, with Sgt. Maj. Gilbert Brush as the third candidate. The fact that the unit had a sergeant major shows the split in organization. Hays had simply started out for Mexico with whatever was left of the regiment after Henderson had picked for the frontier and Chevallie had moved out with the original three companies.

Truett was elected the new major, effective October 26, 1847.[29] It was a wise choice and shows once again the Texans' ability to pick good, experienced commanders. He had been a company commander in the old 2nd Texas and served throughout the Monterey campaign.

The election caused several shifts in the command. Lieutenant Handley became captain of Company E. When Sergeant Major Brush became a candidate for major, his position became vacant, with William Hewett (or Hewitt) of Company E assuming this position.[30] Hewitt stayed in the senior NCO position until December 12, when Brush came back. Later, February 17, 1848, Hewitt was appointed quartermaster sergeant. The first change in company commanders had taken place just before the election for major. Stephen Kinsey retired on October 1, 1847, being replaced by Preston Witt, who became captain on October 23, 1847.[31]

While he was plainly disgusted at losing the election, Armstrong went back to Company G. His conduct afterward never did measure up to Ranger standards. However, for the time being, there was nothing to cause any problems. With elections over, and the new men in command, the Texans settled into their duties of chasing guerrillas.

The Rangers were evidently in the field a large part of the time, though their actions did not appear in official reports. There was a scout to check out a *hacienda* belonging to Santa Anna, which resulted in the accidental death of one man. A larger and more successful strike occurred after some volunteers were killed outside Vera Cruz. This time, the Rangers were ordered to chase the guerrillas. Earlier attempts by the Ohio infantry to punish the attackers only resulted in more casualties. Captain Roberts was given the assignment, riding in the direction of Medellin. He returned the following day and asked Ford, the adjutant, to write a report. He casually mentioned they had killed five *rancheros*. When Ford questioned him to receive a more accurate figure, Roberts said no more than twenty-five.[32]

While operating out of Vera Cruz, the regiment formed a special "spy company" of men from each of the companies. While he never said so, Ford may have been the instigator of this idea. John Glanton was lieutenant. The Rangers had the same experience later commands would have with elite units. It drew the best men from the regular companies, and most of the company commanders didn't like the idea. Armstrong was the one who was outspoken in opposition, and the idea was abandoned as the men rejoined their units. The mystery is why Hays ever consented to the idea, since the men had learned how to use their new revolvers and had been tested in numerous scouts and fights. All he had to do to get a special unit was send *any* of the companies.[33]

Scott was sitting in occupied Mexico City, with almost no army, while considerable reinforcements were gathering in Vera Cruz. Childs was cooped up in Puebla, holding out, and *rancheros* and guerrillas were riding freely over much of the interior. Their activities around Vera Cruz, however, had shown a sharp decrease. As Ford mentioned casually, many had come to grief. Strong reinforcements were ordered up from the coast, to relieve Puebla and reinforce the garrison in Mexico City and the surrounding area. It was a task ready-made for the Rangers, one they had been sent to do. They were ordered to join Scott.

They would almost see their old companion, Samuel Walker, captain of the Mounted Rifles. Walker had been in arrest in the Castle of Perote for the second time, having been there as a Mier prisoner. Brig. Gen. Joseph Lane, commanding a relief force that raised the siege at Puebla, ordered Walker's release. He needed his leaders on horseback, not in jail.

Released October 4, 1847, Walker wrote his brother the next day. It was a long letter, containing much of interest to this story. Writing at 10:00 P.M., he told his brother: "I write in haste to inform you that I leave here tomorrow under the command of General Lane in command of three other companies of Cavalry with the expectation of fighting Santa Anna at the pass of Pinon about fifty miles from this place." He went on to explain something of the military situation, then continued: "I think Santa Anna's race is nearly run. Jack Hays will soon be here with his Regt. of Rangers and I have no doubt that Santa Anna will be in a tight place. If I had my revolving pistols I should feel strong hopes of capturing him or killing him. I have written three times to the different officers at Vera Cruz to forward them and two commands have come up since they arrived at Vera Cruz but I have no hopes of getting them until Jack Hays comes up. I have also made repeated applications to go for them but without success."

Walker described how he had trained his company and how he had written several times, but doubted the letters would get through. There is a passage about a servant who was with him and how he was sending money to pay for a Wesson rifle. Then he mentioned he had just received a pair of the new revolvers from Colt. As a postscript he told his brother about his confinement "by Col. F. N. Wyncoop the cowardly creature who was the first to retreat since the commencement of the war and that from an insignificant force of the enemy." This letter did get through and now survives in the Texas State Archives.[34]

A. G. Brackett, a young officer in the Indiana volunteers, wrote one of the key memoirs of this campaign. He was with Lane's brigade from the first, telling of the actions of the 4th Indiana and the 4th Ohio Infantry, as well as the Rangers, who were later included in the brigade.

Lane started from Vera Cruz on September 19, 1847, with 2,500 troops and 200 wagons. The lengthy train was slow, and a wondrous prize. Brackett described how his 4th Indiana and the 4th Ohio slogged along, fighting guerrillas.[35] Hays and the Texans had been assigned to this brigade but did not accompany the infantry on the march. They might have made a difference. The infantry and wagons moved slowly, and there was ample warning of their coming.

Unable to overpower the garrison at Puebla, Santa Anna made one final attempt to add a victory to his string of defeats.[36] He still had a force of over a thousand lancers and made an effort to cut off the wagon train. Lane's column was moving from Jalapa to Puebla and would have to go through a key mountain pass. If the lancers could catch the wagons in the pass they would have an easy time, and the infantry should not be too much of a problem. Lane held up his wagons and kept his infantry moving, sending Walker and three mounted companies ahead to a small town, Humantla, about twenty-five miles from Puebla.

It was October 9, and Sam Walker was back in combat, leading his Company C, Company I, and a volunteer company. They came in sight of the full force of lancers and fell back on the town, trying to regroup before the vastly superior force facing them. Brackett described how the Indiana infantry were almost running, trying to reach the cavalry before the lancers could overrun them. It was no contest, and the exhausted infantrymen watched the lancers sweep into town. A bitter struggle ensued in the streets, and when the infantrymen came up and finally dispersed the lancers, Walker was dead.[37]

There are several versions of how he died. One reported he died from a lance thrust. J. J. Oswandel, who was not there, said he was shot. Brackett evidently saw the body and that of Walker's slave, and agrees he was shot.[38]

Lt. William D. Wilkins, an officer with the 15th Infantry, was in the fighting and wrote his parents about Walker, saying, "We received a reinforcement of Col. Wyncoop's battalion, the celebrated Capt. Walker's Company of mounted rangers and three pieces of artillery." Wilkins described how Walker led a charge that broke a force of lancers and then into town, where he was killed. He finished by saying, "He was, in the opinion of all who knew him, the bravest and most dashing officer in our army."[39]

According to Oswandel, Walker was buried in a secret spot. Brackett agreed, saying it was in a wall.[40] One of the ironies of the burial ceremony was Colonel Wyncoop reading the eulogy. Walker would have appreciated the irony of this. The killing of Walker, though an act of war, made the troops very bitter and incensed Lane. After the enemy force was completely scattered, he turned the town over for plunder, the only time this ever happened. It would later get him involved in a bitter dispute with Colonel Childs.[41]

Hays received orders to proceed to Mexico City, and the Rangers left the coast on November 2, 1847. Ford mentioned they halted for one night at the National Bridge, a famous landmark constructed in 1776. The bridge was a critical feature on the march to the capital and it is surprising that it was not destroyed to hamper Scott's march inland. Ford and Hays and probably many others slept under the arches, with the adjutant fighting a chill.[42]

For the first time, Hays began having open trouble with Armstrong. The disgruntled captain fell behind and seemingly turned his company over to Lieutenant Evans, as he rode along talking with several officers from other units. Hays sent Ford back to ask him to keep up with the column, but it did little good.[43] The Ranger colonel was a strict disciplinarian, but he seemed to feel sorry for Armstrong's losing race for major and took no further action.

There were no big fights on the march inland, though there were evidently some guerrilla encounters. The Rangers came into Puebla with at least one prisoner, much to Oswandel's amazement. He didn't think they took prisoners. As they passed through Jalapa, American troops lined the roadside and cheered Hays and the Rangers.[44] The Texans were well known, and the troops probably thought they would start doing something about the incessant guerrilla attacks. The Rangers camped a few miles beyond Jalapa, while Hays and two companies went on to Puebla to report to Brig. Gen. Joe Lane.[45]

In the main plaza in Puebla the Rangers decided to show the troops and the citizens of the city that the Texans were in town. Going from a trot to a gallop, the Rangers circled the plaza, yelling, leaning down and snatching sticks from the cobbles. One would drop a handkerchief and another would gallop up, hang suspended, and snatch the cloth from the dust. Some would drop down, at a gallop, touch their feet on the ground and bounce over the backs of their horses, or hang from their horses' necks while supposedly shooting at an enemy. One big fellow rode about the plaza standing on his saddle, with a revolver in his hand. When it was over, Puebla knew the Rangers had come to their area.[46]

General Lane took a liking to the Texans and became especially fond of Hays. The two men were much alike and worked well together. While an infantry commander, with two fine volunteer infantry regiments, Lane did some of his best work with the Rangers. He understood them and may have secretly envied their free and wild style. Later, Lane was given some form of command over what mounted units were operating out of Mexico City. Part of the new 3rd Dragoons was there, with at least Company I of the Mounted Rifles. The Ranger companies would make up the bulk of the loose organization, occasionally called the Cavalry Brigade.

The regular cavalry officer who figured most often with the Rangers was Maj. William H. Polk. Polk was the brother of the president and was newly appointed to his position. There were plenty of political appointees in the war who made poor showings, but Polk was not one of them. He served in a gallant fashion, working closely with the Texans. From time to time, a few volunteer mounted companies served with the Rangers. Their numbers were few, and throughout the central Mexico campaign the Mexicans enjoyed a marked superiority in cavalry units.

There was enough action for all on the march toward Mexico City. The Rangers had acquired two Mexican spies, identified by Ford only as Miguel and Vincent.[47] He stated that they learned of Mexican troops at a town called Izucar de Matamoros, probably from one or both of their agents. Lane decided to attack the place and took some of the Rangers, plus an artillery detachment and a company of Louisiana Dragoons. Lane's report numbered the mounted men at about 135, which would indicate most of Captain Roberts's company was along.[48] The force made a hard night march and surprised the enemy at dawn. In a brief fight the Americans scattered the Mexicans and recaptured fifteen American prisoners, plus a large store of weapons and many horses.

The column spent most of the day in town, loading the captured stores in wagons. Ford mentioned that many horses had been rounded up in the fighting, and when matters calmed down, Lane ordered that they be returned to their owners. Once again the claiming of ownership began. Most of it was legal enough, but one Mexican brazenly claimed Chaplain Corley's mount! The black horse was famous throughout the command; the amused Rangers watched as the man recited how he had raised the animal from a colt. Finally, even the Reverend could no longer stand the lying and suggested he would fight before turning his own horse over to such an unmentionable character. Ford thought this was one of the best jokes of the season.[49]

The column started marching early the next morning, advancing over a road that was ankle deep in water from rain the previous day. They were going by way of Atlixco, returning to Puebla. As usual, the wagons were in rear of the column, with a guard, while scouts and an advance guard led the way. The sodden trail was more than the wagons could negotiate, and they were continually getting stuck. The column was slowing to a dangerous degree. Lane gave orders to destroy the weapons and ordnance stores, but the word did not get to the main body. As the wagon escort dumped the muskets and ammunition and tried to build fires to burn the stocks, the advance and main body got ahead. All at once the ammunition began exploding, and there was a wild alarm; some of the Rangers dismounted and ran back through the mud and water to repel what they thought was a guerrilla attack.

The next day, November 24, the march started again. Miguel was ahead, with an advance guard commanded by Lt. James G. Gaither from Roberts's company. Galaxa Pass was near, and the lancers and guerrillas had selected the battleground with care. Miguel came riding for his life, chased by 200 lancers, and soon the advance guard was fighting desperately. Hays, near the head of the column, heard the firing and galloped up, followed by some forty men from Roberts's unit. Hays yelled charge, and they rushed the lancers, using their revolvers with good effect. The surprised lancers turned and ran, with the Rangers in close pursuit. The chase carried them a mile, over a crest, where they saw at least a thousand horsemen in a long line. The retreating lancers broke through the line and caused it to waver. Ford remembered that some of the Rangers wanted to charge the entire force, but Hays was too smart for this type of bravado.

Hays called for his men to wheel and retire on the rest of the force; they had expended most of their revolver rounds. As they started to turn, the entire Mexican line opened fire. The Rangers were almost in the enemy ranks by now, and the fire was accurate. Lt. Henderson Ridgely and a private of the regular artillery were killed instantly. The Rangers were shaken and fell back. Roberts's horse was killed and the Ranger was thrown to the ground. He jumped up and started running from the advancing horsemen. The Ranger horsemanship again showed its worth. Seeing their captain down, several Rangers wheeled and galloped back. George White reached him first, with James Carr covering; others fell in to screen them. Roberts grabbed one of White's stirrups and began running beside the horse. Leaning down, White grabbed him and swung him up behind on the horse. They all galloped off.

By now, most of the Rangers had empty weapons and there was some confusion as Hays ordered them to fall back and reload. He had a charged revolver and stayed to cover the withdrawal. Hays waited and shot the first two lancers who rushed him, and the others fell back to get away from the revolver. In his official report, Lane singled out this act for special mention, stating the withdrawal was necessary as the Rangers did not have sabers and could not resume fighting until they reloaded.

In short order, Hays had them ready for the fight, and the Rangers charged the superior force. Despite the numbers, they broke the line and cleared the field and the pass.[50] Lane's report is extremely complimentary and this action established the Texans in central Mexico. It was the last action of any moment before the Rangers and Lane's brigade gathered at Puebla, with the Rangers and some of the brigade going on to Mexico City.

The Texans entered Mexico City on December 6, 1847.[51] The altitude, cold weather, and size of the place would not inhibit the Rangers. In the ununiformed column, with rifles, revolvers, knives, slouch hats, and every form of coat and blanket, the bearded men looked more like monsters than humans. Their reputation had preceded them, and people watched from windows and rooftops, or while clustered in the streets. The column rode at a walk through the city to the main plaza and halted while they were being assigned quarters.

This group of Rangers was not too different from the ones who had served in the north under Taylor. In fact, some served in both campaigns, though the number was small. There are several descriptions of the second regiment, and all give the impression of huge men, most six feet tall and solidly built. The lack of any uniform struck all who left accounts, and many misinterpreted it. Brackett remembered: "I watched them closely as they passed silently by me, and could distinguish no difference between the officers and men. They carried no sabers."[52]

Others thought the Rangers dressed this way so that people would not mistake them for regulars or other volunteers. They, of course, dressed the way they did because it was simply the way they dressed. As before, Brackett commented on the broad-brimmed hats, which he described as both low and high crown, with some Panamas; they also were wearing black leather caps to some degree. This was a change from the Rio Grande campaign. Even Hays is mentioned wearing this headgear. He still seems to have been the only one without a beard and the only one who still didn't look like a commander of the wild Texans.

Spectators in Mexico City noticed revolvers and suggested that all Rangers had this weapon. Brackett described five-shooters, so this old favorite was in use, in addition to the new Walkers. And they all carried rifles; their deadly use of this arm was stressed by all who wrote about them.

There was some change in horses. In central Mexico, observers mentioned the varied mounts ridden by the Texans. Like most cavalry units, they lost horses coming south to Vera Cruz, and they had to refit with whatever they could find after landing. They still favored their thoroughbreds and crosses, but as battle losses would mount, they made do with what was available.

Memories of the entrance into Mexico City vary. One said the Texans rode silently, and they evidently did for a time. Other versions describe how they put on one of their shows.[53] They began riding about the plaza, yelling and demonstrating their horsemanship. Men pushed to get closer, while the women pretended to be frightened and rushed back inside. Trying to see what was going on, more people pushed into the plaza. Some American officers came to investigate, thinking it was a riot, but Lt. Col. Ebenezer Dumont of the 4th Indiana, now accustomed to his brigade companions, assured the regulars that the Texans were quite all right. Dumont, like his commander, Lane, took a warm view of the Rangers and found them patriotic and brave.

The wild riding attracted enough attention, but following incidents were not so happily remembered. One of the Rangers was buying candy from a street peddler and kept asking for more of the sweets. Apparently, the vendor thought he was not going to be paid and picked up some pebbles and started stoning the Ranger. He was immediately shot. Ford recounts this story, explaining that the Ranger would have paid. They were harsh men, but none of the Rangers thought much of a thief.

There was another firing of a weapon, this an accident. In all the hard riding, a revolver fell to the ground and discharged, striking a spectator in the leg. The curious crowd scattered and ran, trying to get away from the Texans, thinking the Rangers were starting to kill everyone in sight. Men were crushed, knocked into the gutters, and smashed against the walls. Ford thought as many as 10,000 people had crowded into the plaza to view the Texans. Whatever the number, they showed more interest and speed in leaving than they had in coming.

Also that night, one of the street people snatched a handkerchief from a Ranger and ran. He was ordered to stop (in Spanish) and kept running. The Ranger shot him and recovered his property.[54] Until the Texans arrived, there was little control in the city. The people who doubted the reputation of the Rangers were in for a terrible time. By the end of the month, the correspondent for the *Picayune* reported that

Scott had been asked to get the wild men out of the city or only allow them out with army guards.[55]

This probably fell on deaf ears. Scott was already furious with the continuing guerrilla and *ranchero* activities. He was not satisfied that his commanders were doing enough to stop the attacks, and he probably felt the Rangers were the ones who understood how to handle this problem. On December 12 he published an order directing each post to begin active patrolling and push out and keep the guerrillas moving. A significant sentence in the order stated there would be no quarter to guerrillas or *rancheros*.[56]

For the most part, the Rangers were quartered in Mexico City when not on patrol. The year ended on a somber note. Because he was sick, Isaac Ferguson could no longer command Company I. While the roll listed his age as forty-four, he was at least seventy. The old man served with distinction, but the campaign was too much. He died the first day of 1848. Ephraim M. Daggett assumed command and was promoted to captain on January 17, 1848.[57]

The fighting to relieve Puebla was the last regular combat of the war, but there was no more peace in central Mexico than there had been in the north after Monterey or Buena Vista. The mountainous country was ideal for guerrilla warfare, and the Mexicans took full advantage of the terrain. Two of the leaders of these bands, Gen. Mariano Paredes and an ex-priest, Celedonia de Juarata, were especially troublesome and became prime targets for the Rangers.

When the Rangers heard that Juarata was in a town called Otumba, Hays took a detachment and started out to kill or capture the priest.[58] Ford says there were sixty-five men in the column, obviously from Company I, as Captain Daggett was along. Mike Chevallie accompanied the expedition, as did Ford. Departure date is uncertain, but it had to be in early January 1848, just after Ferguson's death. This was a lot of extra rank for such a small command, and Daggett could have handled the matter, but everyone wanted a shot at Juarata. They spent the first day trying to find the way and hiding in a large ranch to avoid spies.

During the night they passed near a town and heard firing. Someone suggested looking for one of the men. It was discovered that a man Ford remembered as Julius Roach and two others had slipped away and tried to rob someone in the town and been fired upon. After all the years, Ford was embarrassed by the incident and mentioned that Roach was not a Texan by birth. There is a Roach on the rolls, but not with this first name.

The Rangers reached Otumba about daylight, having ridden sixty miles in the two days of hide-and-seek. They were told by people in town that the *padre* had gone and was in San Juan Teotihuacan, twelve miles back toward Mexico City. They turned and rode off, trying to rest their horses. The ride took three hours; the Rangers entered town exhausted, after no sleep in two nights.

Teotihuacan was much as other Mexican towns, with a large main plaza surrounded by houses, generally of stone. The Rangers took over a large, solid building with several stables. This series of structures occupied one side of the plaza.

Ford was sick and all the others were tired; soon most were asleep. It was one of the few times they did not have adequate security. They tended to their horses, which took precedence over anything, then fell asleep. Suddenly, men were yelling and shots were being fired from all directions. Large numbers of Mexican infantry had gotten on top of some of the houses and opened fire. Horses could be heard in the streets leading to the plaza, and a force of enemy cavalry rushed the main door of the building.

Captain Daggett and a few men awakened and began firing, stopping the charge for a moment. Juarata rallied his horsemen and rushed the door again. By then, more men were awake, and Daggett had fifteen or more Rangers ready. They didn't wait to receive the charge. Rushing outside, they deployed and started firing with their Colts. Several of the lancers were hit, and the rush halted. The lancers lowered their weapons and waited, expecting the Rangers to rush them on foot. One of the officers suddenly yelled and rushed the Texans. Chevallie shot him once, and the man fell forward over his horse's head.

The entire Ranger detachment was awake now, and Hays had men firing at the infantry on the roofs. The fight began to go the other way. Juarata made one final rush, leading the attack, sword in hand. He made quite an impression on the Texans, who admired bravery. But that didn't keep them from shooting him. They saw the priest fall and several of his men run to rescue him.

Ford is the source for most of this account, which gives credit to Daggett for stopping the initial rush. Later, Daggett wrote a short version of the fight, without great overall detail, as he was fighting at the gate most of the time.[59] He described how they hid in the ranch during the day and tried to catch Juarata by night. Daggett later learned some of the secrets of the priest and how he evaded capture on so many occasions. The man never spent the night in the same spot, always moving at least once during darkness.

When the Rangers failed to find him, they moved to San Juan, arriving dead tired, their horses too exhausted for further travel. They took shelter in the stone buildings, as Ford described, and went to sleep. During the night Juarata was reinforced by a lancer force and came charging in on the sleeping Texans. Daggett recalled that he was trying to rest on a bench just off the ground. For a time he heard rumbling sounds and finally got up and asked an old woman what it was. She quickly reassured him it was the Ranger horses fighting in the *cuartel* nearby. This worried him and he looked out the gate. Several people were running away from the buildings, with the rumble now clearly identified as galloping horses. Daggett said he started yelling like a Comanche, but the Rangers seemed dead to the world:

> So I quickly got my two revolvers, but did not have time to buckle the belt before in came the guerrilla chief. I shot him in the wrist and his sword fell. His lieutenant then shot into my face, which powder-burnt me, but I kept my six-shooter playing at random, and got a bullet into the chief's beef steak and another ball into the lieutenant's right shoulder. By this time our men on the roof commenced firing, and Juarata went out, bleeding before and behind. The guerrillas tried to rally, but had no leader.
>
> This was my first time when I fought without hope. I did not expect to live but a few moments; and if the feeling I experienced at that time were the feelings of bravery, all brave men are to be pitied. I had made up my mind never to surrender to a Mexican; I knew what that involved.

Daggett admitted that he was frightened, as any sensible man would have been. He made no claim to having played the key role in saving the command. Instead, he gave credit to the new Colts: "One thing that contributed to save our command in this affair was the holy awe and superstition entertained by the untutored greaser in regard to the 'revolver'."

There is some variation between the two versions of the fight. Daggett stressed mounted actions, but there were many infantrymen attacking the Rangers. Ford's version is longer and more detailed, but they agree on the main point: When Juarata was wounded, the fight ended.

Proud of their marksmanship, several of the Rangers almost fought each other over who had hit some of the attackers. Ford tells one story on himself, where he and Daggett each fired on an attacking horseman. The man went down and they started claiming the prize. While they were arguing, the man got up and ran away. Two others fired on the same target and almost came to blows over who had dropped the sniper. It was a long shot and a difficult mark. Each man staked his claim — one a shot in the head, the other a breast shot. After the fight was over they checked the corpse and found a bullet in the head and one in the chest.[60]

When Juarata was hit, his followers broke off the fight and fled. Accounts of his losses varied, but they were light, maybe twenty killed or wounded. The Rangers had no casualties, but this was due as much to luck as hard fighting. Had not Daggett and a few men been awake, or awakened quickly and held the door, the detachment would have suffered.

Later, the Ranger spies reported that there was a force of 500 guerrillas nearby. This was probably the same group, but the Rangers, low on ammunition, decided against going after this group. They started back to Mexico City, being followed part of the way by strong cavalry units. They reached the capital without incident. Ford was rather proud of their action and would always think that it was never officially reported.

Actually, Scott mentioned the affair in a dispatch, No. 43, January 13, 1848.[61] He reported a spy company had returned from Vera Cruz and on the way up had a big fight, capturing forty men. He continued: "Col Hays, with a detachment of Texan rangers, returned last night from a distant expedition in search of the robber priest. In a skirmish, without loss on his part, he killed some eight of Jarauta's *[sic]* men, and he thinks the priest was carried off among the wounded."

The spy company mentioned by Scott was Dominguez and his band of outlaws. He not only carried dispatches and guarded trains on this occasion but also engaged in a pitched battle and captured several officers, including three generals. He treated them so miserably that the Americans interceded.

The Rangers made another scout later in January. According to some accounts, Scott himself sent them to capture Santa Anna, who was rumored to be in Tehuacan.[62] Lane was in command, with Hays along, as well as Chevallie. Adjutant Ford missed this foray, as he was sick. His accounts are second-hand, but David Wooster, M.D., was along and recalled the scout.[63]

As before, the Rangers hid out during the day in a large *hacienda*, allowing no one to leave. After dark they started out in a single file, the rear guard waiting until the column had vanished before they rode out. This tactic was used so that people in the place had no idea where the Rangers were heading. The secrecy was necessary and proved successful. After some time, the scouts captured a large coach, drawn by a team of fine mules. Inside was a Mexican gentleman who produced a supposedly safe conduct pass signed by Gen. Persifer Smith.

Hays and Lane came up and carefully examined the pass by what light they could find. It appeared to be in proper order. Lane was for releasing the man, while the Ranger argued against it. He knew the moment the coach was out of sight, a messenger would be on the way to warn Santa Anna. The Mexican had freely admitted the wanted man was in the town, probably no more than fifteen miles down the road.

Lane's staff wanted to hold the coach for a few hours and let the man go, a solution favored by Hays and the Rangers. However, the general was adamant about respecting the pass, telling them it would damage the good name of the army if they did not allow the man to proceed. Finally, Hays agreed, if he was so ordered, and Lane gave them a direct order. The coach drove off in the darkness.

The Rangers formed again and continued along the road, moving carefully in the darkness. By sunrise they were in sight of Tehuacan. Soon they rode into the streets, with rifles across saddles; those with revolvers had their weapons drawn and cocked. There was no resistance, little more than amused civility. A few houses had foreign flags displayed from the balconies. Most of the remaining houses and buildings had large, white cloths prominently hanging from railings or windows.

Disgusted, the Rangers had a long ride back to Mexico City and sore behinds for their trouble and caution. Dr. Wooster said it was Lane's only mistake in the campaign. The gentleman in the coach had cut loose one of his mules and a rider and had them on the run to warn Santa Anna before the Texas rear guard was out of sight. The Texans never did convince the regulars that it was one thing to fight the Mexicans, and quite another to try to negotiate with them.

The Rangers had been close. They found out how close when they entered the house where Santa Anna and his family had been staying.

Candles were still burning; the table was set. By count, seventeen trunks were piled near the patio, abandoned in the wild rush. It was scant consolidation to open the trunks and poke through the belongings of the man they hated most. According to Dr. Wooster, many of the trunks contained clothing of Doña Santa Anna — dresses by the hundreds, shoes, toilet articles — which Lane sent on to the lady.

A dress coat that weighed fifteen pounds, most of this weight in gold decoration, was sent to the state of Texas. A gold-decorated sash went to another state. Finally, some of the Rangers found a cane belonging to the Napoleon of the West. This object was heavily inlaid, studded with all manner of jewels. The Rangers agreed to let their colonel have this. Hays accepted it, but later sent it to President Polk, saying it was from the Texans.

It was on this scout that one of the few really funny incidents of the war took place. Ford mentioned this, though he he did not see it.[64] Mike Chevallie was along and had tried to bargain with an Englishman for a saddle. Evidently, there was a complete misunderstanding about the term of the transaction, as the Englishman came complaining to Lane. He informed the general that Major Chevallie had been beating him, and Lane showed sympathy and interest. He asked if Chevallie had beaten him badly, and the man said it was so. Lane then was reported to have said: "Then be careful, or he will do it again."

Chevallie evidently was one of the Rangers who was as skillful with his fists as he was with weapons. In his position of civilian-along-for-a-fight, he could get away with this kind of conduct.

Mexico City was supposedly an occupied place, but it was sometimes difficult to tell the captives from the captors. While there was not another armed uprising, the American troops were subjected to constant attack. Any soldier by himself, especially after dark, or any drunken soldier, was fair game. If he was lucky, all that happened was a robbery. Usually, though, it was murder. Scott was forced to order all saloons closed by 6:00 in the evening to cut down on losses and keep drunken soldiers alive.[65] Sometimes the inhabitants played it safe and merely shoved an American officer into the gutters, apologizing profusely. The Mexican police made token efforts to maintain the peace, and the American provost guard tried, but they were outnumbered and could not be every place at once.

If the Texans had a reputation when they came to Mexico City, they added to the legend while there. Quartered in town, they could not help but have run-ins with the local citizens. Certainly, they made no effort to avoid confrontations, and the Mexicans probably tried to see how much they could get away with against the hated Rangers. Some of the incidents seem like unwarranted force, even deadly force, but the Rangers made little distinction between petty thievery and serious attempts on their lives.

The worst incident occurred when one of the Rangers was killed. Ford remembered the man as Adam Allsens of Roberts's company.[66] (There was an Adam Alsans, or several other spellings, in that company.)[67] In a bad section of town, called Cutthroat by the troops, Alsans was riding through one afternoon and was jumped by an unknown number of men. His horse brought him out and he rode slumped over until they reached his company area. By some miracle he was still alive, though slashed to pieces. Ford says his heart could be seen beating through his exposed ribs. A tough man, he lived for hours, dying that night. Company rolls show this as February 13, 1848.[68]

He was buried the following day with their version of honors. Ford, writing later, said the Rangers were strangely quiet. He knew something was afoot, as did Hays, but they didn't know what was going to happen. The day passed quietly enough, with the enlisted Rangers answering questions politely, but the horseplay and banter were missing.

Around 10:00 in the evening, Ford was in Hays's quarters with one of the regulars when they heard shots. After a time, the officer suggested they were six-shooters. Hays thought probably it was the Marines, who had been drilling outside the walls. The clearly controlled firing went on for an hour, then another hour. Hays got up and left, in case Scott would try to stop whatever was happening. By then they had some idea, but not until the next morning, when they got reports from the military patrols, did they understand how the Rangers had avenged the murder of their comrade.

No one ever knew which companies took part, or how many from each company, but it was a large party. They formed up and went through Cutthroat, dropping any man they saw. There is some suggestion that the military patrol went to check on the firing and joined in the sweep. By early morning, fifty bodies had been brought to the morgue. At nightfall there were at least eighty. These were people who had no one to claim their bodies. How many were carried away is unknown.[69]

Although an uproar was made over this, nothing happened. There was, however, a slowdown of the killing of soldiers. A few following incidents showed the event was not one of a kind. A group of men gathered a pile of rocks on the roof of one of the houses and stoned a party of Rangers. There was a burst of fire from the street, with six of the rock throwers killed. Hays was questioned by Scott, who accepted his explanation. Earlier the general had been extremely angry with Hays about the killing of two Mexicans as the Rangers entered the city. Hays reportedly informed his commander that the Texans were not in the habit of being insulted without "resenting" it. Scott seemed to take this as excuse enough.

There was one final incident. Two of the Texans were alone, seemingly unarmed. It was winter and they had on bulky garments, with their six-shooters hidden. By then no sane Ranger went out unarmed. Seeing what they thought were two unarmed Rangers, a crowd started throwing stones and rushed them with knives. Pete Gass, an interpreter, and Van Walling drew their weapons and dropped four or five before the survivors could run. Ford added, somewhat unnecessarily, that this and the Cutthroat sweep pretty well stopped attacks on American soldiers in the city.[70]

There was a major personnel change in late February, when Captain Armstrong resigned. The captain's performance of duty had not been acceptable, but Hays did little to remedy the situation, probably hoping the situation would work itself out and not involve severe disciplinary action. In fact, Armstrong all but turned his company over to the senior lieutenant, and the Rangers performed in fine fashion. Finally, on February 29, 1848, Armstrong solved everything by resigning. He was replaced next day by Alfred Evans, who commanded Company G until they were mustered out of service.[71]

The Rangers were active December through February, though there is almost nothing of an official nature to show what they were doing. They definitely were not sitting around in Mexico City. Again, checking muster rolls gives some hint of activity. It is clear that the various companies were seldom used as units.

Company K was sent to San Angel, not too far south of the capital, on December 19. The unit stayed there for a long period of time, probably being used to control the area. A number of men died from natural causes while in the town.

Company E records show a man dying in Jalapa on January 30, 1848, while two died in Mexico City the same date. Obviously, elements of the company had been operating as far south as Jalapa, where the ill man was left when he could no longer ride.

Company F lost two men to sickness in Mexico City on January 29; later one died in Puebla on March 6. Company G was in Tacubaya during January and February, as men died there during these months. The company also lost Rangers to sickness in Mexico City during this time. Company I was operating between Jalapa and Mexico City during January, based on sickness and death records.

All five companies show movement, besides the actions listed in combat reports. In fact, Hays used only part of his command in any scout, keeping the others on courier or escort duty, or sweeping the countryside. It was not very glamorous work, but it was their specialty.[72]

There must have been times when a company or part of a company was in a locality for some period of time, long enough to get to know people. Daggett tells of making friends with a priest and giving the man a pair of pistols and a belt — muzzle-loaders, naturally, not the Colts. Daggett even gets in a bit of public relations for his command: "He called on me frequently while I was with him to praise the honesty of my company, and declared that he did not believe a company of Mexicans could be found who could keep from taking something they had as good chance as my men had."[73]

The final big fight of the war took place in mid-February. This expedition, directed by Scott to clear the northern and northeastern area, was a major strike. The Rangers played a key role in the sweep. Hays said he had all five companies, though considerable portions of each company must have been on other service. The Ranger force consisted of 250 men, including Hays, Truett, Sergeant Major Brush and others of the regimental staff, as well as dependable Chevallie, never one to miss a fight. Major Polk had 130 men from the 3rd Dragoons, plus a company of riflemen, and Dominguez had a considerable contingent. Ford thought they had a thousand men, but this was wildly inflated.[74] Joe Lane was in overall command.

The column left Mexico City on February 17, going up to scout the mountains north of the Rio Frio. Most of the movement was at night, the departure being after 8:00 in the evening. After going on the Vera Cruz road for some time, Lane turned them back and cut across country toward Tulancingo. Information from spies indicated

General Paredes and Juarata would be there, as well as Almonte, another guerrilla leader.

They pushed hard, testing their horses severely. The Dragoons had to resaddle often, and several of their horses broke down. There was no way to leave the troopers, and mounts were taken from ranches. Going over the high passes in the dark was cold business. Most of the time the column was at a gallop; keeping the units closed up and collecting stragglers was difficult. Somewhere, in replacing horses, spies must have spotted the move.

At daylight, February 22, the head of the column was on a mountain, some nine miles from the town, which could barely be seen. Lane was eager to surprise the place and ordered Major Polk to rush the town. Polk was at the head of the column at the time. Taking some of his men, he made the open country as fast as his horses could move; Adjutant Ford was with him.

Lane and Polk were certain they had the fox in the trap. Major Polk asked some people in the street where the general lived and they pointed out a house, explaining it belonged to Paredes. The Dragoons rushed the place, following their guides up the stairs, and captured a man, who admitted he was Paredes. It occurred to the Americans that he was very cheerful for a wanted guerrilla. They found out why he was so amused: he was Paredes's brother. While they were arresting him, his brother was escaping.

As Ford wrote, the laugh was on Major Polk. Lane, in his report, played down their chagrin: "General Parades alone remained and escaped by a mere miracle and our ignorance of the localities of the place."[75]

The horses had been pushed too hard and rest was necessary before the command could continue. Already they had covered over ninety miles, much of it at a gallop. Early the next morning Major Polk and a small detachment went to a large ranch several miles away to find horses. It was common knowledge that the guerrillas used the place to water and feed and obtain fresh mounts. Polk brought back a number of fresh horses, but after some discussion Lane had them taken back and purchased mounts for the men who had lost horses.

Once again, spies brought positive information that Juarata was in Sequalteplan, about seventy-five miles north of Tulancingo. Lane had a number of sick men and some with weak horses, so he sent them back to Mexico City with Dominguez and his company. This reduced his command to the Dragoons and the Rangers. There might have been as many as 500 men awaiting them, but no one seemed to mind the odds. They started out, taking a mountain road rather than the usual route. It was another forced march, with few halts, made at night. The way through the mountains was a mule path, with the column riding in single file. On this march the Rangers led, while the Dragoons and rifle company brought up the rear. About sunrise on February 25, the Ranger scouts saw Sequalteplan.

As quickly as he could, Hays brought his men into a column. Then, with Lane, they charged. Just at the suburbs they began receiving fire, followed by shots from a barracks on their right. Many of the Texans broke off and started returning the fire with their rifles. Lane dropped off one company to handle the barracks, while the rest resumed the attack, galloping into the main plaza.

This part of the action became Lane's fight; several other areas of town became battlefields as other commanders came under fire. Lane ran through the fire in the plaza with his aide and Lieutenant Hays, as well as a Lieutenant Haslet and several of the Rangers. Three hundred yards farther on, his small party came under fire from another barracks and ran into a large group of lancers. By then he had been joined by Captain Daggett and a handful of Rangers, but he was afraid they might be cut off and surrounded. He sent his aide for whatever help could be found.

There had not been time to make any plan before they charged the city. Everyone was so intent on getting into the streets before Paredes could escape again that they simply rushed in and found they had kicked over a beehive. But it was the kind of fight the Rangers loved. A party rode up with Lane's aide, dismounted, and began using their rifles on the snipers in the barracks. Lane decided to charge the building and yelled for a rush, which was made, driving the defenders from the walls about the barracks. The guerrillas had no time to get set, as the Rangers forced the doors and got inside with revolvers and knives. This became a bloody affair; thirty defenders were killed and some made prisoners, though many escaped through a back door.

There were several tense moments during the fight. For a time, Sergeant Major Brush was defending the door of the building single-handedly, using his revolver, knife, and sheer determination to keep the enemy contained. He was wounded during this struggle. As they rode up to the building and started firing, Lane was targeted by a sniper who had his *escopet* pointed right at the general's breast. Lane thought he was dead. However, one of the younger Rangers rode beside him, lifted his revolver, and shot the sniper just as he fired at Lane. The Mexican jumped and the ball passed through Lane's hat. Brackett mentioned that the youngster was later taken under Lane's charge.[76]

While Lane was engaging this force, Hays was fighting at the first barracks and in the plaza. In his report, he described how they charged into town and came under fire from a barracks that had been hidden from view until they entered town. There were fifty or sixty infantry in the building, all firing on the Rangers. Hays ordered Major Truett to take a small force and clean out the barracks. Ford was ordered to assist.

The reports and Ford's recollection place the number of men with Truett at fifteen to eighteen, who now dismounted in an open lot and began fighting the Mexican infantry. They drove them from the open into the barracks and the other buildings, where the firing continued. One of the buildings was a large, wooden structure with a stone house adjoining. A palisade ran before the buildings; about thirty yards away and roughly parallel was a stone fence, where the Rangers took cover. Both sides were firing, the Mexicans as rapidly as possible, the Rangers with care, taking longer to reload their rifles. In a short time it became clear that any infantryman who exposed himself over the fence or on the roof was as good as dead. The Mexicans began loading and lifting their muskets and firing them blindly without showing themselves.

Fighting became general all over town, and the Rangers and the Dragoons went wherever they heard firing. Truett had started with fifteen men, but he now found he was fighting at least sixty enemy infantry with a half dozen Rangers and Adjutant Ford. Some of his men came back and their rifle fire began to cripple the men in the house; a growing number began slipping out through the pickets on the right of the Ranger line.

Seeing this, Ford suggested that he should go and stop the retreat. Truett agreed. Taking Jacob M. Horn, Ford ran along the top of the stone wall, exposed to fire from the buildings. They were no more than thirty yards from the enemy, firing as they ran. At the end of the wall, they opened on a retreating group, killing several and driving the rest back inside the house. Horn was hit in the chest, falling back and calling out to Ford that he was killed. The adjutant told him the wound was too high to be fatal and kept shooting. There is no doubt that the use of their Colts enabled them to hold this part of the line and cut off the enemy retreat.

Fortunately, Chevallie rode up, under fire from all sides, dismounted, and joined the fight with Ford. Despite being exposed for some time, he was not hurt; the only ball that struck him was a spent round. In a moment Lt. Dan Grady and two privates reinforced the hard-pressed Ford. With the breather, Ford found he had seriously wounded Colonel Montagna, one of the major commanders of the enemy troops.

A messenger had come from Hays, fighting in the main plaza, asking to send whatever men could be spared. Even though his own fight was now more severe than before, Truett broke off with some men and went to join Hays, leaving Ford in command. Ford found he was now reinforced by Pvt. G. M. Swope. He and a few others found a barred gate in the Mexican right rear and forced it open. They discovered that they could sweep a long gallery along the front of the building and command a window that had been used as a firing station. They settled down and opened fire; after a few minutes it was impossible for a sniper to show himself without being killed.

Truett had gone to the plaza and found that action there had died down. He returned in time to see a white flag being cautiously dangled from the house. Truett's report says the wounded colonel and twenty infantry surrendered. Ford recalled they captured forty, but time plays tricks on the memory.

Sequalteplan was a series of small battles, most taking place at the same time. When Lane and his party charged through the town, Hays had followed and dropped off Truett to contain the barracks. Hays then rode into the plaza and found the street to his left was filled with lancers and infantry. Hays divided his forces and took the major portion and charged this force, before they could retreat to another barracks in their rear. Despite considerable firing from the barracks and buildings on the plaza, the Rangers broke up the mounted force and chased the lancers for a half mile down a road. This, again, was close work with the six-shooters and resulted in thirty dead lancers.

Gathering his scattered men, Hays turned back into town and rode into the plaza. He was met there by Lieutenant Hays, who told about Lane being under heavy attack. Hays immediately dispatched Daggett and his company, as was noted earlier. They helped Lane finish his part of the fight. The mopping up which followed, running down stragglers, rounding up prisoners, was not any easier. Hays reported that the Mexicans fought with bravery and determination, trying to hold back the Rangers and Dragoons, taking advantage of every shelter.

The lancers were trying to break to the west of town, and in chasing them in that direction Hays met Major Polk and some of his troopers, also engaged in running down stragglers. While in this area they captured a prisoner who told them the good *padre* had quarters in the church on the main plaza. They turned back and rushed the church and had another skirmish with the remnants of the lancers, scattering them and killing a few more. As always, Juarata was a few moments ahead of them and vanished in the confusion. The last fighting was probably his men covering his escape with their lives.

While the main action was carried by the Rangers, it would not be fair to overlook the work done by the regular cavalry. This force was commanded by Maj. William H. Polk and consisted of E and G Companies of the 3rd Dragoons and Company I of the Mounted Rifles. The brother of the president, Polk may have been a political appointee, but he was a fine officer and a gallant fighter. When the column approached town his command was in the rear. As he stated in his report, they were strung out and their horses were tired. It was necessary for Polk to halt his men to close up and give a brief rest in the growing light. By the time he had things under control, the Rangers were fighting in the outskirts of the town.

When the regulars reached town, the main fight had moved ahead, but they came under fire from another barracks, and Polk dismounted the rifles and cleared this structure. The Dragoons then advanced into town and met some scattered fire from the church on the main plaza. They rushed through the streets to a hill on the outskirts and turned back, as the enemy forces in this area had broken into small groups. Coming in slower, Polk had kept control of his companies and broke them into squads to check the various streets. By then Lieutenant Walker with Company I of the Mounted Rifles had taken the church. The Rangers under Hays came up, and the fighting was over, though they would pick up an occasional prisoner for some time.

During the fighting by Ford and Truett at the first barracks, Private Swope and his comrades had managed to start a fire in one of the thatched roofs. No one had time to fight a fire, and the blaze spread, as Lane reported, over a large part of town.

Juarata never recovered from this fight. It was estimated that he had 400 lancers and about 50 infantry in the town when the fighting broke out. Most accounts place the guerrilla loss at 150, with a considerable number wounded, though there was no accurate count made. Fifty prisoners were taken, including three American deserters. Ford mortally wounded Colonel Montagna at the first barracks. Hays's group killed a Padre Martinez, Juarata's lieutenant, in the fight near the plaza, and three other officers were in the ranks of the prisoners. A considerable number of horses were captured — a boon, as the mounts of the command were exhausted. The guerrilla losses were severe enough, but the most damaging thing was the knowledge that there was no place that was safe.

The fight was not casualty-free. Despite Ford's assurances, Jacob Horn was mortally wounded. The Rangers fixed a litter and the prisoners took turns carrying him on the return to Mexico City. They finally dropped him off about forty miles from the capital, but there was no way to remove the ball from his chest, and he died. Peter Gass was wounded slightly, as was Brush. Lieutenants Harris Davis and Thomas Greer were severely wounded, but all reached Mexico City and survived.

Back in Mexico City, on March 2, 1848, Lane, Hays, Polk, and Truett wrote reports on the scout.[77] These are the last combat reports of the war. The three accounts show the scattered nature of the fighting, really three separate battles. Truett is the only one who mentioned the use of Colt revolvers. After describing his part of the battle, he added this paragraph: "The engagement lasted upwards of half and hour; and but for Colt's six shooters, we could not have held our own, much less have driven Montagna from his position. This is certainly the most effective fire-arm in use."

He finished by commending Ford, Chevallie, Horn, Gass, Elliott, and William Williams. Ford was also mentioned by Hays, as was Major Truett. Much as he had earlier at Monterey, Hays did not go into lengthy detail about individual actions, merely stating his pride in the performance of his entire command.

General Lane praised the Rangers, mentioning Hays and Truett by name, but he covered only the actions he personally observed or commanded. In a previous report, that on the actions at Orizaba and Tehuacan, Lane had also been very generous in his praise of the Texans. He had singled out Chevallie on this earlier report: ". . . Major Chevallie, late of the Texas rangers . . . also have my thanks for their attention."

Chevallie was always listed as Major, no matter what position he held, and this report shows he was formerly with the Rangers. No one seems to have minded, and certainly he did not. When there was a fight, he was there. It was a rather irregular operation. Hays signed his report "Col Texas Rangers." Truett signed "Major 1st Regiment Texas cavalry." The names didn't matter. The work did.

Sequalteplan was the last battle, fought after the war was over. Ironically enough, even the death of Alsans in Mexico City was after the Treaty of Guadalupe Hidalgo was signed on February 2, 1848. It took weeks to get copies from capital to capital, and the treaty was not ratified in Washington until March 10. It was May 30, 1848, before it was returned to Mexico City. American troops started to leave at once, with the Rangers departing Mexico City on April 20, 1848.[78] The last American units were ready to leave by June 10.

The Texans were ordered down to Vera Cruz, working down the long road in stages. They knew the war was over, but they were still in the guerrilla-hunting business. If the war was over for the regular Mexican army, the *rancheros* and those who were merely bandits kept active. Ford recounted how a young man who looked after Hays's horses caused a lot of commotion with his galloping up and down the column. Mike Chevallie grumbled that he wished the guerrillas would get the fellow. Next morning they could not find him and started marching, locating him down the road, dead. The shaken Chevallie swore he would never make such a wish again.[79]

This action took place at Rio Frio. Ford thought Hays left Major Truett and two companies to work over the area for a time, while the rest moved on. He remembered a rather notable event at a place called San Carlos. In the fighting, Sgt. Maj. William Hewitt saw several guerrillas some distance away. He took his Walker Colt, aimed carefully, and shot three of them. When the fight was over, someone paced the distance. It was 120 yards! Ford understated that "Hewitt was one of the best shots with a pistol the writer ever saw."[80]

The Rangers camped for a time at a place called Tepejahuilco. While there they heard of a gang in a town some six miles away. Hays sent Ford and fourteen men to check the report, accompanied by their guides. They must not have known the country very well; the distance was closer to sixteen miles when they finally rode into San Juan de los Llanos. It was a fairly large town, with most of the population gathered in the main plaza.

The small group of Texans rode into a crowd of several thousand sullen people, arriving at dusk on a Saint Day. They were in a tight place. Ford was afraid to fall back, as this might lead the crowd to rush them. He decided to brazen it through and had the interpreter ask for the *alcalde*. Apparently, the chief of police ran the town, and Peter Gass asked for food and rations.

There was no immediate reply, but they were led to a large house on one side of the plaza. It was a typical well-to-do dwelling, with rooms surrounding an interior courtyard. The Rangers placed their horses in the courtyard and tried to figure out what to do next. Then a delegate arrived and said there would be no rations or food. Ford took Gass and went to the chief's quarters and demanded to know why they had been refused. He was told that American deserters had been roaming the countryside and making demands for food and shelter.

Ford played his bluff to the limit. He told who he was and all about Hays and his regiment. Quite likely he suggested that the rest of the Rangers were close by and that anything they were provided would be paid for in full. The bluff worked, and the prefect agreed to furnish everything they needed. He also invited Ford and any guests to dine with him at 9:00. They were not free by any means. Any hesitation would have invited a rush. Ford recalled there were enough men in the plaza to kill the Texans with stones.

Back in the house, Ford assigned each man a station and told all of them to fight to the death if attacked. Then he took Gass and Miguel and went to dine. It was a meal that staggered them, accustomed as they were to what they could buy on the road. The meal was served in numerous courses on fine silver. They would have enjoyed it more if they had not been so busy watching the servants. Gass sat with his revolver in his lap, as did Ford. Somehow they got through the meal and returned to their quarters.

Back in the courtyard they described everything and learned that one Ranger knew they had been murdered and almost talked the others into making a run. Calmer heads took over, and they waited until Ford came back. They spent a restless night, what was left of it. Vincent, one of two spies with the Rangers, had been roaming the streets and came in and told Ford there were only four guns in the town, and this was why they had not been attacked. It wasn't enough to make up for several thousand hostile townspeople. By daylight, Ford had them up and gone, taking the prefect as a guest-hostage until they were clear of town.

Ford mentioned briefly here that one of the guides lived a few miles away from the town and asked to visit his family. He was given permission and rode away — and vanished. Everyone but Ford thought he had deserted, but after ten days or so he came up to the column. On his way back he had been intercepted by guerrillas and barely escaped, having to hide for days. There is no doubt the two Mexicans served the Rangers efficiently and faithfully. What happened to them later is unknown, just as why they agreed to serve is a mystery.

The command continued to Jalapa once again and camped near the town.[81]

There were no more real fights, but a final incident was more interesting than most skirmishes. The Texans finally met Santa Anna — and lived, which was more than most could say. What was more incredible, Santa Anna lived!

Several people wrote about the meeting; the versions differ somewhat. Ford recalled that rumors came down the road that Santa Anna was leaving the country and would pass near their camp. He and Major Truett were in Jalapa when several Rangers rode in and told them they had better get back to camp, since the Rangers had decided to kill Santa Anna when he passed. Hays and some of his officers had ridden up the road to see the Mexican general at a ranch where he was supposed to eat. Ford and Truett had ridden into Jalapa to watch any demonstration the people might stage in honor of Santa Anna.

Alarmed by what he heard, Truett turned and he and Ford galloped back to camp. They found the messengers had not exaggerated. The camp was in turmoil.

It is difficult today to appreciate the way the Rangers felt. Santa Anna represented everything that was evil. This was the man who saw there were no survivors at the Alamo. When the men of Goliad surrendered under promise of safe conduct, Santa Anna gave orders they be killed — and they were. He may not have been personally responsible for the deaths and suffering of the Santa Fe and Mier prisoners, but it was his policy that was being followed. He may not have led the raids that killed settlers, but it was his policy. Some of the men in camp had lost friends or relatives to this policy. All knew families who had suffered. Now they had the opportunity to balance the scales.

Ford and Truett knew enough not to issue orders or make threats. This was not a military situation. In battle these same Rangers would have attempted anything commanded. This was not a battle; this was a matter of honor. Orders meant nothing here. And that was the way Ford and some of the other officers finally handled the matter.

One thing that made these men so fierce in battle was their pride in their country, their locale, and in themselves. It was the only way he could appeal to them. Ford says he explained that Santa Anna had been condemned for killing prisoners, that the world detested him for his actions. He showed how the Texans after San Jacinto had been commended for sparing his life and the Mexican soldiers taken captive. If they killed him, they were no better than he was.

A few of the Rangers pointed out he was not a prisoner. Ford explained that he was — almost. He was as good as a prisoner, being forced to flee his country by his own countrymen. They began to waver. Finally, he said, "You will dishonor Texas."

They nodded agreement, and the matter was settled. They lined the road and waited. Some wanted to talk to the general, wondering just what kind of man could do what he had done, but instructions went out to not speak or cheer — no jeering, just silence.

And that was the way it was when the coach came in sight. They had been warned by a courier galloping by and watched as the coach and escort arrived. Santa Anna's wife and daughter were with him, the wife smiling and waving to people along the roadside. Not a word or sound was heard as the coach and escort passed. Ford thought Santa Anna seemed startled for a moment when he realized the men lining this section of road were Texans, but he never turned his head or made a sound. The escort stared straight ahead, and it was over; the coach was down the road and soon out of sight. The Rangers broke up and drifted back to camp.[82]

It was one of their finer hours.

The regiment camped at Encerro, a *hacienda* owned by Santa Anna, another fourteen miles closer to Vera Cruz. It was probably the last camp before being mustered out. Ford remembered the trouble they had with the major-domo who was running the place for the departed general. As usual, he was charging as much as possible for the cheapest beef he could find. It got so bad the Rangers went out and "helped" him find decent cattle to slaughter, having him pay for the animals. They, in turn, paid him.

It was probably while here that they had time on their hands and conducted some experiments with the Walker Colts and the Standard rifle, the Model 1841, now beginning to be called the Mississippi

Rifle, after Jeff Davis's regiment. The Colt fired a bullet a greater distance than did the rifle.[83]

Each day they passed the time as best they could. Someone suggested they take up a collection for the chaplain, and the amazing sum of $500 in gold was gathered together and presented to the surprised minister. He had been a friend to every man in the command, as well as unit chaplain. The gift, characteristic of the Rangers, enabled him to pay his debts. Reverend Sam Corley was in every respect a Ranger.[84]

Then they were on the way to Vera Cruz, turning in what government property they had. Capt. John Williamson, USA, reported to Lieutenant Colonel Talcott, chief of ordnance, that the discharged Rangers had turned in 191 of the 280 pistols issued less than a year before. Some of the weapons had been lost in combat, but most had been lost to mechanical failure. Of the 191 turned in, only 82 were serviceable.[85]

The companies were mustered out, but Hays and Ford stayed on active duty to bring back the records.[86] When they left the steamer in home port, each thought the other had brought off the records and reports of the regiment, and the box was left aboard and lost. Not forgetting his experiences as a journalist, Ford had written long letters to his old paper in Austin when he found time. He did not feel too bad about losing the unit records when he thought of his articles covering the unit history. When he came back to Austin and went to check on the papers, he was told the letters were so long they had been thrown away.[87]

The second regiment came home by ship and in increments, but there were enough of them together to be given heroes' welcomes in several towns. There were parades and parties and speeches, and then they scattered to their homes.

That war was over.

Afterword

A surprisingly large number of Texans volunteered for service in the Mexican War. Some names appear several times on muster rolls, and many served in more than one unit, giving over 8,000 listings. If the duplicates and various spellings are dropped, something over 7,000 is a more reasonable figure.[1] This from a population of 150,000 or less is a fine showing. Considering that most of the companies were in combat, the showing becomes more remarkable. The men believed in this struggle, and they had more of a stake in the fight than did other states.

The Texas volunteers came from most areas and from wide social and economic levels. It was not a poor man's war, though most of them *were* poor. There are all manner of names, including Spanish, on the rolls, and they would rise in protest if any one group tried to claim they were best, or most — just as they would protest if they were left out. They were all Texans.

Most of the Rangers went home and picked up their old pursuits or found new ones. Not all were weary of service. Jacob Roberts gave up his old company in central Mexico and accepted command of a newly formed company to protect the frontier. John Glanton became a first lieutenant in a second company. Unfortunately, conditions had changed. The federal government had authorized Ranger companies for the duration of the war, and the war was over. Roberts and Glanton were no sooner in their new positions than they were mustered out.[2]

Glanton liked the wild life too much to return to family and humdrum living. He went back to Mexico and signed on as a contract scalp hunter. The Mexican government found that one way to combat the Indian raids was to pay bounty hunters for scalps. Glanton organized a detachment of kill-for-pay drifters. There were others. Michael Chevallie was active, a sorry ending to a fine career. They offered Ben McCulloch a contract, but he turned them down.[3] Killing Indians to protect the frontier was one thing; killing them for money was another matter, even in those days.

McCulloch did not serve as a Ranger again. He went to California, as did many, to find fortune and ease and found neither, though he did better than most. After several years he returned to Texas. A federal marshal and several times applicant for an army commission, he joined the Confederate army when the Civil War began. Ben and his brother Henry became brigadier generals in the new army. McCulloch had considerable success in earlier fighting, but his luck ran out. He was killed in 1862 while on a scout of enemy lines, preparing for a new battle.[4]

Jack Hays went back to Texas as a national hero. He joined an expedition to discover the best route from San Antonio to El Paso. It was the only scout or fight of his that was a failure. Not even Hays could outfight the desert country of the Big Bend. When he returned, Hays left for California. He remained there, living until 1883.[5]

Walter Lane stayed away from military life until the Civil War, when he went into service and also became a brigadier general in the Confederate army.[6] Considerable numbers of the old Rangers reentered service in this struggle, too many to list.

George Wood left his 2nd Regiment and returned to his plantation and politics. He was a hero to his friends in East Texas and to enough others throughout the state to be elected the second governor. He and J. Pinckney Henderson became embroiled in a silly dispute over who had done the most at Monterey, a political fight that kept Wood from being reelected.[7]

There had been numerous connecting links between the Republic Rangers and the Rangers of the Mexican War. Only one Ranger bridged the war and postwar periods. With Texas a state, the U.S. Army had the responsibility for protecting the frontier. It was more than the small force could handle; by 1849 the Texans were beginning to turn to their own resources for defense. John Ford, Hays's adjutant, had acquired a feeling for military life and headed one of the new Ranger companies. During the next decade he would become the premier Ranger commander, as well known in the fifties as Hays had been in his time.[8]

First with Comanches, and later with Mexican bandits, Ford fought from the Rio Grande to the northern reaches of Texas. He joined the Confederate army and served throughout the war and afterward. Troops under his command fought the last battle of the Civil

War in the southern tip of the state. They won, but it made no difference, as the war was over. Ford had the distinction of fighting in the last battle of the Mexican War and of the Civil War, both fights after peace had been declared. After the war Ford engaged in more peaceful pursuits, in education and writing. He became one of the leaders in historical studies of Texas.

Interestingly enough, one of the Ranger enemies, Juan Seguin, returned to Texas after the war. He asked permission to do so; passions had cooled and an earlier hero came home in peace. Seguin outlived nearly all the men who chased him. When he died in 1890, he was as respected as he had been in his earlier years.[9]

Manuel Dominguez also moved to the States after the war. There was a price on his head, and Colonel Hitchcock felt responsible for him and took him back with his family to New Orleans. For a number of years Hitchcock tried without success to get Congress to provide some form of pension for the ex-guerrilla. The veterans of the Mexican War never did get much from a grateful country for their services. In the 1880s, Gen. Joe Lane had to turn down a request to appear at a Mexican War reunion in Philadelphia because he was too poor to make the trip.[10]

General Taylor became President Taylor, though he did not live long enough to fully enjoy the honor. It is generally accepted that he was a better soldier than statesman. Winfield Scott tried for the office, as did several other Mexican War generals, but none were elected. Scott went back to his old job as head of the army. When the Civil War broke out he was still in the position, a mountain of a man, far too old and heavy to take the field. His mind was still as sharp as ever, though. Today, people think only of the great ones who finished the conflict, but Scott developed the strategic plan that would eventually win the Civil War.

Of all the men who took part in any way in the Mexican War, none profited more than Samuel Colt. The Texans had shown the value of his new revolvers; Colt never forgot, giving them full credit for his fame and fortune.

He had been working on a new contract while finishing the delivery of the 1847 Model. His second army revolver, the 1848 Dragoon, was a slightly smaller Walker, easier to handle and much better constructed.[11] He returned to the workmanship and materials that had marked the first Colts, and the Dragoons were soon satisfying even army inspectors. This arm came out in several versions, with many being sold to civilians. Colt began turning out revolvers designed for civilian use. When gold was discovered in California, there was a tremendous move westward, with a vastly expanded market for revolvers. The army trade had reestablished Colt; the civilian trade made him wealthy. He soon opened a factory in England. Colt and revolver became the same in the public mind. In time, others would design revolvers, some better than those of the old master, but to this day the name Colt is synonymous with revolver.

Few modern historians find much connection between the Rangers and cavalry tactics. There is no doubt that contemporary observers, military and civilian alike, were impressed by the use the Texans made of the new handguns. Following the war, more than seventy units or individual commanders requested the arming of their troops with Colt revolvers. Only the 1st Dragoons seem to have been unimpressed.[12] While the tide had turned in favor of repeating firearms for mounted units, the army did not give in gracefully. In 1855 the army issued a single-shot muzzle-loader, probably the best single-shot martial pistol ever manufactured. It was just a generation outdated. As late as the 1870s, efforts were made to return to single-shot pistols. Fortunately, the troopers would have nothing to do with throwbacks.

It is just as easy to give the Rangers credit for a revolutionary influence as it is to ignore them completely. As late as the 1850s, inspectors visiting the forts in Texas suggested the units should design their own holsters for the revolvers, rather than using old-style holsters on the saddle.[13] Only a few regiments — the 2nd Cavalry, for example — had been in contact with the Plains Indians. It would not be until the great campaigns of the 1870s that the cavalryman would adopt the Ranger system of mounted fire, leaving his saber in camp.

During the Civil War this system was followed to a large extent, though many commanders were still infatuated with European concepts of lance and saber. In combat between mounted units using the saber and those relying on revolvers, the casualty lists were heavily weighted in favor of firepower. It is one of those little ironies of history that the last U.S. mounted charge was in 1916, near Parras, Mexico, where the Rangers had shown what the revolver could do. This time the troopers attacked, firing the new Colt Automatic, Model 1911.

The introduction of the revolver was not an unmixed blessing. It enabled the Rangers, and later the cavalry, to fight the Plains Indians, but it also created a new class of civilians. With the new weapons, any little man could tower over his neighbors — until they were armed.

Then the man with greater skill could rule them all. Thus was created another great myth: the Western gunfighter. The Rangers were indirectly responsible for this monster, and they would eventually be called upon to destroy him in Texas. When they were reorganized in 1874, the Rangers were the old quasimilitary force fighting invaders, Indian or Mexican. Almost at once they also had to contend with heavily armed outlaws who had virtually taken over the state. They outfought them, as they had the others, but that is another story.[14]

Much has been made about the revolver, but the Ranger use of rifles also had an impact. Contemporary observers mentioned the Ranger marksmanship even more than their use of revolvers, for *every* man had a rifle. Until then, rifles had not been too favorably considered for military use, and there were good arguments for this bias. In 1841 a rifle for the infantry was issued, but this was not equipped with a bayonet.[15] Riflemen were light troops, scouts, skirmishers, those not meant for the solid business of mass fighting. The Texans made deadly use of rifles in varied situations. When technical advances made loading a rifle as easy as loading a musket, there was no reason to fight the change. In a few years the army was completely equipped with rifles, the way eased by the Rangers.

Most of the observers in the war did not understand the Rangers; nor do all contemporary writers. It is usually assumed that the commanders of the Texans were the toughest and roughest, the best shots. It has been stated that Hays simply pointed his men and yelled at them to charge. But most agree the Rangers were a successful combat force — mean, even harsh, but effective. Compared to most volunteer outfits, they were amazingly successful. In their own field of mounted reconnaissance, screening, and counterguerrilla operations, they were unexcelled. Not even the regulars came close to them, or even tried.

What made the Rangers different?

Again, it is easiest to say they had the hard background. Yet, in the 1840s most of the men who entered military service came from farms, and they were all tough. Another answer is better weapons. Here, there is more justification, as the Rangers all had rifles and knew how to use them. They also had revolvers, and they knew how to use them. Had the other volunteer cavalry regiments been armed as the Rangers were, it is likely they would have achieved about the same results they did with their standard arms.

The Ranger success was due also to superior leadership, not just better weapons. All volunteer commands elected their officers. As a general rule this often led to disaster, with company and regimental voting taking on the character of a county election, with free drinks, favors, promises, and bribery. Training and experience usually played no part in a man being a colonel or captain. Since few men standing for command had any previous military experience, it usually came down to who could make the most promises or put up the most cash, drinks, or food. Occasionally a Jefferson Davis, an experienced soldier, was chosen to head a regiment, but not often. Unfortunately, there were all too many who had no concept of commanding a regiment.

The Texans had a large pool of experienced frontier fighters to serve as commanders. The men who made up the companies knew the best men, and they voted them into office. A number of times the man picked the company. When quotas came to a county or town, someone like Ben McCulloch or Eli Chandler or R. A. Gillespie started forming a company. Elections, if held, were mere formalities. The men in the companies did not vote for a man to lead them because he was popular, or could whip any man in the outfit. They chose someone they thought could lead them in a fight. Their selections were amazingly good. Only one captain was allowed to resign for cause. Lieutenants also were selected with care, a number becoming captains and serving with distinction. Walter Lane, for example, was a lieutenant in the Monterey campaign. He signed up again as a captain in Chevallie's Battalion and then became major and commander when Chevallie resigned.

There was not this much success with noncommissioned officers. The rolls show that many of the original sergeants and corporals resigned or were replaced as the campaigns progressed. It took some time for the true junior leaders to emerge.

As to being the best physically, the toughest, the best shot, a commander had to be all these, as well as a fine horseman, but this was not enough to command. One could not whip these Texans into doing anything. Regular army lashing and gagging and tying to a wheel would not have been tolerated one minute by the lowest private.

Those who saw the Rangers in a fight, with their wild yells and aggressive manner, easily believed they simply rushed ahead, no matter the cost, whatever the odds. But these men were brave, not stupid. A lot of what seemed foolish bravado was based on experience. Usually, in a meeting engagement, especially in low visibility, a sudden rush would overrun the enemy, breaking up larger formations by surprise. The Rangers used this trick time after time. Yet there are numerous examples, both in central Mexico and before Monterey, when they rushed so far and pulled back before vastly superior formations. They used trickery if required, bluffing to the last card or bullet. A single scout confronted by enemy troops would turn and wave and yell, as though signaling to his command to join him. A few Rangers in a hostile town would ride arrogantly through the streets, daring anyone to take action, and demand the *alcalde,* ask for food, or do *anything* but look uncertain.

And they had one final edge: They really believed they *were* better. They were Texans. Their people believed in them, and they were not going to let them down. It was that simple.

In 1856 the bodies of Sam Walker and R. A. Gillespie were recovered and brought back for reburial in San Antonio. J. C. Wilson gave a eulogy on April 22, describing these two men.[16] In his long, beautiful bit of nineteenth-century oratory, he concluded with some remarks that sum up much of this story:

> Walker . . . if he had any one characteristic on which I could fix as particular prominent, it was the ardent, the enthusiastic love he bore to the country of his adoption . . . but Texas — the Texas for which he suffered — was inexpressibly dear to him.

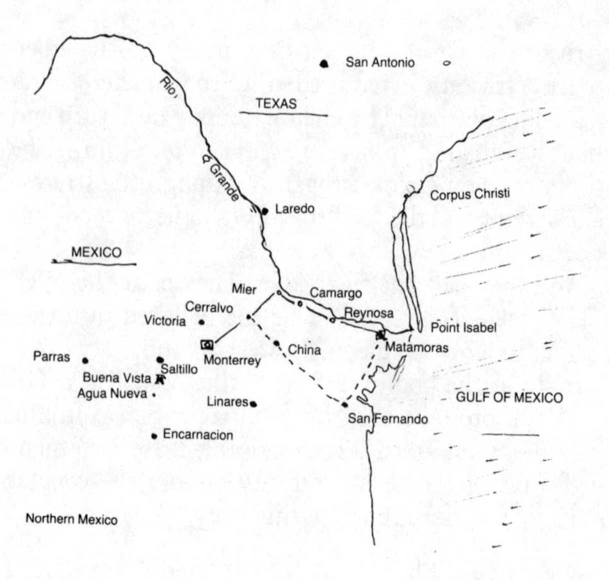
San Antonio
TEXAS
Rio Grande
Corpus Christi
Laredo
MEXICO
Mier
Camargo
Cerralvo
Victoria
Reynosa
Point Isabel
Matamoras
Monterrey
China
Parras
Saltillo
Buena Vista
Agua Nueva
Linares
GULF OF MEXICO
San Fernando
Encarnacion
Northern Mexico
Taylor's March
Hay's Route

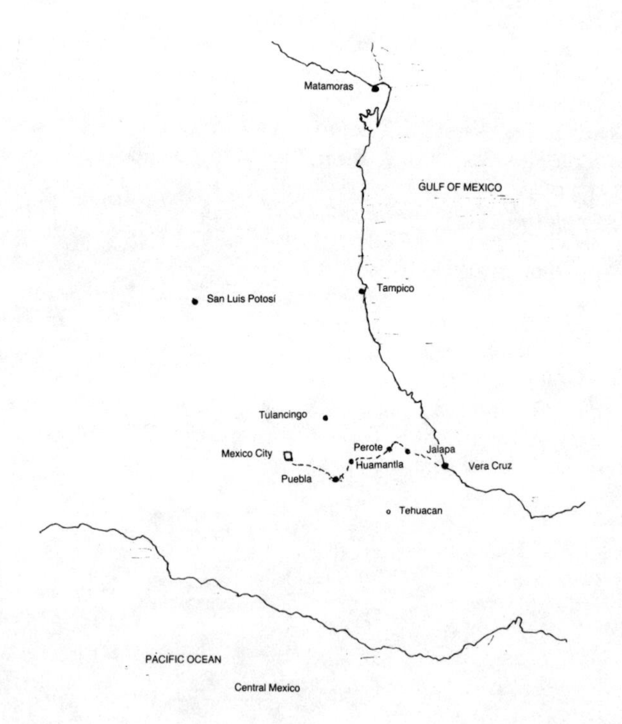
Matamoras
GULF OF MEXICO
Tampico
San Luis Potosí
Tulancingo
Perote
Jalapa
Mexico City
Huamantla
Vera Cruz
Puebla
Tehuacan
PACIFIC OCEAN
Central Mexico

Notes

Chapter 1

1. Eugene C. Barker, *The Life of Stephen F. Austin,* 102–106. Austin hired and paid ten men for protection — the first who could be called Rangers. The first fights were with the Karankawas.

2. Webb and Carroll, eds., *Handbook of Texas,* 2:554.

3. John G. W. Dillin's *The Kentucky Rifle* is the classic study of this weapon. It was the premier weapon in Texas during the settlement and revolutionary periods.

4. The full story of this epic struggle is outside the scope of this book. It is covered by T. R. Fehrenbach in *Comanches: The Destruction of a People.*

5. Walter Prescott Webb, *The Texas Rangers,* 23–25.

6. As early as April 1837, a "corps" of mounted gunmen had been authorized. Other units were authorized through 1838. H. P. N. Gammel, *Laws of Texas,* 1:1113–1114 and 1134–1135. None of the early units bore the name Ranger. They were spies or, more often, mounted gunmen.

7. Donaly E. Brice, *The Great Comanche Raid.* This is the best modern account of the raid and shows the Mexican influence. The raid would be another cause of growing ill will between the two peoples.

8. John Holland Jenkins, *Recollections of Early Texas,* 62–68.

9. Mirabeau B. Lamar, *The Papers of M. B. Lamar,* 5:409 ff.

10. John T. Price is another. A letter from Price to the secretary of war, January 23, 1840, mentions Hays as another captain. (*Journals of the House of Representatives of the Republic of Texas, Fifth Congress, First Session.* Appendix, 444.)

11. There are numerous authoritative studies of the Colt revolver. Charles T. Haven and Frank A. Belden's *A History of the Colt Revolver* was used for this book because of the vast amount of source material — newspaper accounts, diaries, letters, advertisements, etc. — bearing on the use of Colts in Texas or by the Rangers.

12. Belden and Haven, 253.

13. *Ibid.*

14. *Ibid.*, 264.

15. *Ibid.*, 264–265.

16. William B. Edwards, *The Story of Colt's Revolver,* 93–101.

17. Belden and Haven, 34.

18. *Ibid.*

19. Louis A. Garavaglia and Charles G. Worman, *Firearms of the American West,* 100–103. The use of revolvers in the mountains is traced in this study. While the trappers and

traders on the Santa Fe Trail used Colts earlier than the Texans, their infrequent use had no lasting impact. It was somewhat like the Vikings discovering America.

20. Jenkins, *Recollections,* 171–174.

21. *Telegraph and Texas Register,* November 18, 1840.

22. Garavaglia and Worman, 63, reproduce an early photo that may be some of the Mier prisoners and Mexican guards, one holding what is probably a Colt rifle.

23. See Charles E. Hanson, Jr., *The Plains Rifle.*

24. Jenkins, *Recollections,* 200. In this passage, Jenkins mentions his weapons: a rifle, a Bowie knife, a tomahawk, and a derringer pistol. Not many others mention any form of ax, and most carried the larger pistol. He also mentions he traded 300 acres of land for his rifle — and most thought he got a bargain.

25. *Ibid.*, 96–100.

26. Lamar, 4 (Part I): 233–234. A later fight on the Llano showed much the same pattern of close engagement (234–235).

27. John E. Parsons, *Samuel Colt's Own Record,* 9.

28. *Journals of the House of Representatives of the Republic of Texas, Ninth Congress,* 313.

29. Report of the Secretary of War and Marine, November 30, 1844, in appendix to the *Journals of the Ninth Congress,* 28.

30. Parsons, 10.

31. Appendix to the *Journals of the Ninth Congress,* 32–33. Hays's report is brief, considering the engagement. As he would show later, Hays did not waste words, whether in writing or speaking.

32. Mary Ann Maverick, *Memoirs of Mary A. Maverick,* 81–82.

33. Dorman H. Winfrey and James M. Day, eds. *The Indian Papers of Texas and the Southwest, 1825–1916,* 2:72–73.

34. Samuel C. Reid, Jr., *The Scouting Expeditions of McCulloch's Texas Rangers,* 109–111. This version was the first to be printed in book form (1848) and had wide circulation. It was obviously based on accounts of participants he met during the Mexican War. For all the contemporary accounts, this key battle has been pretty well forgotten.

35. Jenkins, *Recollections,* 145–146.

36. *Journals of the Ninth Congress,* following p. 34.

37. Adjutant General Papers, Archives Division, Texas State Library.

38. This account is based on Jenkins, *Recollections,* 195–198.

39. Adjutant General Papers.

40. John Salmon Ford, *Memoirs,* typescript in Texas State Library. Ford may have copied these reports from newspapers, as he did not take part in the action.

41. See Webb, *The Handbook of Texas,* Vol. 2 and Vol. 3, for an updated account of Seguin.

42. See Thomas J. Green, *Journal of the Texian Expedition Against Mier,* for the classic account.

43. In a letter of July 1844, he mentioned he had spies checking on a reported force of 600 Mexicans assembled to invade Texas. (Army Papers, Texas State Library.)

Chapter 2

1. U. S. Grant, for example, writing his memoirs years later, still felt strongly about the "plot" to annex Texas. (U. S. Grant, *Memoirs,* 1:53–54.)

2. *Zachary Taylor* by Brainard Dyer is one of several excellent biographies of the general.

3. William Addleman Ganoe, *The History of the United States Army,* 191–201.

4. *House Executive Document No. 60,* Thirtieth Congress, First Session, 83. Hereafter cited as *HED* No. 60.

5. Grant, 67; Ganoe, 199.

6. These are too numerous to cite and not pertinent to the main theme of this book. It is interesting to note, however, that young Grant was among the few junior officers who appreciated Taylor. His comparison of Scott and Taylor is a model for evaluating different styles of dress, command, and attitude and how they have absolutely no bearing on what makes a field commander. (Grant, 138–139.)

7. George B. McClellan, *The Mexican War Diary of General George B. McClellan,* 18–19.

8. *Ibid.,* 19.

9. *HED* No. 60, 88.

10. *Ibid.,* 101.

11. *Ibid.,* 106.

12. *Ibid.*

13. Henry W. Barton, *Texas Volunteers in the Mexican War,* 7. This was the first company to be designated Ranger. As will be seen, there was no standard listing for the Texas volunteer units.

14. C .D. Sporlin, *Texas Veterans in the Mexican War,* 200.

15. Taylor has been castigated by some for inactivity, but he evidently kept the troops as busy as possible. In his *Memoirs* Grant mentions drilling, arranging for food and supplies, etc. (70–71).

16. *HED* No. 60, 90–91.

17. *Ibid.,* 123–125. Taylor's report makes more of the incident than most observers do. Looking back at the crossing, Grant remembered it as a few enemy buglers who were trying to create the impression of large numbers (87–89).

18. *HED* No. 60, 132–133. Taylor was camped by the next day and had a battery placed to command Matamoros.

19. See Lester Dillon, Jr., *American Artillery in the Mexican War.*

20. Trahern was one of the Texans of the legends: young, loud, a teller of tall tales, and a fighter. A short version of his exploits has been used for this book. ("George Washington Trahern," by A. Russell Buchanan, in *Southwestern Historical Quarterly* 58.)

21. Taylor had authority to muster units under the letter of August 6, 1845, as cited earlier. He did not have authority to sign men for three months, a fact that would plague him the rest of the war. While eventually large, the company initially had only twenty-six privates. Capt. W. S. Henry in his *Campaign Sketches of the War with Mexico,* 85, noted the formation of the company and how additional men joined on April 25.

22. Possibly the only remaining copy of this booklet is in the Walker Papers in the Texas State Library. Walker was a pretty keen observer of things military and had some unkind things to say about army commanders.

23. Belden and Haven, *A History of the Colt Revolver,* 272. Many of Walker's copies of issue and turn-in slips are in the Walker Papers. They give us an idea of how his company used army supplies to supplement their own equipment and weapons. Walker was probably the only Texan who understood the army supply system and kept good records.

24. Barton, 12.

25. *HED* No. 60. 132–133.

26. Grant, 89. Grant also mentions Mexican activity and losses by the Americans in

the bush and when trying to move supplies. A. Russell Buchanan, in "George Washington Trahern" (*Southwestern Historical Quarterly* 58:70), said the Rangers started scouting early, so there must have been considerable guerrilla activity that did not get into official reports.

27. David Nevin, *The Mexican War,* 28.

28. *HED* No. 60, 140–141.

29. Buchanan, 71. Contemporary observers did not place much importance on the incident, though some modern writers describe it as the defeat of the entire company.

30. *HED* No. 60, 288–289.

31. Henry, 85.

32. Buchanan, 77.

33. Ford didn't help by describing them. None of the Texans left any mention of how they dressed. They either did not consider it of importance or assumed people knew. Fortunately, the outsiders did remark on dress, equipment, and weapons.

34. Brantz Mayer, as quoted in Smith and Judah, *Chronicles of the Gringos,* 41. Mayer agrees to some degree with contemporary accounts, especially on weapons, but he says the Rangers' hunting shirts and leggins were buckskin. He seems to be describing earlier Texans.

35. This material is from Linda Ayres, "William Ranney," *American Frontier Life: Early Western Painting and Prints,* 79–108.

36. *HED* No. 60, 292. Taylor reported this in a dispatch on May 5, 1846, which also contains details of the following action.

37. Grant, 92. It was his first exposure to the sound of hostile fire. He did not like it. Like most commanders, Grant had no love of war.

38. *HED* No. 60, 292.

39. *Ibid.,* 294.

40. Walker Papers. Walker, or his clerk, kept careful records. Twelve Colt revolvers, with accessories, were lost in the attack on his camp, as well as six belts, some long arms, a spring vise, even some arms chests.

41. Walker Papers. In a letter on May 13, 1846, citizens of New Orleans expressed their admiration for Walker's daring and sent him a five-year-old bay gelding named Tornado as a replacement for a horse he had lost.

42. John E. Parsons, *Samuel Colt's Own Record,* 6–7.

43. Grant, 93–96.

44. According to W. S. Henry, 90, Walker and his scouts found the enemy camp deserted. On the following day Walker and some Dragoons confirmed that the Mexicans had retreated.

45. Buchanan says they took part in Resaca de la Palma and captured Francisco Mejia (71). Mejia was a senior commander, the man who had refused to kill all the Mier prisoners when ordered by Santa Anna.

46. *HED* No. 60, 297.

47. *Ibid.,* 299. Taylor evidently considered Walker's company as apart from his call for Texas volunteers, or considered the short enlistment term of the unit.

48. *Ibid.,* 300.

49. Henry, 113.

50. Walker spent some time in Matamoros during May, as he wrote his brother a letter from the city. He felt bad about not writing. Surprisingly enough, he had nothing to

say about the war. He apologized for not making money and wondered if a cousin still felt the same way about the course Walker had taken. It was a strange letter from a man who had just become a national hero (Walker Papers).

Chapter 3

1. Henry W. Barton, *Texas Volunteers in the Mexican War,* 15.

2. *Ibid.*, 17.

3. C. D. Sporlin, *Texas Veterans in the Mexican War,* 21–22.

4. Barton, 31. Henderson was basing his instructions on Taylor's orders for mounted regiments to assemble at Point Isabel. Until units reached the assembly point and were mustered into the army, they were state troops and responsible for their own pay, supplies, etc.

5. Sporlin, 18–20.

6. *Ibid.*, 25–27.

7. Barton, 32–33.

8. Sporlin, 30–31.

9. *Ibid.*, 211–214. The unit was mustered into service as Benjamin McCulloch's Company of Texas Militia on June 13, 1846.

10. For a full account of McCulloch see Victor M. Rose, *The Life and Services of Gen. Ben McCulloch.* A brief account by Jack W. Gunn, "Ben McCulloch: A Big Captain," is in the *Southwestern Historical Quarterly* 58.

11. Samuel C. Reid, Jr., *The Scouting Expeditions of McCulloch's Texas Rangers,* 38–42.

12. *Ibid.*, 42.

13. Zachary Taylor, *Letters of Zachary Taylor from the Battle-Fields of the Mexican War,* 24–25.

14. *HED* No. 60, 321.

15. Reid, 26.

16. *Ibid.*, 108.

17. *Ibid.*, 104.

18. As examples: On June 15 a lieutenant from McCulloch's company was directed to draw funds for the unit (*HED* No. 60, 523.) On August 3, the quartermaster was directed to turn over to Hays necessary funds to buy supplies (*HED* No. 60, 526.)

19. B. F. Scribner, *A Campaign in Mexico,* 26.

20. *Ibid.*

21. Reid, 34.

22. *Ibid.*, 33.

23. Unfortunately, few of these wild tales were written down. Reid remembers one about a man chasing a prairie fire, trying to cook a steak, and another about a dying German girl who was brought back to life by a plate of sauerkraut.

24. Sporlin, 211–214.

25. *HED* No. 60, 522.

26. Sporlin, 200.

27. *Ibid.*, 190–192.

28. *Ibid.*, 31–33.

29. *Ibid.*, 33–34.

30. *HED* No. 60, 479.

31. *Ibid.*

32. Sporlin, 17–34.

33. W. S. Henry, 118, also noted the arrival of the Texans.

34. Sporlin, 34.

35. See Webb, *Handbook of Texas,* 2:929–930, for a brief sketch of Wood.

36. James K. Holland, "Diary of a Texan Volunteer in the Mexican War," *Southwestern Historical Quarterly* 30. This is the only diary, as opposed to memoirs or letters, written by one of the Rangers.

37. *Ibid.,* 1–10.

38. Sporlin, 1–16.

Chapter 4

1. *HED* No. 60, 304. This company was not with Taylor, being part of the force mustered in to protect the frontier against Indians. Some of these Rangers had acted as scouts and guides with the Dragoons on patrols to the Nueces River and down to the Presidio of the Rio Grande.

2. *Ibid.,* 323–325.

3. *Ibid.,* 526.

4. *Ibid.,* 550.

5. Samuel C. Reid, Jr., *Scouting Expeditions,* 43–51. The narrative of the Linares scout is based largely on Reid.

6. W. S. Henry, *Campaign Sketches of the War with Mexico,* 122, 137. Like Reid, Henry mentions the high prices paid for food and the care taken not to steal or molest the inhabitants. Henry, like others, also felt it would not change any opinions.

7. Reid, 44.

8. From a dispatch, quoted by Reid, 51–52.

9. *Ibid.*

10. Several hundred pages of *HED* No. 60 are filled with requests for steamers, contracts, specifications, claims and defenses, explanations as to why no steamers were available, or how they were doing all possible. Much the same is true for wagons. Taylor carried on one war with the Mexicans and another with the supply people in Washington.

11. Reid, 54.

12. *Ibid.,* 55.

13. Holland, 11–12.

14. Reid, 56–58.

15. *Ibid.,* 58–60.

Chapter 5

1. *HED* No. 60, 329.

2. James K. Holland, "Diary of a Texan Volunteer," *Southwestern Historical Quarterly,* 30:12.

3. *Ibid.*

4. Samuel C. Reid, Jr., *Scouting Expeditions,* 61.

5. *Ibid.*

6. *Ibid.,* 62.

7. Zachary Taylor, *Letters,* 24. These letters, written by Taylor to his friend Surgeon R. C. Wood, are frank and contain opinions he would never express in his official papers. In an earlier letter on June 30, 1846, Taylor wrote "in regard to the outrages committed by the Texas volunteers on the Mexicans and others." Just what outrages is not specified,

and what "others" can only be guessed. Taylor said he couldn't do anything about it anyway, which seems strange. He concludes: "I fear they are a lawless set" (22).

8. Reid, 62–63.

9. Holland, 15.

10. *Ibid.*, 16.

11. *Ibid.*, 16–17.

12. *Ibid.*, 17.

13. *Ibid.*

14. *Ibid.*, 18.

15. *Ibid.*

16. *Ibid.*

17. Buchanan, 73.

18. Holland, 20.

19. *HED* No. 60, 321.

20. Photocopy in McCulloch Family Papers, Library of the Daughters of the Republic of Texas, San Antonio.

21. Henry W. Barton, *Texas Volunteers,* 44.

22. Photocopy in McCulloch Family Papers.

23. Reid, 66–74.

24. Barton, 44.

25. *HED* No. 60, 402.

26. Reid, 78–88, is the basis for this account.

27. U. S. Grant, *Personal Memoirs,* 105–106. Grant also describes his adventures with pack mules, which were becoming the main method of transporting supplies.

28. *HED* No. 60, 408.

29. Taylor was trying to get his forces concentrated as rapidly as possible. On July 28, 1846, he had ordered Hays and Johnston to move their regiments to Matamoros as soon as possible. (*HED* No. 60, 527.)

30. *HED* No. 60, 498.

31. Taylor reported this move later in the month to the adjutant general. He stated that Hays was checking out a new area of the country. There was evidently no contact between Hays and the rest of the army during this swing. (*HED* No. 60, 412.)

32. Reid, 106–108.

33. W. S. Henry, *Campaign Sketches,* 160.

34. The original is in the Walker Papers. One can only guess why it did not go to Washington with the rest of the regimental records and muster rolls.

35. *HED* No. 60, 498.

36. Taylor, 41–44.

37. *HED* No. 60, 412. By then, Hays was already in China and on his way to Camargo. Taylor glosses over the mustering out of the Texas foot. The regiment had been well trained by Col. Albert Sidney Johnston, himself a trained soldier. Taylor may have led to some of the problem by his manner when talking to one of the infantry delegations. He was wonderful one-on-one, but was not always effective when speaking to groups. In a vote to reenlist or disband, 318 went home and 224 stayed and were reassigned to other units, mostly with the mounted units. This is considerably different from the regiment being "mustered out." See Charles P. Royland, *Albert Sidney Johnston,* 131.

38. Reid, 91–103.

39. This is according to Reid. He does not appear on muster rolls.

40. Reid, 102–103. He mentions the review, as did others, because it was the largest assembly of troops any had ever seen (Henry, 155).

41. F. L. Olmsted, *A Journey Through Texas,* 302. Olmsted mentions the Rangers a number of times. By then (1857) the Rangers were already becoming a legend.

42. C. D. Sporlin, *Texas Veterans,* 17–18.

43. *HED* No. 60, 500. Taylor, faced with lack of transport, which limited supplies, had to make some tough decisions about who went to Monterey. He sent what he considered the best troops.

44. *Ibid.,* 527.

45. Royland, 136.

46. Based on Reid, 116–122.

47. Henry, 160, mentions the march and the role of the two Texas regiments.

48. Reprinted by Reid, 119–120.

49. As cited earlier.

50. Sporlin, 17.

51. See muster rolls of the 2nd Texas, Sporlin, 34–35.

52. Holland, 13–14.

53. Sporlin, 33–34.

54. C. W. Smith and S. Judah, *Chronicles of the Gringos,* 318–350.

55. *HED* No. 60, 504.

56. Holland, 20.

57. Reid, 126.

58. *Ibid.,* 129.

59. *Ibid.,* 131, quoting a Mr. Haile.

60. *Ibid.,* 132–136. Most of this section is based on dispatches of Kendall, quoted by Reid.

61. *Ibid.,* 141.

Chapter 6

1. James K. Holland, "Diary of a Texan Volunteer," *Southwestern Historical Quarterly,* 30:24–25.

2. *HED* No. 60, 506.

3. *Ibid.*

4. Samuel C. Reid, Jr., *Scouting Expeditions,* 141.

5. *Ibid.,* 192.

6. *Ibid.*

7. *Ibid.,* 143.

8. Luther Giddings, *Sketches of the Campaign in Northern Mexico by an Officer of the First Ohio Volunteers,* 143–144.

9. Holland, 25.

10. S. Compton Smith, *Chile con Carne,* 82.

11. Reid, 143. Reid does not have details, but he outlines the overall reconnaissance plan.

12. Walter P. Lane, *The Adventures and Recollections of General Walter P. Lane,* 43.

13. Reid, 143–144.

14. *Ibid.,* 151. Reid's account is backed up by the official reports and other participants. This was a regular force, for the most part, and Taylor could have sent the 1st Texas because he considered them more experienced than Wood's command.

15. The following is based on Reid, 152–153.

16. Lane, 44.

17. Reid, 154.

18. Hays's official report of Monterey, printed in Mirabeau Lamar, *Papers of,* 138–140.

19. Reid, 155.

20. The following is based on Reid, 156–168. Also, Hays's report. Lt. Edmund Bradford, quoted in Smith and Judah, *Chronicles of the Gringos,* 85–89, and George Wilkins Kendall, *The War Between the United States and Mexico,* 6–9: Lane, 45–48.

21. Kendall is the only one who mentions the use of revolvers at the fence line (6). Texan observers probably took it for granted.

22. All accounts vary, probably because some were describing all Mexican losses and some were listing only the lancer casualties. Kendall said 40 of the squadron were killed and 100 wounded (6).

23. Reid, 160.

24. *Ibid.,* 162.

25. *Ibid.,* 163.

26. *Ibid.,* 164.

27. *Ibid.,* 167.

28. Lane, 46.

29. Kendall, 8.

30. As usual, Reid has a fine account of the fighting on Independence Hill. This account is based on 181–186.

31. Most of the contemporary observers fought in the eastern part of town. Thorpe, Grant, Henry, and Giddings fought there and left vivid accounts of the bloody fighting. Reid also devoted a chapter to the fighting there (168–181). This summary is based on their combined accounts.

32. Holland, 25.

33. Some historians have criticized Taylor for his seeming lack of cooperation with Worth. There was a considerable distance to be covered between the two forces, blocked by large enemy forces. Kendall is the only observer who noted that Taylor's strong feint to support Worth became a major attack, causing the Mexicans to think Worth was the feint. They did not detach strong forces to fight Worth, and this contributed to the easier fight in the western sector.

34. Lamar, 136–138. Lamar's papers contain Wood's report. This section is based on his account of the fighting.

35. Holland, 26.

36. T. B. Thorpe, *Our Army at Monterey,* 76.

37. Kendall is the only one to mention this fact, citing the fighting at San Antonio in 1835 and the Mier fighting (9).

38. Worth's Report, *House Executive Document No. 4, 24th Congress,* 103 ff.

39. Hays's report, along with Reid (190–199), are the basis for this account of fighting in the west on the twenty-third.

40. For the most part, the Texans fought through the walls and across the roofs, avoiding the streets. The bulk of the army fought in more conventional fashion along the streets, which caused their heavier losses. S. Compton Smith was another observer who commented on the Rangers boring through the walls (93).

41. Holland, 26.

42. S. Compton Smith, 93–95.

43. W. S. Henry, *Campaign Sketches,* 206–209, describes the fighting in the east on the twenty-third.

44. Lane, 47–48, covers the rest of the fighting in the west.

Chapter 7

1. Samuel C. Reid, Jr., *Scouting Expeditions,* 203–205. Lane generally agrees (*The Adventures and Recollections of General Walter P. Lane,* 48).

2. Taylor to AG, September 25, 1846, quoted by Reid, 203–204. As might be expected, Polk and his cabinet refused to accept the terms (James K. Polk, *The Diary of,* 181).

3. Parts of this letter, written January 6, 1847, are quoted by Reid, 205–206. Jefferson gave a spirited and reasonable explanation for Taylor's decision.

4. A lot depended on the observer. Grant remembered them as scrawny with small horses. His only emotion was pity (U. S. Grant, *Personal Memoirs,* 117–118). Kendall observed the retreating forces were well-dressed, other than wearing sandals (quoted in Reid, 211).

5. James K. Holland, "Diary of a Texan Volunteer," *Southwestern Historical Quarterly* 30:27.

6. William A. Ganoe, *The History of the United States Army,* 213.

7. Luther Giddings, *Sketches of the Campaign in Northern Mexico,* 221–222.

8. His report is extensive. *House Executive Document No. 4, 29th Congress,* 103 ff.

9. As cited.

10. Mirabeau B. Lamar, *Papers of,* 136–138.

11. *Ibid.,* 138–140. Hays's report is not much longer than the account of Wood, despite being in combat three days. He covers all phases of the fighting, but he was not a man to waste words, either in writing or speaking.

12. *HED* No. 60, 424.

13. C. D. Sporlin, *Texas Veterans in the Mexican War,* 17, 31.

14. Reid, 216–218.

15. *Ibid.,* 225.

16. *Ibid.,* 226.

17. *Ibid.,* 227. This agrees with Trahern and others who visited with Taylor during off-duty moments.

18. *Ibid.,* 232. Reid, of course, did not witness this incident, as he was on his way home. There is independent verification, as will be explained later. Reid evidently kept in touch with his former comrades.

19. *HED* No. 60, 508.

20. Holland, 27.

21. *HED* No. 60, 508. Order No. 124, October 1, 1846, directed the discharge of the two Texas regiments the following day, except for the companies of McCulloch and Gillespie, already mustered out.

22. *HED* No. 60, 430.

23. S. Compton Smith, *Chili Con Carne,* 301.

24. *HED* No. 60, 430.

25. *Ibid.*

26. Samuel L. Chamberlain, *My Confession,* 176.

27. *HED* No. 60, 512–513.

28. Smith, 294.

29. *HED* No. 60, 431 ff.
30. C. D. Sporlin, *Texas Veterans in the Mexican War,* 22 (Company D muster roll).
31. *Ibid.,* 31 (Company H muster roll).
32. *Ibid.,* 33 (Company K muster roll).
33. Giddings, 96–97.
34. English translation in Reid, 215–216.

Chapter 8

1. As cited earlier.
2. Walker Papers, Archives Division, Texas State Library.
3. Henry W. Barton, *Texas Volunteers in the Mexican War,* 85.
4. Walker to James Gridley, Walker Papers.
5. In an address given in London, November 25, 1851, Colt said Taylor had sent Walker to get more, or new, revolvers. (Frank Belden and Charles Haven, *A History of the Colt Revolver,* 317.) There is nothing to support this, as will be discussed later.
6. Belden and Haven, 25–26. These writers were among the first to dispute the accuracy of stories that Walker visited Colt in 1839, tracing the origin of the myth to the memorial volume in 1865.
7. Colt patented this feature, as well as other improvements, in Letters Patent No. 1304, August 29, 1839.
8. James K. Polk, *The Diary of James Knox Polk,* 2:252.
9. John E. Parsons, *Samuel Colt's Own Record,* 7–9. The letter is undated, but it is obviously in November 1846, based on Walker's reply.
10. *Ibid.,* 9–10.
11. *Ibid.,* 10–11.
12. *Ibid.,* 11–12.
13. Belden and Haven, 273.
14. *Ibid.*
15. Parsons, 12–13.
16. Belden and Haven, 274.
17. Belden and Haven have an entire section on this correspondence. *Samuel Colt's Own Record,* edited by Parsons, is a small book and does not contain material in Belden.
18. Parsons, 24–27.
19. Belden and Haven, 278–279.
20. Louis A. Garavaglia and Charles G. Worman, *Firearms of the American West,* 145. This is based on the report of the ordnance officer who accepted the turn-in of Walker Colts at the end of the war.
21. Belden and Haven, 279.
22. *Ibid.,* 280.
23. *Ibid.,* 284.
24. *Ibid.,* 282–283.
25. *Ibid.,* 284–285. Walker to Colt, February 19, 1847.
26. *Ibid.,* 285. Talcott to Walker, March 20, 1847.
27. *Ibid.,* 284–285.
28. *Ibid.,* 285.
29. Barton, 84–89.
30. Parsons, 56–57.
31. *Ibid.,* 49–51.

32. Belden and Haven, 285.

33. Parsons, 74–76. This was Walker's last letter to Colt.

34. Belden and Haven, 288.

35. *Ibid.*, 289.

36. Parsons, 81–82. This was some time before he finished his contract. He was obviously turning out extras, either for advertising or as a hedge against a new contract.

37. *Ibid.*, 84–85.

38. Belden and Haven, 301.

Chapter 9

1. James K. Polk, *The Diary of James Knox Polk*, 181.

2. *HED* No. 60, 355–357.

3. *Ibid.*, 329.

4. *Ibid.*, 369.

5. *Ibid.*, 373.

6. *Ibid.*, 377.

7. *Ibid.*, 383.

8. This is generally accepted. It could have happened — must have happened — but there is no hard evidence to support the assumption.

9. *HED* No. 60. 1098–1099.

10. *Ibid.*

11. Samuel C. Reid, Jr., *Scouting Expeditions*, 233.

12. Henry W. Barton, *Texas Volunteers in the Mexican War*, 81.

13. Frank Belden and Charles Haven, *A History of the Colt Revolver*, 304. G. H. Tobin wrote about the fight and the recovery of the Colt in a letter to the inventor.

14. Barton, 81.

15. See P. B. Clark, *History of Clarksville and Old Red River Country*. The letter was sent to a relative of the writer and kept until the publication of the book, when it was included as an appendix. Along with McCulloch's letter, *The Democratic Telegraph and Texas Register* for August 2, 1847, has a lengthy account of the actions of McCulloch's spies. Reid has a section, 236–237, probably based on correspondence with his old companions. All these accounts agree to a remarkable degree, other than in dialogue. This version is a composite.

16. Clark, *History of Clarksville*, 246.

17. C. D. Sporlin, *Texas Veterans in the Mexican War*, 198.

18. McCulloch, 255; Reid, 236, quotes it as: "Very well, Major, that's all I wanted to know. I am glad they did not catch you."

19. Scribner, 59, for example, mentions May's scout. McCulloch also said they left with the Dragoons and then split for their own scout.

20. Clark, 257–258, is the only real source for actions during the battle. W. S. Henry, *Campaign Sketches*, 310–311, has an account of the scouts, as do others. It was generally agreed that the Rangers played a key role in the way the battle developed.

21. Trahern only appears on Walker's company roll. His account of Monterey is very brief; he may not have even been in the fight. His recollection of Buena Vista is long and fairly accurate. It appears he was engaged in the contracting business and willingly served as a scout and courier when needed. (A. Russell Buchanan, "George Washington Trahern," *Southwestern Historical Quarterly*, 58:73–74.)

22. David Lavender, *Climax at Buena Vista,* is a good short account of the campaign in the north and the final battle.

23. Sporlin, 203–206.

24. Barton, 83.

25. Sporlin, 198.

26. Barton, 83.

27. *Ibid.* Actual discharge was on June 14. The mustered-out Rangers must have met the incoming replacements as they rode home.

28. *HED* No. 60. 1176.

29. *Ibid.,* 1186.

Chapter 10

1. Samuel E. Chamberlain, *My Confession;* 175–176; S. Compton Smith, *Chili Con Carne,* 161–162, also describes this massacre.

2. Chamberlain, 175–176.

3. As described in Chapter 2, Gray was a strange character. He had come to Texas with the first of Austin's settlers and fought at San Jacinto, certainly no latecomer as Smith said. He had the most mixed reputation of any of the Ranger commanders. See *Handbook of Texas,* 1:723.

4. Henry W. Barton, *Texas Volunteers in the Mexican War,* 76.

5. *Ibid.*

6. Smith, 294–295. Smith has several references to the Texans. Like most observers, he commented on their love and care for their horses (265). His general opinion was that they were an intelligent group, adventurous, with many professionals looking for excitement (268). Other than his castigation of Gray, his comments are highly favorable.

7. Chamberlain, 177.

8. On April 4, 1847, Canales declared unrestricted guerrilla warfare against the Americans, supposedly for hanging twenty-five men at Rancho Guadalupe. This agrees with Smith's account to some degree. Canales imposed the strictest penalties for any Mexicans selling food or supplies or cooperating in any way with the Americans. The proclamation suggested that guerrilla warfare was a protest against the hanging, when in fact guerrilla warfare had been in effect since the beginning of the invasion. By then, both sides had resorted to whatever was necessary or could be accomplished. Canales proclamation is quoted in Mirabeau B. Lamar, *The Papers of,* 167–168.

9. Smith, 100–101.

10. *Ibid.,* 102–119. The following account is based on Smith. While the incidents of the action seem typical, Smith is off on the date — late December 1846. McCulloch and his spies didn't come down until February 1847.

11. C. D. Sporlin, *Texas Veterans in the Mexican War,* 193–196.

12. Lamar, 159–160. Lamar to Taylor, March 1, 1847.

13. Barton, 80.

14. Lamar, 159–160.

15. *Ibid.,* 161–162.

16. Sporlin, 70–88.

17. Henderson did better than this. Most of the time he was able to keep at least eight Ranger companies on the frontier and had as many as ten at times. (Barton, 101.)

18. This is not fully documented. The recruiting situation at this time was very confused. The Texans still did not want to enlist for the duration, or even a year, and raising

the companies for a new regiment did not go smoothly or quickly.

19. Walter P. Lane, *The Adventures and Recollections of General Walter P. Lane,* 49. Lane doesn't give much explanation about why they left when they did. He said he waived his rank as senior captain so Chevallie could be elected major.

20. Sporlin, 151.

21. *HED* No. 60, 1131.

22. Lane, 52.

23. *Ibid.*

24. *HED* No. 60, 1178.

25. Sporlin, 151–167.

26. *Ibid.*

27. It would be tedious to cite each listing. The summaries are based on the notations following each name: died from battle wounds, died from natural causes, deserted, transferred, changed in grade. There are few combat actions mentioned during this time, either in official reports or contemporary accounts. Smith has a casual mention of an Indian fight involving Lane in the Parras region, claiming they killed half the Indians involved (352) and an even briefer mention of a fight involving Reed's company (54). It is difficult to match these with any casualties in the muster rolls.

28. *HED* No. 60, 1180.

29. *Ibid.,* 1187.

30. This is another action that cannot be pinned down with any certainty. Taylor was not the man to falsify reports, especially to protect the Texans. The Rangers were not the type to be driven away and take it. They would have come back in force and destroyed the guerrilla nest.

31. This is another conflicting event, or nonevent. Tablas and Sablas could be the same location. Smith was going on second- or third-hand talk and could easily have confused the names. It is also possible Baylor split his company and fought two actions the same day, but it seems unlikely.

32. *HED* No. 60, 1185.

33. Lamar, 176–177.

34. *Ibid.,* 177–178.

35. *HED* No. 60, 1194.

36. Sporlin, 151.

37. *Ibid.*

38. Lane, 52–53.

39. *Ibid.,* 52–53. There is another mention of this incident by a member of a Missouri regiment who witnessed the execution. He said it took place in late May. (Isaac George, *Heroes and Incidents of the Mexican War,* 135–136.)

40. Lane, 56–59. The following account is based on Lane.

41. Sporlin, 93 and 153. Company rolls show Glanton transferred without any mention of why.

42. Lane, 60–61.

43. *Ibid.,* 62–63. This was a favorite Mexican trick. It will reappear again in the campaign in central Mexico.

44. *HED* No. 60. 1195.

45. *Ibid.,* 1201.

46. *Ibid.,* 1212.

47. Zachary Taylor, *Letters of Zachary Taylor,* 148–149.

48. *HED* No. 60, 1221.
49. Lane, 64–67.
50. *Ibid.*, 67–68.
51. Smith, 282–291.
52. Lane, 69.
53. *Ibid.*, 73–74.
54. Sporlin, 151–167.

Chapter 11

1. Scott's campaign is outside the scope of this work. The brief outline is based on William A. Ganoe, *The History of the United States Army*, 219–224.

2. *HED* No. 60, 1171.

3. J. J. Oswandel, *Notes on the Mexican War*, 147–153.

4. G. W. Smith and S. Judah, *Chronicles of the Gringos*, 221–223.

5. Albert G. Brackett, *General Lane's Brigade in Central Mexico*, 186. Admitting he did good work, Brackett still considered him a traitor.

6. Oswandel, 171–172.

7. Walker's service record and a letter to his brother, quoted in Frank Belden and Charles Haven, *A History of the Colt Revolver*, 293.

8. John S. Ford, *Rip Ford's Texas*, 61.

9. Taylor wrote from Monterey, July 27, 1847, saying he had received Hays's report of July 13, with the news that the War Department had ordered Hays to join him. Taylor gave Hays some leeway in defending the Texas frontier, but he specified that Hays bring at least five companies with him when he rejoined the army of occupation. (*HED* No. 60, 1185.)

10. C. D. Sporlin, *Texas Veterans in the Mexican War*, 88–112.

11. Ford later wrote his memoirs, containing over a thousand handwritten pages, now in the University of Texas Library. A typescript copy is in the Texas State Library. These versions contain much of the history of Texas that was outside Ford's personal experience. An edited version, containing only his personal actions, is *Rip Ford's Texas*, edited by Stephen B. Coates, paperback 1987. This version is used for this book.

12. Ford, 61.

13. *Texas Democrat*, September 16, 1847.

14. These events have been covered earlier.

15. Ford, 62.

16. *The American Flag*, September 1, 1847, quoted by Henry W. Barton, *Texas Volunteers in the Mexican War*, 110.

17. Ford, 63–64.

18. The same John Glanton who had been slipped from camp by Walter Lane, saving him from Taylor's wrath. Company muster rolls show him dropped from Lane's command and picked up by Hays — all without question. (Sporlin, 93 and 153).

19. Ford, 65. Ford says he resigned to join his old friend. There was, of course, more to the story.

20. *Ibid.*

21. *Ibid.*, 66. See 66–68 for the following action.

22. *Ibid.*, 68.

23. *Ibid.*, 69–70.

24. Brackett, 194–195. Brackett had several opportunities to observe Hays, as did

Reid, and was not making a guess or taking another opinion as his own.

25. Ford, 107.

26. *Ibid.*, 70.

27. Correspondence on this topic has been discussed in the chapter on the Walker Colt. Just why the Rangers were issued the new weapons is unclear, but it was probably because they were the ones who knew the most about their use. In a letter on March 31, 1847, Colt wrote Walker he thought Hays would get a large part of the order, even though the revolvers were already stamped for the Mounted Rifles. (John E. Parsons, *Samuel Colt's Own Records,* 62–64.) There must have been talk about the Rangers getting some of the Walkers, as Walker wrote Colt and said he understood Hays had the promise of the new arms. (*Ibid.*, 74–75.) We have seen how the initial 220 Walkers were sent to Vera Cruz, supposedly for Walker's company. At least sixty more were shipped to make up the Ranger allotment.

28. Brackett, 107, in his description of the Rangers.

29. Sporlin, 91. There is some confusion over the spelling of his name, as with many others. Truit and Truitt are seen. The spelling of Truett is based on an official report he filed.

30. *Ibid.*, 93.

31. *Ibid.*, 108.

32. Ford, 72.

33. *Ibid.*, 73 and 76.

34. It is reprinted in Belden and Haven, 292–293.

35. Brackett, 53.

36. J. J. Oswandel tells of this struggle for Puebla in great detail. It is the basis for most of his book.

37. Brackett, 92–96.

38. *Ibid.*

39. Smith and Judah, 169–170.

40. Oswandel, 305. Whatever the location, the grave was marked, as Walker's remains were recovered later and reburied in San Antonio.

41. Brackett, 211–217.

42. Ford, 76–77.

43. *Ibid.*, 76.

44. Oswandel, 382.

45. Ford, 77–78.

46. Brackett, 173–174. Lt. Col. Ebenezer Dumont, second in command of Brackett's regiment, also observed the Ranger entrance and became a good friend of Hays. He sent home accounts of the Rangers, which were later reprinted in the *Democratic Telegraph and Texas Register,* February 14, 1848.

47. Ford, 78.

48. This report was written in Puebla on December 1, 1847. *House Executive Document No. 1, Thirtieth Congress, Second Session,* 86–89.

49. Ford, 78.

50. Brackett was not in this fight, but describes it (190–192). Ford (78–80) has details, including part of Lane's report.

51. The entrance into Mexico City is based on Ford, 81–82. Dumont's letter, reprinted in the papers in Texas, has details. E. A. Hitchcock also noted the arrival of the Rangers, 310.

52. Brackett, 174.

53. Dumont stressed the wild riding of the Texans, quoted in Ford, 81.

54. *Ibid.*, 81–82.

55. *Ibid.*

56. Reprinted in Brackett, 220–222. The order was published December 12, 1847.

57. Sporlin, 105.

58. Ford's account is given in *Rip Ford's Texas,* 86–89.

59. Daggett later wrote a short account of the fight from his personal viewpoint. "Adventures with Guerrillas," part of Isaac George's *Heroes and Incidents of the Mexican War,* 210–213.

60. Ford, 88.

61. *HED* No. 60, 1067.

62. Brackett is authority for this (234–235). He says they left Mexico City on January 18, 1848.

63. Printed in George, 218–221.

64. Ford, 90.

65. Oswandel, 83–85.

66. Ford, 83–85. The following account is based on Ford. Dumont also mentions this incident in the letters cited earlier.

67. Sporlin, 96.

68. *Ibid.*

69. Ford, 84.

70. *Ibid.*, 85.

71. Sporlin, 99.

72. This summary is based on notations after the names on each muster roll. It is not an exact record, but all we have to go on when there were no official reports or accounts in memoirs.

73. George, 213.

74. Ford, 92.

75. From Lane's report, to be cited later. This account is based on the reports of Lane, Hays, Major Polk, and Major Truett. Ford's version is from his book (91–98).

76. Brackett, 266–267.

77. These reports are printed in *Executive Document No 1, House of Representatives, Thirtieth Congress, Second Session.* Lane's report, 95–98. Hays's report, 98–100. Major Polk's report, 100–101, and Major Truett's report, 102–103. This report, incidentally, is the basis for the spelling of Truett's name.

78. Barton, 116.

79. Ford, 100.

80. *Ibid.*, 101.

81. *Ibid.*, 101–102.

82. *Ibid.*, 103–104.

83. *Ibid.*, 105.

84. *Ibid.*, 106.

85. This turn-in has been discussed earlier.

86. Hays was considered still in command of the part of his regiment guarding the Texas frontier. His five companies were mustered out of the army in Vera Cruz.

87. Ford, 109.

Afterword

1. Henry W. Barton, *Texas Volunteers in the Mexican War,* 118.

2. This was the beginning of a very troubled period in Texas history. The state assumed the national government would protect the frontier, though they were willing to furnish troops if the U.S. paid them. In time, Texas would have to go back to the earlier Ranger system. The government was not unwilling to defend the new frontiers; the task was too great for the few mounted regiments. Even creating new cavalry regiments in the 1850s did not solve the problem.

3. See Webb, et. al., eds., *Handbook of Texas,* 1:693–694, for Glanton. Samuel E. Chamberlain, *My Confession,* 267–288, has a long account of his adventures with Glanton. This has to be treated with extreme caution, however. The information on Chevallie and McCulloch was generously shared by a candidate for an advanced degree.

4. Webb, et. al., eds., *Handbook of Texas,* 2:106.

5. *Ibid.,* 1:789.

6. *Ibid.,* 2:24–25.

7. *Ibid.,* 2:929–930.

8. See John S. Ford, *Rip Ford's Texas,* for a full account of the 1850s and his Civil War service.

9. Branda, ed., *Handbook of Texas,* 3:868, has new material on the life of Seguin.

10. Isaac George, *Heroes and Incidents of the Mexican War,* 200.

11. See Frank Belden and Charles Haven for the continuation of the Colt story.

12. Louis A. Garavaglia and Charles G. Worman, *Firearms of the American West,* 146.

13. *Ibid.,* 148–149.

14. See Webb, *Texas Rangers,* for post-Civil War Ranger history.

15. This rifle was popularly known as the Mississippi Rifle, the weapon made famous by Jefferson Davis and his riflemen at Monterey and Buena Vista.

16. The Walker Papers, Texas State Library.

Bibliography

Manuscripts

Adjutant General Papers. Archives Division, Texas State Library. Austin.

Ford, John Salmon. *Memoirs*. Typescript copy in Archives Division, Texas State Library. Austin.

McCulloch Family Papers. Library of the Daughters of the Republic of Texas. San Antonio.

Walker Papers. Archives Division, Texas State Library. Austin.

Documentary Sources

Texas:

Journal of the Fourth Congress of the Republic of Texas, 1839–1840. Edited by Harriet Smither.

Journal of the House of Representatives of the Republic of Texas, Fifth Congress.

Journals of the Ninth Congress of the Republic of Texas. Washington. 1845.

United States:

House Executive Document No. 1. Thirtieth Congress, Second Session. Serial No. 537.

House Executive Document No. 4. Twenty-ninth Congress, Second Session. Serial No. 497.

House Executive Document No. 60. Thirtieth Congress, First Session. Serial No. 520.

Articles

Buchanan, A. Russell. "George Washington Trahern." *Southwestern Historical Quarterly* 58.

Gunn, Jack W. "Ben McCulloch: A Big Captain." *Southwestern Historical Quarterly* 58.

Holland, James K. "Diary of a Texan Volunteer in the Mexican War." *Southwestern Historical Quarterly* 30.

Newspapers

Morning Star (Houston)

Semanario Politico del Gobierno de Nuevo Leon

Texas Democrat (Austin)

The American Flag

The Democratic Telegraph and Texas Register

The Telegraph and Texas Register (Columbia)

Books

Axelrod, Alan. *American Frontier Life: Early Western Paintings and Prints.* New York: Abbeville Press, 1987.

Barker, Eugene C. *The Life of Stephen F. Austin.* Austin: University of Texas Press, 1985.

Barton, Henry W. *Texas Volunteers in the Mexican War.* Wichita Falls, TX: 1970.

Belden, Frank, and Charles T. H. Haven. *A History of the Colt Revolver.* New York: Bonanza Books, 1940.

Brackett, Albert G. *General Lane's Brigade in Central Mexico.* Cincinnati: H. W. Derby, 1854.

Brice, Donaly E. *The Great Comanche Raid.* Austin: Eakin Press, 1987.

Chamberlain, Samuel E. *My Confession.* Lincoln: University of Nebraska Press, 1984.

Clark, P. B. *History of Clarksville and Old Red River Country.* Dallas: Mathis, Van Nort and Company, 1937.

Dillin, John G. W. *The Kentucky Rifle.* Washington, D.C.: National Rifle Association of America, 1924.

Dillon, Lester R., Jr. *American Artillery in the Mexican War, 1846–1847.* Austin: Presidial Press, 1975.

Edwards, William B. *The Story of Colt's Revolver.* Harrisburg: 1953.

Fehrenbach, T. R. *Comanches: The Destruction of a People.* New York: Alfred A. Knopf, 1974.

Ford, John Salmon. *Rip Ford's Texas.* Edited by Stephen B. Coates. Austin: University of Texas Press, 1963. Paperback 1987.

Gammel, H. P. N. *The Laws of Texas.* Vol. 1. Austin: The Gammel Book Co., 1898.

Ganoe, William Addleman. *The History of the United States Army.* New York: D. Appleton and Co., 1924.

Garavaglia, Louis A., and Charles G. Worman. *Firearms of the American West.* Albuquerque: University of New Mexico Press, 1984.

George, Isaac. *Heroes and Incidents of the Mexican War.* Greensburg, PA: 1903. Reprinted Hollywood, CA: Sun Dance Press, 1971.

Giddings, Luther, *Sketches of the Campaign in Mexico by an Officer of the First Ohio Volunteers.* New York: Putnam, 1853.

Grant, U. S. *Personal Memoirs of U. S. Grant.* New York: Charles L. Webster & Company, 1885.

Green, Thomas J. *Journal of the Texian Expedition Against Mier.* New York: Harper, 1845.

Greer, James Krimmins. *Colonel Jack Hays.* Revised edition. College Station: Texas A&M University Press, 1987.

Gregg, Josiah. *Commerce of the Prairies.* Edited by Max L. Moorehead. Norman: University of Oklahoma Press, 1954.

Hanson, Charles E., Jr. *The Plains Rifle.* New York: Bramhall House, 1960.

Henry, W. S. *Campaign Sketches of the War with Mexico.* New York: Harper and Brothers, 1847.

Hitchcock, Ethan Allen. *Fifty Years in Camp and Field, Diary of Major General Ethan Allen Hitchcock.* Ed. by W. A. Croffut. New York: Putnam, 1909.

Jenkins, John Holland. *Recollections of Early Texas, The Memoirs of John Holland Jenkins.* Edited by John Holmes Jenkins III. Austin: University of Texas Press, 1987.

Kendall, George Wilkins. *The War Between the United States and Mexico.* New York and Philadelphia: Appleton and Company, 1851.

Lamar, Mirabeau Buonaparte. *The Papers of.* Austin: Von Boeckmann-Jones Company, 1921–1927.
Lane, Walter P. *The Adventures and Recollections of General Walter P. Lane.* Austin and New York: Jenkins Publishing Co., 1970.
Lavender, David. *Climax at Buena Vista.* Philadelphia and New York: J. B. Lippincott Company, 1966.
Mansfield, Edward D. *The Mexican War.* New York: A. S. Barnes and Company, 1849.
Maverick, Mary Ann. *Memoirs of Mary A. Maverick.* Edited by Rena Maverick Green. San Antonio: Alamo Printing Co., 1921.
McClellan, George B. *The Mexican War Diary of General George B. McClellan.* Edited by William Starr Myers. New York: Capo Press, 1972.
Nevin, David. *The Mexican War.* Alexandria, VA: Time-Life Books, 1978.
Olmsted, Frederick Law. *A Journey Through Texas.* New York: Dix Edwards and Company, 1857.
Oswandel, J. J. *Notes on the Mexican War, 1846–47–48.* Philadelphia, 1885.
Parsons, John E. *Samuel Colt's Own Record.* Hartford: The Connecticut Historical Society, 1949.
Polk, James Knox. *The Diary of James Knox Polk.* Milo Milton Quaife, ed. Chicago: A. C. McClurg and Company, 1910.
Reid, Samuel C., Jr. *The Scouting Expeditions of McCulloch's Texas Rangers.* Philadelphia: John E. Potter and Company. Undated. This edition has been used. There are several other editions and publishers.
Rose, Victor M. *The Life and Services of Gen. Ben McCulloch.* Philadelphia: Pictorial Bureau of the Press, 1888.
Rossi, Paul A., and Avid C. Hunt. *The Art of the Old West.* Secaucus, NJ: Castle Books, 1985.
Royland, Charles P. *Albert Sidney Johnston.* Austin: University of Texas Press, 1987.
Scribner, B. F. *A Campaign in Mexico.* Philadelphia, 1847.
Smith, G. W., and S. Judah. *Chronicles of the Gringos.* Albuquerque: University of New Mexico Press, 1968.
Smith, S. Compton. *Chile con Carne.* New York: Miller and Curtiss, 1857.
Sporlin, C. D. *Texas Veterans in the Mexican War.* Victoria, TX: 1984.
Taylor, Zachary. *Letters of Zachary Taylor from the Battle-Fields of the Mexican War.* Rochester, NY: The Genesee Press, 1903.
Thorp, T. B. *Our Army at Monterey.* Philadelphia: Carey & Hart, 1848.
Webb, Walter Prescott. *The Texas Rangers.* Boston, New York: Houghton Mifflin Company, 1935.
Webb, Walter Prescott, and H. Bailey Carroll, eds. *The Handbook of Texas.* 2 vols. Austin: Texas State Historical Association, 1952. Vol. 3 edited by Eldon Stephen Branda. 1976.
Winfrey, Dorman H., and James M. Day, eds. *The Indian Papers of Texas and the Southwest, 1825–1916.* Austin: Pemberton Press, 1966.

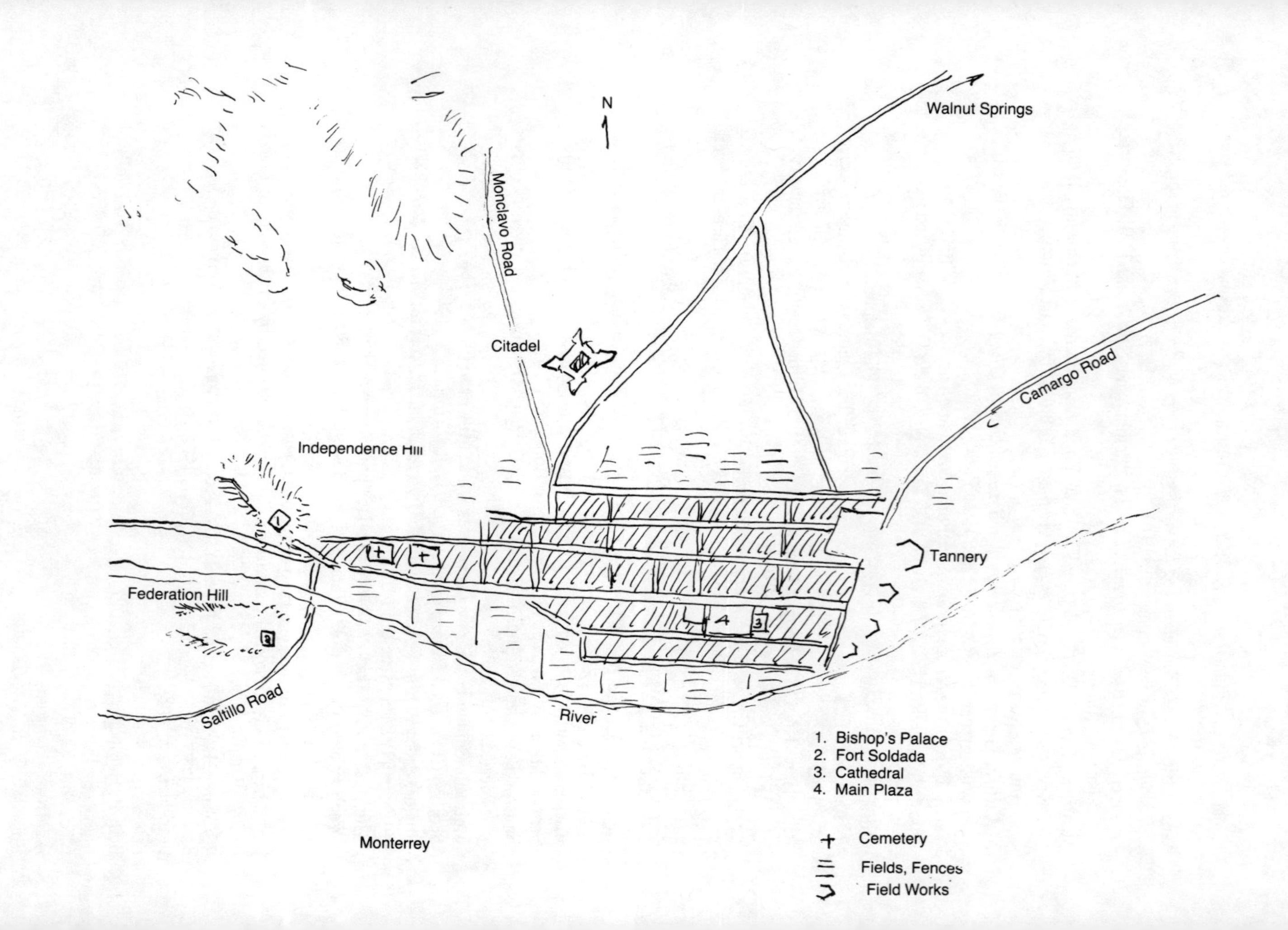
N
Walnut Springs
Monclavo Road
Citadel
Camargo Road
Independence Hill
Tannery
Federation Hill
Saltillo Road
River
1. Bishop's Palace
2. Fort Soldada
3. Cathedral
4. Main Plaza
Cemetery
Fields, Fences
Field Works
Monterrey

Index